PARKS AND PEOPLE

George,
I... hope the book is useful and that our paths will cross again soon.

Bob

PARKS AND PEOPLE
Managing Outdoor Recreation
at Acadia National Park

ROBERT E. MANNING

University of Vermont Press

BURLINGTON, VERMONT

PUBLISHED BY UNIVERSITY PRESS OF NEW ENGLAND

HANOVER AND LONDON

University of Vermont Press
Published by University Press of New England,
One Court Street, Lebanon, NH 03766
www.upne.com

Printed in the United States of America
5 4 3 2 1

Library of Congress Cataloging-in-Publication Data
Manning, Robert E., 1946–
Parks and people : managing outdoor recreation at Acadia National Park / Robert E. Manning.
    p. cm.
Includes bibliographical references and index.
ISBN 978-1-58465-791-0 (pbk. : alk. paper)
1. Outdoor recreation—Research—Case studies. 2. Outdoor recreation—
Environmental aspects—Maine—Acadia National Park—Management.
3. Acadia National Park (Me.)—Management. I. Title.
GV191.6.M3137 2009
796.509741'45—dc22   2009016154

 University Press of New England is a member of the Green Press Initiative. The paper used in this book meets their minimum requirement for recycled paper.

Contents

Preface

Visits to the U.S. national parks total nearly 300 million annually. Over two million visits per year are accommodated at Acadia National Park alone. While we should celebrate the popularity of national parks as a clear reflection of the enjoyment they generate and their importance in society, this popularity also presents a growing challenge: Parks are to be protected as well as enjoyed. Moreover, the quality of the visitor experience also must be maintained for parks to be appreciated fully and to foster the public support that ultimately is needed to ensure park protection. Use of parks and related areas can cause impacts to natural and cultural resources, including trampling of fragile vegetation, soil compaction and erosion, water pollution, disturbance of wildlife, and loss of cultural artifacts. Visitor use also can degrade the quality of the park experience through crowding and congestion, conflicting uses, and the aesthetic implications of the damage to park resources as noted above. How much and what types of visitor use can be accommodated in national parks and related areas before impacts to park resources and the quality of the visitor experience become unacceptable? This fundamental question is a vital component of managing parks and often is addressed under the rubric of "carrying capacity."

Several frameworks have been developed to help guide analysis and application of carrying capacity as applied to parks and related areas. While subtle differences may be found among these frameworks, they all incorporate a management-by-objectives approach that involves (1) formulating management objectives or desired conditions and associated indicators and standards of quality, (2) monitoring indicator variables, and (3) managing park resources and visitors to ensure that standards of quality are maintained. This conceptual approach can help guide analysis of carrying capacity and management of outdoor recreation more broadly. Application of this approach can be supported and "informed" by a program of research.

Acadia National Park has been a leader in applying this management-by-objectives approach, and has supported a program of natural and social science research as a foundation for this work. This book describes elements of this program of research, including its research and management implications. While the methods, findings, and implications of this research apply directly to Acadia, the lessons learned extend to the broader system of parks and related areas.

This book draws heavily on the work of many people. Authors of each chapter are found in the table of contents. John Daigle at the University of Maine along with his student Min Kim and colleagues Carole Zimmerman and James Pol have conducted a series of studies on the increasingly important issue of planning and managing transportation at Acadia and parks in general, as well as a study of visitor-caused impacts to vegetation on the summit of Cadillac Mountain. Jeff Marion of the U.S. Geological Survey and Virginia Tech University along with his students Kerri Cahill, Jeremy Wimpey, and Logan Park have conducted inventories and assessments of visitor-caused impacts to soils and vegetation on park trails and campsites, and explored visitor preferences applied to alternative management practices. Margaret Littlejohn of the University of Idaho conducted a baseline survey of park visitors as part of the National Park Service (NPS) Visitor Services Project. Steve Lawson of Virginia Tech University, along with his student Steve Bullock, studied the visitor experience at the summit of Cadillac Mountain.

I have been pleased to conduct a long-term program of research at Acadia under the auspices of the University of Vermont's Park Studies Laboratory. This work has been conducted with several colleagues, including Bill Valliere, Wayne Freimund, Dave Lime, Jeff Marion, Steve Lawson, and Laura Anderson, as well as graduate students Ben Wang, Jim Bacon, Steve Lawson, Peter Newman, Megha Budruk, Daniel Laven, Jeff Hallo, Rebecca Stanfield McCown, Carena van Riper, Dan Abbe, Kelly Goonan, Ben Minteer, Jennifer Morrissey, and Logan Park.

None of the work of the Park Studies Laboratory would have been possible without the strong and progressive leadership of NPS staff at Acadia. The park provided much of the needed research funding, but also provided logistical support and, most importantly, contributed in substantive ways to the design, execution, and interpretation of this program of research. Special appreciation is expressed to Charlie Jacobi, my colleague and friend, who has vigorously led the program of outdoor recreation management at the park for many years. I am also grateful for the support and advice of David Manski, John Kelley, Len Bobinchock, and Superintendents John Reynolds, Paul Haertel, and Sheridan Steele.

Finally, several people assisted me with production of the book. Marcie Newland and Bill Valliere of the University of Vermont helped produce the manuscript. Dave Lime provided helpful comments on an initial draft of the manuscript. Phyllis Deutsch of the University Press of New England skillfully guided the manuscript through the publication process.

Acknowledgments

Most of the chapters included in this book are edited versions of journal articles, conference proceedings, and technical reports. Appreciation is expressed to the following authors and publishers (listed in the order of their appearance in the book).

Margaret Littlejohn. *Acadia National Park Visitor Study: Summer 1999.* U.S. National Park Service Visitor Services Project Report 108. Moscow: University of Idaho, Cooperative Park Studies Unit, 1999.

Robert Manning, Charles Jacobi, William Valliere, and Ben Wang. "Standards of Quality in Parks and Recreation." *Parks and Recreation* 33 (1998): 88–94.

Charles Jacobi and Robert Manning. "Crowding and Conflict on the Carriage Roads of Acadia National Park: An Application of the Visitor Experience and Resource Protection Framework." *Park Science* 19 (1999): 22–26.

James Bacon, Robert Manning, Steven Lawson, William Valliere, and Daniel Laven. "Indicators and Standards of Quality for the Schoodic Peninsula of Acadia National Park." *Proceedings of the 2002 Northeastern Recreation Research Symposium.* USDA Forest Service General Technical Report NE-302, 2003: 279–285.

Jeffrey Marion. "Development and Application of Trail and Campsite Monitoring Protocols in Support of Visitor Experience and Resource Protection Decision Making at Isle au Haut, Acadia National Park," Blacksburg, Va.: USDI, U.S. Geological Survey, Virginia Tech Field Station, 2007.

Jeffrey Hallo and Robert Manning. "Transportation and Recreation: A Case Study of Visitors Driving for Pleasure at Acadia National Park." *Journal of Transport Geography* (forthcoming).

Kelly Goonan, Robert Manning, and William Valliere. "Research to Guide Trail Management at Acadia National Park." *Proceedings of the 2008 Northeastern Recreation Research Symposium.* USDA Forest Service General Technical Report NRS-P-42, 266–74. 2009.

Laura Anderson, Robert Manning, and William Valliere. "Indicators and Standards of Quality Across Space and Time." *Proceedings of the 2008 Northeastern Recreation Research Symposium.* USDA Forest Service General Technical Report NRS-P-42, 170–76. 2009.

Robert Manning. "Do Parks Make Good Neighbors?" *Park Science* 11 (1990): 19–20.

Carole Zimmerman, John Daigle, and James Pol. "Tourism Business and Intelligent Transportation Systems: Acadia National Park, Maine." *Transportation Research Record: Journal of the Transportation Research Board* 1895 (2004): 182–187. Transportation Research Board of the National Academies, Washington, D.C. Reproduced with permission of TRB.

Robert Manning, William Valliere, Ben Minteer, Ben Wang, and Charles Jacobi. "Crowding in Parks and Outdoor Recreation: A Theoretical, Empirical, and Managerial Analysis." *Journal of Park and Recreation Administration* 18 (2000): 57–72.

Robert Manning and William Valliere. "Coping in Outdoor Recreation: Causes and Consequences of Crowding and Conflict among Community Residents." *Journal of Leisure Research* 33 (2001): 410–426.

Robert Manning and Wayne Freimund. "Use of Visual Research Methods to Measure Standards of Quality for Parks and Outdoor Recreation." *Journal of Leisure Research* 36 (2004): 557–579.

Robert Manning, William Valliere, Ben Wang, and Charles Jacobi. "Crowding Norms: Alternative Measurement Approaches." *Leisure Sciences* 21 (1999): 97–115.

Robert Manning, Jennifer Morrissey, and Steven Lawson. "What's Behind the Numbers? Qualitative Insights into Normative Research in Outdoor Recreation." *Leisure Sciences* 27 (2005): 205–224.

Ken Hornback and Robert Manning. "When Is a Visit Really a Visit? Public Use Reporting at Acadia National Park." *Park Science* 13 (1992): 13, 23.

Ben Wang and Robert Manning. "Computer Simulation Modeling for Recreation Management: A Study on Carriage Road Use in Acadia National Park, Maine, USA." *Environmental Management* 23 (1999): 193–203. With kind permission from Springer Science and Business Media.

Jeffrey Marion, Jeremy Wimpey, and Logan Park. "Monitoring Protocols for Characterizing Trail Conditions, Understanding Degradation, and Selecting Indicators and Standards of Quality, Acadia National Park, Mount Desert Island." Blacksburg, Va.: USDI, U.S. Geological Survey, Virginia Tech Field Station (forthcoming).

Min Kim. "Monitoring Vegetation Impact Using Remote Sensing Technology: Cadillac Mountain Summit, Acadia National Park." Ph.D dissertation, University of Maine, 2009.

John Daigle and Carol Zimmerman. "Alternative Transportation and Travel Information Technologies: Monitoring Parking Lot Conditions over Three Summers at Acadia National Park." *Journal of Park and Recreation Administration* 22 (2004): 82–103.

Logan Park, Robert Manning, Jeffrey Marion, Steven Lawson, and Charles Jacobi. "Managing Visitor Impacts in Parks: A Multi-Method Study of the Effectiveness of Alternative Management Practices." *Journal of Park and Recreation Administration* 26 (2008): 97–121.

Jeffrey Hallo and Robert Manning. "Use of Computer Simulation Modeling to Support Analysis of the Social Carrying Capacity of a National Park Scenic Road." *International Journal of Sustainable Transportation* (forthcoming).

Kerri Cahill, Jeffrey Marion, and Steven Lawson. "Exploring Visitor Acceptability for Hardening Trails to Sustain Visitation and Minimize Impacts." *Journal of Sustainable Tourism* 16 (2008): 232–245.

Steven Bullock and Steven Lawson. "Managing the 'Commons' on Cadillac Mountain: A Stated Choice Analysis of Acadia National Park Visitors' Preferences." *Leisure Sciences* 30 (2008): 71–86. Reprinted by permission of the publisher (Taylor & Francis Group, http://www.informaworld.com).

John Daigle and Carole Zimmerman. "The Convergence of Transportation, Information Technology, and Visitor Experience at Acadia National Park." *Journal of Travel Research* 43 (2004): 151–160. Reprinted by permission of Sage Publications.

Robert Manning. "An Experiment in Park Traffic Patterns." *Parks and Recreation* 24 (1989): 6–7, 64.

Introduction
Outdoor Recreation Research and Management
at Acadia National Park

Managing national parks and related areas presents both opportunities and challenges. Opportunities include protecting the substantial natural, cultural, and recreational values of these areas, and providing for public enjoyment and appreciation of these special places. Challenges include optimizing both of these opportunities simultaneously and balancing the inherent tension between them. When people visit national parks and related areas, they can impact park resources and the quality of the visitor experience. How much and what types of visitor use can be accommodated in parks without unacceptable impacts?

Acadia National Park is a quintessential example of these issues. Acadia is one of the "crown jewels" of the national park system. Moreover, its location in New England and the broader Northeast makes it easily accessible to the nation's largest concentration of population. Consequently, Acadia has moved ahead deliberately in its attempt to balance park use and protection. This process has been guided by the National Park Service's recently developed Visitor Experience and Resource Protection (VERP) framework, and has been supported by a program of natural and social science research designed to inform its application.

This chapter provides an introduction to the program of outdoor recreation research and management at Acadia. First, we describe the park briefly, including its natural and cultural history and its contemporary visitor use patterns. Second, we outline the VERP planning and management framework, along with its application at Acadia. Third, the chapter briefly describes the program of natural and social science designed to support and "inform" park planning and management. Finally, the organization of this book is outlined briefly.

ACADIA NATIONAL PARK

More than three thousand islands comprise the vast Maine archipelago, but only one stands out as the largest, the highest, and surely the prettiest of the fleet. The virtues of Mount Desert Island (MDI) attracted visitors as early as the 1840s, when Hudson River School artist Thomas Cole rambled about, recording its scenic wonders on canvas. As word of these wonders spread, well-to-do families began their summer migrations from Boston, New York, and Philadelphia to MDI to escape the cities and enjoy the beautiful land and seascapes. By the late 1890s, threats of development and logging turned these summer residents into conservationists to protect their tranquil retreat, and thanks to them, today we know MDI as the principal home of Acadia National Park, established in 1916 for all to enjoy as the first national park east of the Mississippi River.

Acadia now protects in perpetuity over 35,000 acres of land. Most of this land is located on MDI, where half of the island is in park ownership. An additional 2,700 acres are found on Isle au Haut, 15 miles to the southwest of MDI, and 2,300 are found on the mainland at Schoodic Peninsula, 5 miles to the east of MDI. Also included in the park are all or part of fourteen other islands, and 208 conservation easements totaling nearly 12,800 additional acres.

Most of these lands were donated by those early conservationists, and while park founders and superintendents pieced together lands as best they could, by 1980 the geography of the park on MDI consisted of a few large areas with convoluted boundaries and many isolated parcels scattered about the island. In 1986, legislation finally established a permanent boundary for the park on MDI and at Schoodic, easing relationships with local towns regarding property taxes. The federal government then began consolidating lands within that authorized boundary through purchases and divesting itself of the separate parcels with low park value; this lands program continues today. Separate legislation passed in 1982 established an authorized park boundary on Isle au Haut.

Park Mission

The mission of Acadia, articulated most recently in the park's 1992 General Management Plan, is derived from the 1916 National Park Service Organic Act and the park's own enabling legislation and associated documents:

The National Park Service at Acadia National Park protects and preserves outstanding scenic, natural, scientific, and cultural values for present and future generations through programs, facilities, and services. It also provides programs and opportunities for nonconsumptive, resource-based recreation and education for an increasingly urban population. (National Park Service 1992)

At the time of its establishment, park proponents, including President Woodrow Wilson, signer of the original proclamation, cited the area's rich history, landscape beauty, scientific interest, topography, geology, flora, fauna, and recreational values. Nearly one hundred years of seasoning have only underscored the importance and relevance of these values. Today, this rich combination of natural, cultural, and scenic resources—together with a host of exceptional scientific, educational, and recreational opportunities—contribute to the significance of Acadia, still the only national park in New England.

Natural and Cultural History

Acadia is located in the midst of a broad transition zone between southern deciduous and northern coniferous forests. The moderating effects of a maritime climate (especially fog), the range in elevations, and a glacial history enhance the diversity of habitats within the park. Fifty-three distinct vegetative communities are recognized by ecologists. These varied habitats range from subalpine summits and coastal headlands to forested wetlands, deep-water lakes, and beaver ponds, to saltwater marshes and the rocky intertidal zone. Mature spruce-fir forests, jack pine stands, and a coastal raised peat bog are among the more notable communities. The park's eleven hundred species of vascular plants include fourteen state-listed threatened or endangered species, as well as many of local concern.

Acadia is also home to a typical assemblage of northeastern U.S. fauna. Bird species are abundant, especially migratory song birds and shorebirds. More than 330 species have been identified, and the park protects two important seabird nesting islands. Endangered or threatened species include the peregrine falcon (federal listing) and bald eagle (state listing). Even moose and black bear are occasional island visitors, though habitat for them is limited.

The geology of the park records the history of the last continental glaciation in plain view. Granite-domed mountains and U-shaped valleys filled with lakes and wetlands illustrate this on a large scale. Somes Sound is the only fiord-like feature on the east coast of the United States. On a smaller scale, glacial erratic boulders, striations, chatter marks, and polish are widespread features of the park's exposed granite bedrock.

The cultural heritage of the park is equally important and includes stories and resources related to Native Americans, French and British settlers, and the wealthy Americans of the late 1800s and early 1900s who established summer colonies, founded the park, and contributed to the creation and development of the U.S. conservation movement. The privately run Abbe Museum, located in the park at Sieur de Monts Spring since 1927 and recently expanded into new space in Bar Harbor, preserves artifacts and interprets Native American history. Eastern pioneers like the Gilley family of Baker Island carved a hard living from the sea and the land for nearly a hundred years before Thomas Cole began the summer visitor and resident era that continues today. One of those early summer residents, George Dorr, is credited as the driving force behind the establishment of Acadia National Park, along with Charles Eliot, Sr., President of Harvard University, and oil magnate John D. Rockefeller, Jr. A strong tradition of philanthropy underlies establishment of the park, and thrives today under the direction of Friends of Acadia, one the leading "friends of the parks" groups in the country.

Surviving historic features and designed landscapes, such as the park loop road, hiking trail system, and carriage roads, are recognized for their history, craftsmanship, durability, and uniqueness. All three have been nominated for the National Register of Historic Places. The carriage roads, built under the direction of John D. Rockefeller, Jr., between 1913 and 1940, are often cited as the finest example of broken-stone road construction for horse-drawn vehicles in the United States. The roads and their seventeen beautiful stone bridges were designed and constructed in harmony with the landscape. Summer residents provided design and construction oversight for the hiking trail system as well. The hiking trails are known for their local origins in the Village Improvement Societies and the high level of craftsmanship in the stone work on many of them.

Acadia has been aptly described as a place where the mountains meet the sea, and the combination of topography, geologic history, and seaside location have created an island landscape of scenic beauty unequaled along the east coast of the United States. Cadillac Mountain offers seemingly limitless views in all directions from the highest point on the east coast (and at certain times of the year the first place in the continental United States to witness sunrise). Surrounded by the rocky shore, Sand Beach is an extraordinary example of a pocket beach, and is all the more unusual because it is composed more of shell fragments than sand. Cadillac pink granite, forest green spruce, sparkling blue lakes, and the ever-changing moods of the Gulf of Maine add color and vibrancy to the landscape. The undeveloped shoreline of the park offers great contrast to the developed shoreline of nearby towns and much of coastal Maine, where there is little publicly owned land. It's easy to see how visitors were and still are captivated by this place.

Scientists also recognized the values of Acadia and MDI more than a hundred years ago, long before establishment of the park. Early inventories of flora and fauna contributed to what is now a multidisciplinary database serving as the scientific foundation for extensive ecosystem research and monitoring programs. The Proctor Collection of eight thousand species of invertebrates from MDI is recognized nationally as an exceptional baseline inventory. Acadia is an important site for national air-quality monitoring and research and global climate change research. And as this book describes, Acadia has been a laboratory for research on the ecological and experiential impacts of visitor use on parks and protected areas, a series of studies designed to guide and inform a progressive program of outdoor recreation planning and management.

Acadia also offers excellent opportunities for educating visitors about its significant and varied resources. People of all ages are attracted to a broad spectrum of interpretive activities, including guided walks, amphitheater presentations, environmental education programs, and outreach activities. With the recent transfer to the park of the former Navy base on Schoodic Peninsula and its conversion to a science and education center, even more visitors will have a chance for in-depth learning about the park and the region.

Visitor Use

Acadia National Park is a great place to play. Visitors camp, hike, walk, bicycle, run, rock climb, swim and sunbathe, cross-country ski, snowshoe,

Figure I.1 *Acadia's historic carriage roads are an important cultural resource and are heavily used for hiking and biking.* PHOTO BY ROBERT THAYER

snowmobile, ride horses and carriages, sea kayak, take boat cruises, canoe, birdwatch, sightsee, and simply relax. The most common of these visitor activities are sightseeing, hiking on trails, and walking and biking on the carriage road system. As in many parks, visitation is not distributed evenly over space or time. Most visitors come between Memorial Day and Columbus Day, with the months of July and August sustaining the most intensive use. The most visited spots for sightseers are the summit of Cadillac Mountain, Sand Beach, Thunder Hole, Jordan Pond, and the Seawall area. At times, these places may appear to be congested with vehicles or people or both, while other park areas remain relatively fallow and unexplored. Several of Acadia's primary visitor attractions are shown in figures I. 1–5.

Acadia perennially ranks among the top ten U.S. national parks in visitation. Since new visitor-use estimation methods were adopted in 1990, the park has averaged 2.48 million visits annually, and more than 44 million total visits have been recorded between 1990 and 2007. The highest visitation was 2.85 million in 1995 and the lowest was 2.05 million in 2005. This decline is substantial and similar declines have been recorded in many other parks and protected areas regionally and nationally. However, visitation in 2007 was up again to 2.20 million. On a sunny day in August, more than five

Figure I.2 *Sand Beach is a primary destination for many park visitors. Its two parking lots fill early on most summer days.* PHOTO BY ROBERT THAYER

thousand hikers head for park trails, more than two thousand other visitors are enjoying the carriage roads, and over five thousand visitors find their way to the summit of Cadillac Mountain. Since 1999, the Island Explorer bus has carried many visitors from surrounding communities to park destinations, relieving some of the vehicle congestion, reducing local air pollution, and offering new ways to enjoy the park

On a per acre basis, Acadia may be the most intensively used national park, and park staff have identified visitor management as one of the most critical issues. The sheer numbers of visitors and their concentration over a few months and at a few locations are challenges for managers. Multiple, uncontrolled entry points and easy access from state and town roads further complicate these challenges.

On the other hand, visitors greatly appreciate the accessibility of the park, as indicated in their responses to an annual survey. By accessibility, they mean that the park is small and that the roads, carriage roads, and trails take you most everywhere you want to go in a short amount of time.

Figure I.3 *Acadia has over 100 miles of trails. Hiking is an important recreation activity for park visitors and residents of surrounding communities.* PHOTO BY CHARLES JACOBI

Acadia is not large by national park standards (compared, for example, to Yellowstone National Park's 2.2 million acres). This lack of extensive wilderness or "backcountry" means that visitors generally do not need highly developed skills or even ambition to explore the park. It also means that Acadia offers much to people of all ages and physical abilities. Strenuous cliff-climbing trails offer thrills and a workout, while easy gravel paths and carriage roads allow the less able and willing to explore the further reaches of the park. Few natural areas of similar size offer such a diversity of outdoor recreation experiences.

PARK PLANNING AND MANAGEMENT

Growing concern over the tension between use and protection of parks—often referred to as "carrying capacity" in the scientific and professional literature—resulted in development of the VERP planning and management framework by the NPS in the 1990s (Hof et al. 1994; National Park Service 1997; Manning 2001 and 2007). Like other contemporary park and

Figure I.4 *Thunder Hole is a popular natural feature located along the Ocean Drive portion of the Park Loop Road.* PHOTO BY ROBERT THAYER

outdoor recreation planning and management frameworks, such as Limits of Acceptable Change, developed by the U.S. Forest Service (Stankey et al. 1985), VERP is a management-by-objectives process. As noted above, visitor use of parks and related areas inevitably affects park resources and the quality of the recreation experience. The operative question that must be answered is, how much impact is acceptable? And the answer to this question ultimately must be derived from the management objectives for the park. What degree of resource protection should be maintained? What type of visitor experience should be provided? What type and intensity of management should be applied?

VERP and related frameworks rely on management objectives—sometimes called "desired conditions"—to guide park management. Management objectives are broad, narrative statements that describe desired park conditions, including natural and cultural resources and the visitor experience. Management objectives must ultimately be defined in terms of quantitative indicators and standards of quality, both for purposes of clarity and to enable measurement of the success (or failure) of park management. Indicators of quality are measurable, manageable variables that serve as proxies for management objectives. Standards of quality define the minimum

Figure I.5 *Isle au Haut can be reached only by boat and offers opportunities for remote camping and hiking.* PHOTO BY CHARLES JACOBI

acceptable condition of indicator variables. Once indicators and standards of quality are formulated, indicators variables are monitored to determine the degree to which standards of quality are being maintained. If monitoring suggests that standards of quality are in danger of being violated, then management practices must be applied. Management practices can range widely, including "hardening" park resources (e.g., paving trails, constructing tent platforms), reducing the impacts of visitors (e.g., encouraging visitors to stay on designated trails, substituting public transit for private automobiles), and limiting the amount of visitor use (e.g., limiting the length of stay, requiring a use permit).

Application of this management approach began at Acadia in the early 1990s, starting with the carriage roads. Growing popularity of mountain biking on the carriage roads created concern about the quality of the visitor experience within this iconic area of the park, and the park's 1992 General Management Plan called for development of a plan for the carriage roads. Following development of this plan, VERP was applied to the Schoodic Peninsula and Isle au Haut portions of the park, beginning in 2000 (Jacobi and Manning 1997). In 2001, the park organized a workshop to assess the status and future of this work (Haas and Jacobi 2002). Park staff, colleagues from other agencies, academics, and local community leaders participated in the workshop. This led to application of VERP to the MDI portion of the park (beyond the carriage roads), and this work continues.

A PROGRAM OF RESEARCH

Application of VERP and park management more broadly requires exercise of management judgment. However, this judgment should be as "informed" as possible through a program of research (Manning and Lawson 2002). For example, research can help identify baseline conditions of park resources and visitor use levels and patterns, describe the relationships between park use levels and types and impacts to park resources and the quality of the visitor experience, identify potential indicators and standards of quality for park resources and the visitor experience, develop and test monitoring protocols, measure visitor attitudes toward alternative management practices, and test the effectiveness of management actions.

A substantive program of research has been conducted at Acadia to help inform park and outdoor recreation planning and management and application of the VERP framework. This program of research has incorporated both natural and social sciences and integrated these approaches where possible. A variety of research methods have been applied, including qualitative and quantitative surveys of visitors and other stakeholders, resource inventories and assessments, remote sensing, observation of visitor behavior, and computer simulation modeling. Representative components of this program of research are described in the remaining chapters of this book, along with a discussion of their management implications.

ORGANIZATION OF THE BOOK

The book is comprised of a series of chapters that describe elements of the program of research and management at Acadia. Most of these chapters have been abstracted and edited from the scientific and professional literature. Sources include scientific journals, conference proceedings, and reports prepared for or by the NPS. The original source of each chapter addresses a specific study (or sometimes, a single component of that study), but these sources tend to be isolated in time, space, methods, and findings. Collecting and synthesizing this material in a single volume helps build a body of knowledge through the resulting synergy. In this way, the whole becomes more than the sum of its parts, the seemingly isolated studies are integrated into a "program" of research, and the management implications of this research are more evident.

The book is organized into three major parts, in addition to this introduction and a conclusion. The introduction briefly described Acadia National Park, including its history and geography, the Visitor Experience and Resource Protection (VERP) framework used by the NPS to plan and manage outdoor recreation, and the program of research that has been designed and conducted to help guide planning and management at Acadia.

Parts I through III constitute the body of the book and include edited versions of the papers described above. These parts are organized by the three principal components of the management-by-objectives framework noted above. Part I addresses indicators and standards of quality, and includes fourteen chapters. Chapters 1 through 9 describe a series of studies that explore the role of indicators and standards in guiding management of outdoor recreation and apply this concept to a range of park sites and facilities, including the carriage roads, Schoodic Peninsula, Isle au Haut, the Park Loop Road and Ocean Drive, trails, campsites, and the Island Explorer, and a variety of recreation activities such as hiking, biking, camping, driving for pleasure, or sightseeing. These studies employ both the natural and social sciences, and engage several groups of park stakeholders, including visitors, residents of neighboring towns, and the business community. Chapters 10 and 11 are broader treatments of several pervasive issues in park and outdoor recreation management, including crowding, conflict, and coping behaviors; research at Acadia has helped illuminate these issues. The centrality of these issues to parks and outdoor recreation often demands that related indicators and standards be developed. Chapters 12 through 14 address methodological issues associated with measuring indicators and standards of quality, including normative approaches, visual research methods, and quantitative and qualitative studies, all of which have been applied, tested, and refined at Acadia.

Part II focuses on monitoring indicators of quality and includes six chapters. A wide variety of indicators is addressed, including the number of recreation visits, measures of use density or crowding, visitor behavior, and the condition of soils and vegetation. Monitoring methods include field observation and counts, mechanical counters, visitor surveys, resource inventory and assessment, remote sensing, and computer simulation modeling.

Part III addresses a program of management designed to ensure that standards of quality are maintained and includes six chapters. These studies suggest the range of management practices that can be applied, the efficacy of these management practices, and visitor attitudes and preferences regarding management. The studies employ a variety of research methods, including experiments with associated controls, visitor observation, qualitative interviews, quantitative visitor surveys, and computer simulation modeling.

The final chapter focuses on conclusions that can be derived from the program of research and briefly summarizes the current status of outdoor recreation research and management at Acadia. But this program of research and management at Acadia and elsewhere suggests a series of emerging principles that can guide management of parks and people. These principles are presented, described, and illustrated using examples from the program of research presented in the book. These principles can be seen to apply to Acadia specifically, but to other parks and related areas more generally. The chapter concludes with a consideration of the research implications arising from this series of studies.

PART I   Indicators and Standards of Quality

1 Visitor Use of Acadia National Park

Who are park visitors? Where are they from? Why do they visit the national parks? What do they do in the parks? What do visitors think are the most important management issues in the national parks? Visitor Services Project (VSP) studies are designed to help answer these and related questions. The VSP is a research program administered by the National Park Service (NPS) for the purpose of providing useable knowledge about visitors.

The VSP began in 1982 when the NPS recognized the need to learn more about visitors and their opinions. The VSP works with park staffs to conduct baseline surveys of visitors. Survey questionnaires include "core questions" (those common to all VSP surveys), "common questions" (frequently asked questions), and "customized questions" (questions specifically designed to meet the needs of individual parks). VSP studies provide a snapshot of the visitor population in a park during a seven to ten day study period.

Nearly two hundred VSP studies have been conducted in over 150 units of the national park system including Acadia National Park. This chapter reports selected findings from that study.

STUDY METHODS

The questionnaire for this visitor survey was designed using a standard format that was developed in previous VSP studies. Interviews were conducted with and questionnaires were distributed to a sample of visitors who arrived at Acadia during the peak summer use season. Visitors were sampled at

This chapter is an edited version of the following report: Margaret Littlejohn, *Acadia National Park Visitor Study: Summer 1999*, U.S. National Park Service Visitor Services Project Report 108 (Moscow: University of Idaho, Cooperative Park Studies Unit, 1999).

locations throughout the park, based on the recommendations of park staff.

Visitor groups were greeted, briefly introduced to the purpose of the study, and asked to participate. If visitors agreed, a brief interview was used to determine group size, group type, and the age of the adult who would complete the questionnaire. This individual was given a questionnaire and was asked his or her name, address, and telephone number for the later mailing of a reminder thank-you postcard. Visitor groups were asked to complete the questionnaire during or after their visit and then return it by mail.

Two weeks following the survey, a reminder thank-you postcard was mailed to all participants. Replacement questionnaires were mailed to participants who had not returned their questionnaires four weeks after the survey. Eight weeks after the survey, replacement questionnaires were mailed to visitors who still had not returned their questionnaires. A total of 1,312 visitor groups were contacted, and 1,255 of these groups (96 percent) accepted questionnaires. Questionnaires were completed and returned by 1,065 visitor groups, resulting in an 85 percent response rate.

STUDY FINDINGS

Visitor group sizes ranged from one person to 45 people. Thirty-nine percent of visitor groups consisted of two people, while another 37 percent were people in groups of three or four. Seventy-one percent of visitor groups were made up of family members. Two percent of the visitor groups at Acadia were guided tour groups. The most common visitor age group was 36 to 55 years (42 percent) and another 23 percent of visitors were 15 years old or younger.

Forty-seven percent of respondents were making their first visit to the park while 52 percent had visited the park previously. International visitors to Acadia comprised 5 percent of total visitation. The countries most often represented were Canada (29 percent), England (16 percent) and Israel (9 percent). The largest proportions of United States visitors were from Massachusetts (14 percent), New York (12 percent), Pennsylvania (11 percent), and Maine (10 percent). Smaller proportions of U.S. visitors came from another thirty-nine states and Washington, D.C.

Almost half of visitor groups spent between one and three days on MDI. Another 18 percent spent eight or more days on MDI. Four percent of the groups spent less than a day on the island. Visitor groups were also asked how much time they spent at Acadia. Over half (58 percent) stayed from one to three days. Another 12 percent spent eight or more days visiting the park.

Visitors were asked where they went in the park and in what recreation activities they participated. The most commonly visited places were Cadillac Mountain summit (76 percent), Sand Beach and Thunder Hole (75 percent), Jordan Pond House area (61 percent), the visitor center (59 percent), and the Seawall area (55 percent). The least-visited place was Isle au Haut (2 percent). The most common recreation activities were sightseeing or driving for pleasure (86 percent), hiking on trails (72 percent), and walking or biking on the carriage roads (70 percent).

Respondents were asked, "On this visit, what did you and your group like most about your visit to Acadia National Park?" As might be expected, the most common responses were beauty or scenery and scenic views. Other common responses identified specific places and/or activities and included hiking trails, carriage roads, and the summit of Cadillac Mountain. Respondents were also asked, "On this visit, what did you and your group like least about Acadia National Park?" Crowding and traffic congestion were overwhelmingly the most commonly reported issues. A third question asked, "If you were a park manager planning for the future of Acadia National Park, what would you propose? Please be specific." The most common suggestions were to provide more parking, to preserve park resources, to alleviate crowding and congestion by means of a public transit system, and to limit the number of vehicles and visitors allowed in the park.

Visitor groups were asked explicitly if they encountered traffic congestion and/or parking problems in Acadia or on MDI. In Acadia, 25 percent of visitors said they encountered traffic congestion and/or parking problems. Most of these problems were encountered at park attraction sites, including Sand Beach, Thunder Hole, Jordan Pond House, the Park Loop Road, and the summit of Cadillac Mountain. On MDI, 30 percent of visitors encountered traffic or parking problems. Most of these problems were encountered in the primary "gateway" town of Bar Harbor.

Twenty-one percent of respondents reported that other visitors and their activities interfered with their enjoyment of the park. Primary issues identified by respondents were crowding, traffic congestion, and lack of parking.

Visitor groups were asked to report the park services and facilities they

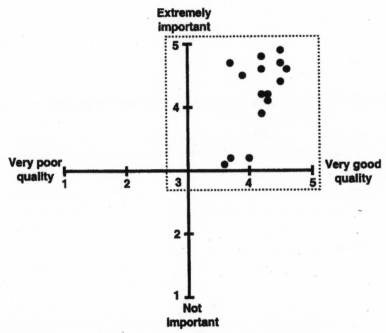

Figure 1.1 *Average ratings of service and facility importance and quality.*

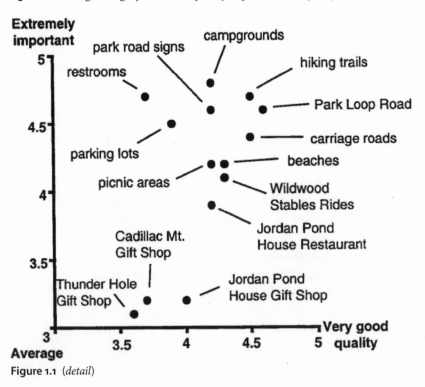

Figure 1.1 *(detail)*

used during their visit to Acadia. The services and facilities that were used most commonly were the Park Loop Road (86 percent), parking lots (82 percent), park road directional signs (82 percent), restrooms (75 percent), hiking trails (69 percent), beaches (52 percent), and the carriage roads (50 percent). Respondents rated the importance and quality of each of the services and facilities that they used, employing five-point response scales. An average score was determined for each service and facility based on ratings provided by visitors who used that service or facility. This was done for both importance and quality, and the results are plotted on the grid shown in figure 1.1. All services and facilities were rated as above average in both importance and quality. Services and facilities receiving the highest proportion of "extremely important" or "very important" ratings included campgrounds (95 percent), hiking trails (95 percent), restrooms (94 percent), and the Park Loop Road (93 percent). Services and facilities receiving the highest proportion of "very good" or "good" ratings included the Park Loop Road (92 percent), hiking trails (91 percent), and carriage roads (90 percent).

CONCLUSIONS

This study provides a snapshot of visitors and visitor use at Acadia. Information derived includes demographic characteristics of visitors, visitor use patterns, visitor evaluations of park services and facilities, and visitor attitudes toward park management issues. This information represents important baseline data that can be used for park planning and management.

Study findings also suggest a number of issues that may warrant special management attention. From the perspective of the visitor, the park includes several attractions that are especially important. These include the Park Loop Road, hiking trails, the carriage roads, Sand Beach, Thunder Hole, Jordan Pond House, and the summit of Cadillac Mountain. These places were reported by respondents as the most often visited and/or the most liked. These results generally are reinforced by the most popular recreation activities reported by visitors, including scenic driving, hiking, and walking or biking on the carriage roads. However, visitors also reported several problems associated with participating in these recreation activities and visiting the attractions noted above. These problems included crowding, traffic congestion, and lack of parking. These problems should be addressed in park planning and management.

2 Standards of Quality in Parks and Outdoor Recreation

Parks are increasingly important in modern society. They protect vital natural and cultural resources and enhance the quality of life by providing opportunities for outdoor recreation to an expanding population. But can parks continue to be successful as they attract more and more visitors? This chapter suggests that setting standards of quality is becoming increasingly important in the management of parks and outdoor recreation.

STANDARDS OF QUALITY

As described in the introduction, contemporary park and outdoor recreation management frameworks such as Visitor Experience and Resource Protection (VERP) rely on formulating indicators and standards of quality. A brief example may help illuminate this approach. Wilderness areas constitute a special type of park and outdoor recreation area where visitors are supposed to find opportunities for solitude (Wilderness Act 1964). But what constitutes "solitude" and how can it be measured and managed? Indicators and standards of quality provide answers to these types of questions. It may be determined through a program of research that the number of encounters with other groups along trails is a key measure of solitude. Thus, number of daily trail encounters with other groups may be a good indicator of quality. Moreover, visitors may report that once they encounter more than three groups per day along trails, they no longer achieve an acceptable level

---

This chapter is an edited version of the following papers: Robert Manning, Charles Jacobi, William Valliere, and Ben Wang, "Standards of Quality in Parks and Recreation," *Parks and Recreation* 33 (1998): 88–94; and Charles Jacobi and Robert Manning, "Crowding and Conflict on the Carriage Roads of Acadia National Park: An Application of the Visitor Experience and Resource Protection Framework," *Park Science* 19 (1999): 22–26.

of solitude. Thus, the standard of quality for the number of trail encounters per day might be set most appropriately at three. Other considerations, of course—including resource conditions and legislative mandates—also can influence indicators and standards of quality: Visitors can trample fragile vegetation, erode soil, pollute water, and disturb wildlife (Hammitt and Cole 1998). Likewise, too many visitors can cause crowding and conflict, degrading the quality of the recreation experience (Manning 1999).

By defining indicators and standards of quality, parks can be managed within their carrying capacity by means of a monitoring and management program. Indicators of quality can be monitored over time and if standards of quality are violated, carrying capacity has been exceeded. At this point, management action is required to ensure that standards of quality are maintained.

THE CARRIAGE ROADS OF ACADIA

The carriage roads, a system of more than fifty miles of unpaved roads constructed at the direction of John D. Rockefeller, Jr., in the early 1900s, represent one of the most significant resources at Acadia. Originally built for horse-drawn carriages, the carriage roads now are used primarily for hiking and biking and have become extremely popular. However, increased use has created concern for the quality of the visitor experience. In response to this concern, a program of research was initiated to help formulate indicators and standards of quality for the carriage road experience.

A first phase of research focused on identifying potential indicators of quality. A survey of a representative sample of carriage road visitors was conducted. Using both open- and close-ended questions, visitors were asked to indicate what added to or detracted from the quality of their experience on the carriage roads. Two types of indicators of quality were identified: One was crowding-related and concerned the number of visitors on the carriage roads; the other was conflict-related and addressed several "problem behaviors" experienced on the carriage roads, including bicycles passing from behind without warning, excessive bicycle speed, people obstructing the carriage roads by walking abreast or stopping in groups, and dogs off-leash.

The first phase of research also documented existing patterns of use on the carriage roads and visitor attitudes toward a variety of management practices. The carriage roads currently support a diversity of recreation opportunities defined both spatially and temporally. Some areas and times are relatively heavily used while other areas and times accommodate relatively light levels of use. Despite the problem behaviors noted above, most visitors supported maintaining the current mix of carriage road users—hikers, bikers, and equestrians. Based on these findings, park management decided to maintain a diversity of carriage road experiences by establishing two types of recreation opportunity "zones" for the carriage roads as defined by location, time of day, and time of year. However, both of these zones would continue to accommodate all types of visitors. The two carriage road zones would be defined by the same indicators of quality, but different standards of quality would be set.

CROWDING-RELATED STANDARDS OF QUALITY

A second phase of research focused on formulating standards of quality. This research also used a survey of a representative sample of carriage road visitors and adopted normative theory and related empirical techniques (Shelby and Heberlein 1986; Vaske et al. 1986; Manning 1986, 1999, and 2007; Vaske and Whittaker 2004). As applied in outdoor recreation, norms generally are defined as standards that individuals and groups use to evaluate social and environmental conditions in parks and related areas (Shelby and Vaske 1991). If visitors have normative standards concerning relevant aspects of recreation experiences, then such norms can be studied and used as a basis for formulating standards of quality.

Because of the relatively large number of visitors on the carriage roads, crowding was measured in terms of persons-per-viewscape (PPV), incorporating a visually based measurement approach. (The issue of visually based measurement approaches is described more fully in chapter 12.) The viewscape for the carriage roads (the length of carriage road that can be seen at any one time) averages approximately 100 meters. A series of computer-generated photographs was prepared that showed a range of 0 to 30 visitors on a typical 100-meter section of the carriage roads. Sample photographs are shown in figure 2.1.

Visitors were shown the photographs in random order and asked to rate their acceptability on a scale from −4 ("Very Unacceptable") to +4 ("Very Acceptable"). Study findings are shown in figure 2.2. This figure is called a social norm curve and represents the aggregate acceptability ratings for the

Figure 2.1 *Alternative levels and types of use on the carriage roads.*

sample of visitors. The norm curve indicates that visitors generally find that it is acceptable to see up to 14 PPV. However, the quality of the experience is very marginal in the upper portion of this range, and visitors prefer to see far lower PPV levels.

A more detailed assessment of PPV was developed through a computer-based simulation model of carriage road use. (Computer simulation modeling of visitor use is described more fully in chapters 17 and 22.) This model was developed using the travel routes that visitors reported in the visitor survey. The model can be run at any total daily use level for the carriage roads and estimates the resulting PPV levels that will occur. The model was validated by comparing model estimates to actual counts of carriage road use.

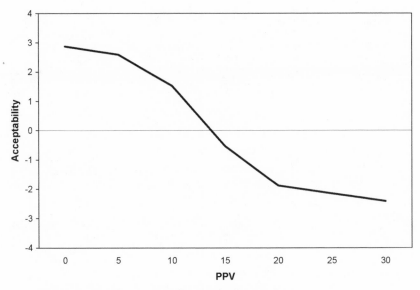

Figure 2.2 *Social norm curve from study photographs.*

Using the model, five hour-long trips on the carriage roads were described in a series of scenarios. These trips represented total daily use levels of 750 to 12,000 visitors. The scenarios described the PPV conditions that would be experienced at each of the five use levels, and visitors were asked to rate the acceptability of each scenario using the response scale described above. Once again, a social norm curve was developed for these data (figure 2.3).

Because the carriage roads are such an important park resource as specified in the park's General Management Plan, it was decided that they should be managed to ensure that most visitors enjoy a high-quality experience. Using this management objective, it was decided that at least 80 percent of visitors should have an experience they rate at quality level +2 or higher on the acceptability scale described above. Data used to develop figure 2.3 indicate that these criteria are met at up to a total daily use level of 3,000 visitors. Moreover, data from the computer simulation model indicate that at a total daily use level of 3,000 visitors, a visitor to the more heavily used portions of the carriage roads (high-use zone) would see 0 PPV at least 31 minutes out of a typical hour, 1 to 5 PPV no more than 27 minutes out of an hour, 6 to 10 PPV no more than two minutes out of an hour, and never more than 10 PPV. A visitor to the less heavily used portions of the carriage roads (low-use zone) would see 0 PPV at least 48 minutes out of an hour, 1

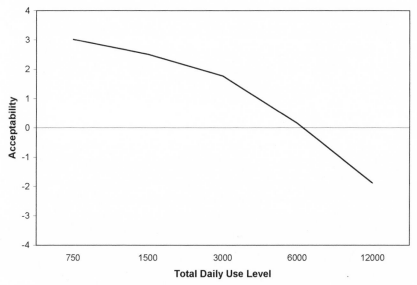

Figure 2.3 *Social norm curve from carriage road trip scenarios.*

to 5 PPV no more than 11 minutes out of an hour, 6 to 10 PPV no more than one minute out of an hour, and never more than 10 PPV.

These detailed use levels, expressed in terms of PPV and the associated total daily use level of 3,000 visitors, have been adopted as crowding-related standards of quality for the carriage roads.

CONFLICT-RELATED STANDARDS OF QUALITY

Standards of quality were also set for the four problem behaviors described above. Visitors were asked to report the maximum number of times it would be acceptable to experience each of these behaviors during a trip on the carriage roads. The resulting norms were used as a basis of formulating standards of quality. As with crowding-related standards, standards of quality for problem behaviors were set somewhat lower than maximum acceptable norms to ensure a relatively high level of quality. And different standards of quality were set for the high- and low-use portions of the carriage roads to ensure that a diversity of experiences was maintained.

For the high-use portion of the carriage roads, standards of quality specify that visitors should experience no more than two instances of bicycles passing from behind without warning during an average trip on the carriage roads, two instances of excessive bicycle speeds, one instance of visitors obstructing the carriage roads, and no instances of dogs off-leash. For the low-use portion of the carriage roads, these numbers should be one, one, one, and zero, respectively.

MONITORING AND MANAGEMENT

The VERP framework requires that indicators of quality be monitored and that management actions be taken when and where standards of quality are violated. (Monitoring and management are addressed more fully in parts II and III of this book, respectively.) This is an ongoing process on the carriage roads. Crowding-related indicators of quality can be monitored in several ways. Total daily use level of the carriage roads can be monitored by means of an electronic trail-use counter that has been calibrated statistically to total daily use. PPV levels can be monitored through estimation by the computer-based simulation model of carriage road use, by a survey of visitors asked to pick the photograph of carriage road use that looks most like what they experienced, and by observations of PPV levels by trained staff. Conflict-related indicators of quality can be monitored by a survey of visitors and by observations of trained staff.

To date, monitoring has indicated that crowding-related standards of quality have not been violated. The current peak total daily-use level is approximately 2,000 visitors. However, data indicate that existing conditions for some problem behaviors may have violated standards of quality. Consequently, park management instituted a number of management actions designed to maintain these standards of quality. These management actions include the development of "rules of the road" that are posted at all carriage road entrances, a liaison with local biking and hiking groups, and "courtesy patrols" on the carriage roads. These are the types of management actions that respondents favored in visitor surveys. Recent monitoring suggests that most of the problem behaviors have declined substantially in the past few years.

CONCLUSION

This study suggests that standards of quality are an important part of park and outdoor recreation management. Standards of quality define the type of recreation experience to be provided and maintained and constitute an informed and empirical foundation for subsequent monitoring and management. While the examples described in this study address the quality of the visitor experience, standards of quality can and should address issues of resource quality as well (Manning et al. 1995; Manning and Lime 1996; Manning, Lime, and Hof 1996). (Standards of quality for soil and vegetation conditions on trails and at campsites are described in chapter 4.)

The research described in this study used relatively sophisticated techniques, including digital photographic editing, computer-based simulation modeling, and visitor surveys to help formulate standards of quality. However, these techniques are not always necessary. Moreover, other sources of information can and should be used to help formulate standards of quality, including legal and administrative mandates, agency policy, historic precedent, interest-group politics, and expert judgment. Even with an abundance of data, some value judgments are still required from park and outdoor recreation managers working to formulate standards of quality. But without thoughtful standards of quality, parks are unlikely to be protected adequately and to realize their full potential to society.

3 Indicators and Standards of Quality for the Schoodic Peninsula

The Schoodic Peninsula of Maine includes an outlying unit of Acadia National Park and is located about an hour's drive north of the main MDI portion of the park. The park's General Management Plan (GMP) states that opportunities for "low-density" recreation should be maintained at the Schoodic Peninsula. In anticipation of some significant land ownership changes at the Schoodic Peninsula, an amendment to the GMP was needed, and a program of research was conducted to support this planning effort. The primary objective of the research was to help identify indicators and standards of quality for the recreation experience and related resource conditions.

STUDY METHODS

An initial visitor survey was conducted at the Schoodic Peninsula during the peak summer season. The purpose of this survey was to gather baseline information on demographic and socioeconomic characteristics of visitors to this area, recreation activities and use patterns, and indicators of the quality of the recreation experience. The survey was administered on ten randomly selected days in July and August. Trained surveyors were stationed at an automobile pullout near the park exit. At the beginning of each sampling day, an interviewer pulled over the first vehicle to exit the park and asked the occupants if they would be willing to participate in the sur-

---

This chapter is an edited version of the following paper: James Bacon, Robert Manning, Steven Lawson, William Valliere, and Daniel Laven, "Indicators and Standards of Quality for the Schoodic Peninsula Section of Acadia National Park," *Proceedings of the 2002 Northeastern Recreation Research Symposium*, USDA Forest Service General Technical Report NE-302, 2003, 279–85.

vey. Respondents were given a copy of the self-administered questionnaire and asked to complete it before leaving the park. At the completion of this process, the next vehicle was pulled over and this process continued throughout the sampling day. Over the ten sampling days, 740 vehicles were pulled over and asked to participate in the survey. A 79 percent response rate was attained, yielding 581 completed questionnaires.

A second visitor survey was administered the following summer. The purpose of this survey was to measure standards of quality for selected indicator variables identified in the initial visitor survey. The survey was administered on ten randomly selected days in July and August. The same sampling procedures were used as described for the initial visitor survey. Over the ten sampling days, 918 vehicles were pulled over and asked to participate in the survey. A 70 percent response rate was attained, yielding 640 completed questionnaires.

STUDY FINDINGS

Indicators of Quality

Respondents were asked several questions to determine potential indicators of quality of the recreation experience at the Schoodic Peninsula section of the park. Questions addressed issues such as what visitors enjoyed most and least; the most important or desirable qualities of the Schoodic Peninsula; perceived resource and social impacts of visitor use; and evaluation of problems or issues at this area of the park. Upon completion of this research, four indicator variables were identified: (1) number of cars at one time along the park road, (2) number of people at one time (PAOT) at Schoodic Point, (3) PAOT at Frazer Point, and (4) level of resource impacts on hiking trails.

Standards of Quality

As outlined above, the second phase of research focused primarily on establishing standards of quality for each of the indicator variables noted above. For each of these indicator variables, a series of five computer-generated photographs were prepared showing a range of use levels or resource impact. (The issue of visual research methods is described more fully in chapter 12.) Study photographs are shown in figures 3.1 through 3.4. For each series of photographs, respondents were asked a standard battery of evalu-

Figure 3.1 *Study photos showing a range of vehicles on the park road.*

ative questions. (The issue of question wording and format related to measuring standards of quality is described more fully in chapter 13.) First, respondents were asked if they had visited the sites in question. If respondents had visited the sites in question, then the remaining questions were administered. In the case of the park road, it was assumed that all respondents had used this facility, since it is the primary form of access to the park. The second question asked respondents to evaluate the *acceptability* of the five photographs showing increasing levels of visitor use or resource impacts at that particular site (called "acceptability"). Acceptability was measured using a nine-point Likert-type scale ranging from −4 ("Very Unacceptable") to +4

Figure 3.2 *Study photos showing a range of PAOT at Schoodic Point.*

Figure 3.3 *Study photos showing a range of* PAOT *at Frazer Point.*

Photo 1

Photo 2

Photo 3

Photo 4

Photo 5

Figure 3.4 *Study photos showing a range of trail impacts.*

35

("Very Acceptable"). The third question asked visitors to indicate the photograph that they *preferred* to see (called "preference"). The fourth question in the series asked respondents to indicate the photograph that showed the condition that would be *so unacceptable that they would no longer visit the Schoodic Peninsula section of Acadia National Park* (called "displacement"). Respondents were given the opportunity to indicate that, "none of the photographs are so unacceptable that I would no longer visit this area." The fifth question asked visitors to select the photograph representing the highest level of visitor use or resource impact they thought *the National Park Service should allow*, or the point at which visitor use should be restricted (called "management action"). Respondents were given the opportunity to indicate that none of the photographs showed a high enough level of visitor use or resource impact to restrict use or that use should not be restricted at all. The sixth and seventh questions referred to existing conditions and visitor expectations. Respondents were asked to indicate the photograph that best represented the condition they "typically saw today." The last question asked respondents to indicate the photograph that looked most like the conditions they expected to see. If they did not know what to expect, they were given the opportunity to indicate that. Findings from this series of questions are presented below for each of the four indicator variables.

Park Road. A summary of visitor responses to the battery of questions referring to the number of cars along a generic section of the park road is shown in table 3.1. Results indicate that acceptability declines as the number of cars increases. This is presented graphically by the social norm curve shown in figure 3.5. Respondents reported that an average of 7.5 cars seen at one time is the maximum acceptable condition for traffic along the park scenic road. However, visitors reported that they prefer to see an average of 2.5 cars at one time. Displacement levels were reported at an average of 12.7 cars. Visitors felt the National Park Service (NPS) should allow no more than an average of 8.5 cars before limiting automobile use. Respondents reported seeing an average of 4.1 cars. Finally, perceived crowding along the park road was measured on a Likert-type scale ranging from 1 ("Not at all crowded") to 9 ("Extremely crowded"). Visitors reported an average crowding rating of 2.5. In other words, crowding levels appear quite low while driving the park road.

Schoodic Point. A summary of findings at Schoodic Point is also shown in table 3.1. Again, results indicate that acceptability declines as the PAOT at

TABLE 3.1 Study findings for the number of cars at one time along the park road, PAOT at Schoodic Point, PAOT at Frazer Point, and resource impacts on hiking trails.

Evaluative dimension	Park road (cars)	Schoodic Point (people)	Frazer Point (people)	Hiking trail (photo number)
Acceptability	7.5	70.1	85.0	3.6
Preference	2.5	22.6	35.3	1.3
Displacement	12.7	102.0	120.8	3.7
Management action	8.5	71.2	89.0	2.7
Typically seen	2.8	30.2	34.7	1.8
Expectation	4.1	38.1	46.5	1.7
Perceived crowding	2.0[a]	2.5[a]		1.6[a]

[a]Scale: 1 = Not at all crowded; 9 = Extremely crowded

Schoodic Point increases. This relationship is illustrated more clearly by the social norm curve in figure 3.6. Respondents reported an average maximum acceptable condition of 70.1 PAOT. Visitors prefer to see an average of 22.6 PAOT, while they would be displaced by an average of 102 PAOT. Respondents reported that the NPS should allow an average of 71.2 PAOT at Schoodic Point before use should be restricted. Respondents indicated that they typically saw an average of 30.2 PAOT, while they expected to see an average of 38.1 PAOT Perceived crowding at Schoodic Point averaged 2.5 (a relatively low level) on the 9-point crowding scale.

Frazer Point. Findings from Frazer point are also shown in table 3.1. The same negative relationship between use level and impact exists here as in the previous indicator variables and is shown in the social norm curve in figure 3.7; as the number of people to Frazer Point increases, acceptability decreases. Visitor responses indicate that the level of use falls into the unacceptable range at 85.0 PAOT. Visitors to Frazer Point prefer to see an average of 35.3 PAOT; they would be displaced at an average of 120.8 PAOT; they feel the NPS should manage for an average of 89.0 PAOT before restricting use; they typically saw an average of 34.7 PAOT; and they expected to see an average of 38.1 PAOT. Respondents were not asked to rate their level of perceived crowding at Frazer Point.

Trail Impacts. The last indicator variable addressed resource impacts on a generic section of hiking trail. A summary of findings is also presented in table 3.1 and the social norm curve for trail impacts is shown in figure 3.8.

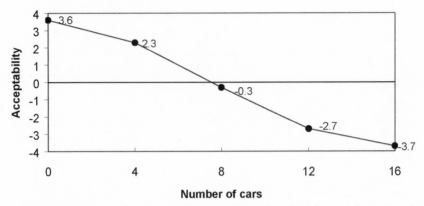

Figure 3.5 *Social norm curve for acceptability of number of cars on the park road.*

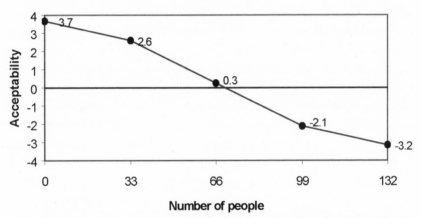

Figure 3.6 *Social norm curve for acceptability of number of people at Schoodic Point.*

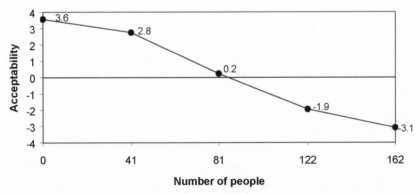

Figure 3.7 *Social norm curve for acceptability of number of people at Frazer Point.*

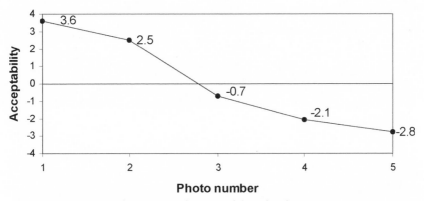

Figure 3.8 *Social norm curve for acceptability of trail impacts.*

Again, as the level of impacts increase, acceptability decreases. Visitors reported that the level of trail impacts falls into the unacceptable range at the conditions approximated by photo 4 (see figure 3.4). Visitors prefer to see conditions as represented by photo 1. Visitors reported that, on average, they would be displaced at levels approximated in photo 4. Respondents felt that the NPS should manage for conditions represented by photo 3 before limiting use of the trails. Existing conditions were, on average, most like the conditions shown in photo 2. Visitors expected to see conditions such as those shown in photo 2 as well. Finally, perceived crowding along hiking trails at Schoodic is quite low, with an average of 1.6 on the 9-point crowding scale.

CONCLUSION

Findings suggest that visitors are receiving a relatively low density and correspondingly high-quality recreation experience at the Schoodic Peninsula section of Acadia as suggested in the park's GMP. In general, visitors are encountering social and resource impacts that are much lower than their minimum acceptable condition and the point at which they would be displaced from the area. Moreover, in most cases the conditions encountered are very close to those they would prefer to see and often higher in quality than what they expected to see.

In addition, this research provides empirical evidence to suggest that visitors are able to provide information on indicators of quality pertinent to the experiences provided at Schoodic Peninsula. Further, visitors are able to make judgments about acceptable conditions for a diversity of indicator variables, and this information can help managers formulate standards of quality. This research provides planners and managers with a set of indicators and standards that are useful in defining the quality of the visitor experience at the Schoodic Peninsula section of Acadia. This information can help planners and managers make more informed decisions about the future of this portion of the park.

This study focused on helping to develop standards of quality across a diversity of indicator variables and incorporated several evaluative dimensions of standards of quality. As has been found elsewhere, study results suggest that standards vary across evaluative contexts. (This issue is addressed more fully in chapter 13.) Standards appear to be relatively consistent and organized in a hierarchical manner across evaluative dimensions such that preferences exhibit the highest standards (lowest level of impact) and displacement exhibits the lowest standards (highest level of impact), with acceptability and management action-related standards falling in the middle of the range. This study suggests that this hierarchical organization holds true across different types of indicator variables, including the number of cars at one time on the park road, PAOT at park attraction sites, and the level of resource impact on hiking trails.

Finally, study data on standards of quality were collected using a visual approach where photographs represented easily quantifiable variables such as number of cars or number of people. However, resource-impact photos did not have quantifiable units associated with them (e.g., percent of vegetation loss), although this approach is in keeping with "impact class" assessment procedures often used in ecological monitoring and management (Brewer and Berrier 1984; Cole 1989). Resulting data represent mean photo numbers and therefore may seem somewhat ambiguous and potentially less useful in a management context. Future research may improve upon this study by developing photographs based on more quantifiable ecological data.

4 | Indicators and Standards of Quality for Trail and Campsite Conditions at Isle au Haut

This chapter describes the results of visitor impact assessment research conducted at Isle au Haut, a small island (6,700 acres) and outlying unit of Acadia located 15 miles southwest of Mount Desert Island (Marion 2007). The NPS owns 2,700 acres on the island, including five camping shelters and twelve trails totaling 20.1 miles. The objectives of this study were to assist the park by (1) identifying appropriate indicators of quality related to hiking and camping, (2) developing monitoring protocols for selected indicators, (3) conducting monitoring to characterize baseline conditions for the indicators, and (4) summarizing data in formats that facilitate formulation of standards of quality for indicator variables.

STUDY AREA

Isle au Haut has received annual visitation of 5,500 to 6,900 day-use visitors and 1,100 to 1,500 overnight camper days over the past decade. Most visitors are transported to the island by commercial ferry or mail boats; others arrive by private boats, including sailboats, motorboats, and sea kayaks. The primary visitor activity on the island is hiking to explore the undeveloped and scenic rocky coastline, wooded uplands, marshes, bogs, and a large freshwater lake.

Camping is permitted only at the lean-to camping shelters, constructed in 1983 just inland from the southern shoreline at Duck Harbor Landing.

This chapter is an edited version of the following report: Jeffrey Marion, "Development and Application of Trail and Campsite Monitoring Protocols in Support of Visitor Experience and Resource Protection Decision Making at Isle au Haut, Acadia National Park." Blacksburg, Va.: USDI, U.S. Geological Survey, Virginia Tech Field Station, 2007.

The five camping shelters each accommodate up to six visitors, so camping is limited to 30 people per night. Associated facilities include a fire ring, food storage box, picnic table, hand-pump for water, and a composting toilet.

Trail Impacts

Resource impacts associated with trampling on trails include an array of problems. Even light traffic can remove protective layers of vegetation cover and organic litter (Cole 2004; Leung and Marion 1996). Trampling disturbance can alter the appearance and composition of trailside vegetation by reducing vegetation height and favoring trampling-resistant species. Loss of tree and shrub cover can increase sunlight exposure, which promotes further changes in composition by favoring shade-intolerant plant species (Hammitt and Cole 1998; Leung and Marion 2000). Visitors also can introduce and transport nonnative plant species along trail corridors, some of which may out-compete undisturbed native vegetation and migrate away from trails (Cole et al. 1987).

Exposure of soil on unsurfaced trails can lead to soil compaction, muddiness, erosion, and trail widening (Hammitt and Cole 1998; Leung and Marion 1996; Tyser and Worley 1992). Compaction of soils decreases soil pore space and water infiltration, which in turn increases muddiness, water runoff, and soil erosion (Manning 1979a). Erosion of soils along trails exposes rocks and plant roots, creating a rutted, uneven tread surface. Eroded soils may smother vegetation or find their way into water bodies, increasing water turbidity and sedimentation impacts to aquatic organisms (Fritz 1993). Visitors seeking to circumvent muddy or badly eroded trail sections contribute to tread widening and creation of parallel secondary treads, which expand vegetation loss and the aggregate area of trampling disturbance (Marion 1994). The creation and use of trails also can degrade and fragment wildlife habitats directly, and the presence of trail users may disrupt essential wildlife activities such as feeding, reproduction, and the raising of young (Knight and Cole 1995).

In summary, most trail-related resource impacts are limited to a linear corridor of disturbance, although impacts like altered surface-water flow, invasive plants, and wildlife disturbance can extend considerably further into natural landscapes (Kasworm and Monley 1990; Tyser and Worley 1992). However, even localized disturbance within trail corridors can harm rare or endangered species or damage sensitive plant communities, particularly in environments with slow recovery rates.

Campsite Impacts

Campsites, or camping shelter sites in the case of Isle au Haut, are also subject to visitor-caused impacts (Leung and Marion 2004). Many camping impacts are caused by trampling and are similar to those previously described for trails. Differences include the nodal configuration of trampling disturbance and campfire-related impacts, including tree damage, fire sites, and offsite firewood-collection trampling and wood removal (Newsome, Moore, and Dowling 2002; Reid and Marion 2005).

Campsites have been found to range in size from several hundred to more than 8,000 square feet (Marion and Cole 1996), generally more than half of which has lost its vegetation cover and more than one-quarter has also lost most organic litter (Leung and Marion 2000; Marion 1995). Large expanses of exposed soil are most susceptible to continuing soil loss through sheet and wind erosion. Soil erosion is a more substantial problem when campsites are located along shorelines, where eroded soil from the site and steeper shoreline-access trails can drain runoff directly into waterways. Other concerns related to the large size of some campsites are the loss of woody vegetation and its regeneration over time. Gaps in forest canopies caused by these sites can alter microclimates and create sunny disturbed locations that allow invasive vegetation to gain a foothold. An additional concern is the extent to which camping activities contribute to vegetation trampling in adjacent off-site areas (Marion and Leung 1997).

STUDY METHODS

A variety of resource indicators were included in this study to maximize flexibility in selection of campsite and trail indicators. Resource assessment procedures were developed, field tested, refined, and applied to the five shelter campsites and 20.1 miles of designated trails. Application of these procedures required one day for the campsites and three days for the trails, which should permit their sustained use by park staff as part of a long-term monitoring program. The following sections outline the campsite and trail assessment methods and analyses used to collect and analyze visitor impact assessment data.

Campsite Assessment Procedures

Campsites were defined as areas of obvious vegetative or organic litter trampling disturbance that in the judgment of survey staff was caused by camping activities. Site size was measured using the variable radial transect method (Marion 1991) and indicator conditions typically were assessed only within the established site boundary. For soil, the percentage of exposed soil was assessed according to a six-category cover-class scale (Marion 2007). The number of trees with moderate to severe root exposure was counted within delineated site boundaries as an indication of soil compaction and erosion. For vegetation, the percentage of ground covered by nonwoody vegetation on-site and off-site was estimated using the cover-class scale. Other indicators included the number of trails extending from a site and the presence of improperly disposed human waste.

Study data were entered into a spreadsheet and several new indicators were calculated. An estimate of the campsite area over which vegetation cover had been lost was calculated by subtracting the midpoint value of the on-site percent vegetation cover category from its off-site (control) counterpart, then multiplying this percentage by campsite size. Area of exposed soil was calculated in a similar fashion. Due to the small number of cases (N=5), data for the campsite impact indicators are presented in tables, and measures of central tendency (e.g., mean/median) are not included.

Trail Assessment Procedures

Trail assessment procedures featured a point sampling method to evaluate selected impact indicators (Marion 2007; Marion and Leung 2001). This method employed a fixed interval of 500 feet, following a randomized start (Leung and Marion 1999b). A trail measuring wheel was used to identify sample point locations. At each sample point, a transect was established perpendicular to the trail tread with endpoints defined by trampling disturbance that contained the majority of traffic. Temporary stakes were placed at these boundaries and the distance between was measured as tread width; maximum depth from a taut string tied to the base of these stakes to the trail surface was measured as maximum incision, an indicator of soil erosion (Farrell and Marion 2002). The cross-sectional area (CSA) of soil loss (square inches), from the taut string to the tread surface, also was measured using a variable interval method (Marion 2007). Trail tread condition characteristics, including vegetation cover, organic litter, exposed soil, muddy soil, water, rock, gravel, and roots, were defined as mutually exclusive categories and assessed across each transect. The number of informal (visitor-created) trails branching from the formal trail since the last sample point also was counted. Informal trails are trails that visitors have created to access features such as streams, scenic attraction features, and camping areas, or to shortcut switchbacks, go around muddy areas or downed trees, or that simply parallel the main trail.

Study data were entered into a spreadsheet and several new indicators were calculated: CSA square inches for each transect and CSA cubic yards, and cubic yards per mile for each trail. The cubic CSA values provide an estimate of total soil loss for each trail. A tread muddiness indicator was calculated by summing the percent cover values for muddy soil and water for each trail transect.

STUDY FINDINGS

Campsite Conditions

Due to the small number of campsites, all campsite-related data are included in table 4.1 by NPS site number. Campsite size ranged from 537 to 1,128 square feet with an aggregate area of disturbance of 3,956 square feet. An estimate of the area over which vegetation has been lost was calculated based on the amount of vegetation cover on paired, environmentally similar control sites. These estimates were highly variable, ranging from 0 to 777 square feet. Vegetation loss is generally highest on sites that receive heavy traffic and/or are shaded by forest canopies. Organic litter is also easily removed by visitor trampling, resulting in exposed soils that ranged from 111 square feet on site 2 to 459 square feet on site 1. On average, soil was exposed over 29 percent of the typical site.

The number of damaged trees was counted only within campsite boundaries to provide an accurate and repeatable measure of this form of impact. Only 2 of the 9 trees found on these sites were rated as damaged. However, 5 of the 9 trees were rated as having exposed tree roots, a measure indicating that soil erosion has occurred at the campsites. Also of concern is the large number of stumps, 33, found within site boundaries, 21 of which were located on site 4. It is possible that the trees represented by these stumps were

TABLE 4.1   Campsite impact data for Isle au Haut.

Impact indicator	Site 1	2	3	4	5	Aggregate impact
Site size (ft²)	537	715	936	1,128	640	3,956
Vegetation loss (ft²)	325	0	777	400	144	1,646
Exposed soil (ft²)	459	111	145	175	243	1,133
Damaged trees (#)	0	0	0	0	2	
Trees w/exposed roots (#)	0	0	30	2	5	
Stumps (#)	1	1	121	9	33	
Trails (#)	7	5	7	10	7	36
Human waste sites (#)	0	0	0	0	0	0

killed by natural causes, or that they were removed by park staff as hazard trees. Further monitoring and tracking by NPS staff is needed to evaluate whether trees are being cut for firewood.

No problems with improperly disposed human waste appeared, probably because of the close proximity of toilets. However, numerous trails, most of which are visitor-created, leave the outer boundaries of the shelter sites. The mean number of trails per site was 7.2, with a total of 36. The findings for this indicator suggest that considerable off-site trampling is occurring in the vicinity of the camping area.

Trail Conditions

Study findings summarizing conditions of all trails are shown in table 4.2. Use data were developed for each trail based on trail use monitoring and simulation modeling conducted in another component of research (Manning, Bacon, et al. 2004). Based on natural breaks in the use data, Isle au Haut trails were classified as low-use (0.3 to 1.0 encounters/mile), moderate-use (4.0 to 6.0 encounters/mile), and high-use (10.0 to 11.0 encounters/mile). Informal "visitor-created" trails diverging from the survey trails ranged from 0 to 17 with a mean of 5.6 and a total of 67. Dividing the number of informal trails by trail length provides a standardized number per mile measure permitting direct comparisons across trails. These data reveal the proliferation of informal trails to be a problem along many of the moderate- and higher-use trails, particularly the Cliff Trail (23.3 informal trails/mile). Mean tread width for the Isle au Haut trails ranged from 18.9 to 39.5 inches with a grand mean of 26.9 inches. Tread muddiness combines

TABLE 4.2   Trail conditions on Isle au Haut.

Trail name	Informal trails (#/mi)	Tread width mean (in.)	Mud mean (%)	Max. incision mean (in.)	Cross-sectional area mean (in²)	Sum, (yd³)	yd³/mi
Low use trails	0.36	21.0	4.3	1.1	10.0	106	13.
Bowditch	0.97	20.0	7.5	1.1	10.2	27	13.2
Long Pond	0.00	20.2	1.5	0.9	7.9	35	10.6
Median Ridge	0.52	21.4	8.0	1.2	8.9	23	11.8
Nat Merchant	0.00	24.1	0.0	1.5	13.6	21	18.1
Moderate-use trails	6.06	27.3	0.0	1.5	16.0	116	26.4
Deep Cove	0.00	20.1	0.0	1.5	31.7	8	50.3
Duck Harbor Mtn	10.66	29.2	0.0	1.7	13.6	22	18.4
Eben's Head	9.09	29.9	0.0	1.6	17.1	19	24.6
Goat	4.48	29.2	0.0	1.4	17.1	53	23.6
Thunder Gulch	2.22	18.9	0.0	1.3	10.3	14	15.1
High-use trails	5.02	38.1	0.3	2.2	40.1	331	48.5
Cliff	23.29	31.1	0.0	2.2	31.9	28	37.7
Duck Harbor	1.00	39.0	0.5	2.1	41.5	214	53.7
Western Head	6.67	39.5	0.0	2.6	40.5	89	54.2
All trails	3.33	28.1	1.9	1.6	20.9	553	27.6

the mud and water substrate categories assessed across each sampled transect. Muddiness is generally not a problem on Isle au Haut trails; as a percentage of tread width at the sample points, muddiness ranged from a mean of 0.0 (for 8 trails) to 8.0 percent for the Median Ridge Trail.

Maximum tread incision, the most efficient (least time-consuming) measure of soil erosion, ranged from a mean of 0.9 to 2.6 inches with a grand mean of 1.6 inches. The cross-sectional area method provides the most accurate measure of soil loss. This indicator ranged from a mean of 7.9 to 41.5 square inches with a grand mean of 20.9 square inches. Trail-wide extrapolations of transect CSA square-inch measures yields cubic measures that provide estimates of total soil loss. Aggregate soil loss for all trails is 553 cubic yards, which equates to 53 single-axle dump truck loads of soil. Soil loss for individual trails ranged from 8 cubic yards for the Deep Cove Trail to 214 cubic yards for the Duck Harbor Trail. These measures are not standardized; both erosion severity and trail length influence their values. Dividing the CSA cubic yard measure by trail length yields a standardized cubic yard per mile measure, allowing direct comparison of soil loss between trails. This measure suggests that the Western Head, Duck Harbor, and Deep Cove Trails are the most substantially eroded trails on Isle au Haut.

GUIDANCE FOR SELECTING INDICATORS AND STANDARDS

A number of critera have been developed in the literature that can help guide selection of indicators of quality for parks and outdoor recreation (Stankey et al. 1985; Merigliano 1990; National Park Service 1997; Manning 1999). For example, indicators should be specific, objective, related to visitor use, sensitive, manageable, efficient and effective to measure, and significant. Based on these criteria, along with study data and professional judgment, several campsite and trail-related indicators of quality are recommended for Isle au Haut.

Campsites

Three campsite indicators are recommended: campsite size, number of tree stumps, and informal trails. Campsite size is perhaps the best single indicator reflecting the total area of camping-related disturbance. Management efforts to minimize the area of trampling disturbance will promote the health of surrounding buffer vegetation, prevent the merging of impact areas from separate sites, and limit the potential for soil erosion. Given that camping has been restricted successfully to five designated shelter sites, there is no need to consider indicators related to the proliferation of visitor-created sites or site density. Furthermore, success in restricting site size would increase trampling intensity and further reduce area of vegetation cover loss and area of exposed soil. Park staff could consider additionally selecting one of these indicators, but both are limited by and strongly correlated with campsite size measures.

Maximum size standards could be set for the size of individual shelter campsites, for an aggregate measure of all five, or both. Given that the shelter capacities and use levels are uniform, there is no reason to vary standards by site. Establishing standards for individual campsites would prevent any single site from growing too large; establishing a standard for aggregate size permits greater flexibility, allowing expansion of one site provided it is offset by reductions in the size of other sites. Given the small number of shelter sites, direct examination of the distribution of sizes provides some guidance for selecting standards. Campsite size ranged from 537 to 1,128 square feet with a mean of 791 square feet and an aggregate area of disturbance of 3,956 square feet. Park staff tentatively selected a conservative standard of 800 square feet as a maximum shelter size. Two sites currently exceed this proposed standard, one by 136 square feet and one by 328 square feet. As an alternative, park staff might consider a maximum shelter site size standard of 900 square feet along with a maximum aggregate size of 3,700 square feet. This would require a small, 36-square-foot reduction in one site, a larger 228-square-foot reduction in another, while freezing the aggregate area of disturbance at the subsequent improved condition levels. The aggregate standard would prevent all the sites from expanding to the individual site standard (900 ft^2 × 5 = 4,500).

Number of tree stumps and informal trails are recommended for consideration as indicators because they characterize site conditions that appear to be problematic currently, in comparison to other possible indicators. The number of stumps ranges from 1 (three sites), to 9 (one site) and 21 (one site). It is possible that the two sites with larger numbers are a response to natural causes (e.g., insects or drought) or hazard-tree removal, so discussion with the knowledgeable NPS staff is recommended. However, if these large numbers are attributable primarily to recreation uses, then focusing management attention on reduction of this "avoidable" impact by establishing standards is recommended.

Standards could be set on the maximum number per site or maximum number per area (all sites). Percentage measures relative to number of campsite trees are problematic; consider the difference between a standard of "fewer than 25 percent of campsite trees have been felled" on sites with 4 trees versus 40 trees. The standard would have to pertain to the number of "new" stumps occurring over a specified monitoring interval and attributable to recreation-related damage (e.g., no more than 1 new stump/site/year). One note of caution is that changing campsite sizes will make this indicator and standard challenging to evaluate, along with the need for evaluations of who cut the tree. An alternate management response might be to prohibit axes and saws and omit this indicator.

The number of informal trails connecting to campsite boundaries ranged from 5 (one site), to 7 (three sites), to 10 (one site). Up to three trails for accessing the site, restroom facility, and water sources should be expected, but more than five trails seems excessive and connotes a substantial amount of trampling damage in adjacent off-site areas. In such cases, it is often common to find two or more informal trails accessing the same area of interest, which represents avoidable impact.

Trails

Trail-related indicators recommended for consideration include tread width, tread incision, cross-sectional area, muddiness, and informal trails. A principal decision that managers must make is whether to assess erosion using the maximum incision or the CSA measure. While CSA requires additional assessment and computation time, it also provides relatively accurate estimates of soil loss for transects, trails, and system-wide. This section presents additional data characterizing the distribution of values for these potential indicators to facilitate management deliberations on selecting appropriate measures and values for standards of quality. Selecting a standard is an inherently value-laden and subjective process. However, presentation of representative data characterizing the distribution of indicator values and their relationship to use levels can greatly assist the process used to evaluate and select standards.

For example, trail use levels on Isle au Haut were related significantly to measures of trail impacts and this provides a potentially important rationale for park managers to consider limiting visitor use where warranted (that is, where trail impacts violate standards that have been established). Moreover, alternative statistical measures of indicators offer potentially important insights into setting standards of quality. Such measures include range, mean, standard deviation, confidence limits, and percentiles. These data can inform the process of selecting standards of quality by describing the existing range of indicator values, their average condition, their level of dispersion, and the probability of finding larger values. Graphic presentations of such data in the form of boxplots and frequency histograms also can be useful.

Finally, note that indicator conditions for trails can be influenced by a variety of factors and may vary substantially over a relatively short distance along a trail. The procedures employed and recommended for continued monitoring are designed to select "representative" points for assessing these indicators, but they may identify atypical locations where any reasonable standard would be exceeded. To some extent, this is a problem inherent in selecting a standard of the "maximum condition" format. A standard could be set for mean values to avoid this problem, provided the trail is sufficiently long or the sampling interval is sufficiently short to generate a robust mean that accurately characterizes typical trail conditions. A problem associated with this option is that exceptionally (perhaps "unacceptably") poor trail conditions can be offset by good conditions elsewhere, particularly if the problem segment is relatively short in comparison to the rest of the trail. One option to address this deficiency is to calculate a "moving average" by calculating an average from a fixed number of consecutive transects, dropping the first and adding another at the end, hence the term "moving" average. This option produces a set of averages that are less sensitive to a single extreme or "outlier" value for an indicator. A standard would be set on mean conditions but evaluated against the moving average values for each trail. An advantage of this option is that standards would be violated less frequently by extreme or atypical conditions associated with a single point. The number of trail points included in the average directly influences the sensitivity of this option; the smaller the number, the more sensitivity to any single point.

CONCLUSIONS

While a variety of recreational uses are clearly appropriate in national parks and related areas, managers must ensure that these areas are spared significant impairment of natural and cultural resources. Park managers must apply professional judgment in evaluating the type and extent of recreation-related impacts when determining what constitutes "impairment." However, the type of research described in this study can help inform such determinations.

This research developed and applied state-of-the-art campsite and trail condition assessment and monitoring procedures and applied them to all Isle au Haut campsites and trails. A variety of campsite and trail condition indicators were identified in consultation with park staff. Protocols were developed, field-tested, and applied with results summarized for use in selecting standards of quality. Park staff participated in the field assessments and received training for future application of all procedures.

Guidance provided on the selection of campsite indicators and standards suggests a focus on campsite size, number of tree stumps, and informal trails. Two park staff should be able to assess these indicators is less than one day. Standards for site size could be established for individual sites and/ or for all sites combined. If the tree mortality represented by the large number of tree stumps is attributable primarily to natural causes or safety concerns, then the tree stump indicator should be omitted. An indicator on informal trails is recommended since survey staff saw several informal trails that were viewed as unnecessary at each site. Some of these appeared to leave the site close to one another and access the same general off-site areas.

For trails, resource conditions assessed by the trail survey are generally good, with a mean width of 28 inches and mean depth of 1.6 inches. However, soil loss as assessed by the CSA measure provided an extrapolated estimate of 553 cubic yards of soil loss for the entire formal trail system. Only 2 percent of the transects were classified as having mud or standing water. The occurrence of visitor-created informal trails branching from the formal trail system was identified as a moderate problem. All of these indicators are recommended and can be assessed by two park staff in three days. Omitting the muddiness indicator (including trail substrate estimates) and the CSA procedures would likely reduce field assessment time to two days.

Trail widening and creation or proliferation of informal trails are the indicators most likely to be related strongly to amount of visitor use. Due to the complexity of the environmental and use-related factors that influence resource conditions along trails, it is difficult for resource-based research to provide specific or credible guidance on what level of reduction of visitor use would be necessary to achieve specified levels of improvement in indicator conditions. Instead, managers should reduce use incrementally (e.g., 10 percent reductions) with subsequent monitoring to evaluate improvement in the conditions of indicators whose standards were violated. Given the park's mandate for low levels of use and associated impacts at Isle au Haut, park staff also should consider experiential factors when evaluating appropriate Isle au Haut use levels. It is likely that experiential qualities for Isle au Haut hikers will degrade and violate their standards of quality sooner than will trail conditions.

5 Indicators of Quality for the Visitor Experience on Ocean Drive

Automobiles are both a form of transportation to and through national parks and a mechanism for experiencing these areas. Park visitors use automobiles to access attraction sites or to travel to a location to participate in an activity. However, studies consistently have shown that large numbers of people in the United States also consider driving a recreation activity (Manning 1999). Recently, "driving for pleasure" was ranked as one of the most popular recreational activities in the United States (National Survey on Recreation and the Environment, 2000–2002). Some NPS units (e.g., national parkways) were established and designed explicitly to provide recreational driving experiences through scenic landscapes (Havlick 2002).

Most studies of vehicle use in national parks have focused on their environmental impacts (Forman et al. 2003). Few empirical studies have examined the recreational driving experience. The study described in this chapter examines the recreational driving experience along Acadia's Ocean Drive, the most scenic portion of the Park Loop Road. Objectives of the study were to (1) determine the importance of Ocean Drive to the "park experience," (2) gather data to help identify indicators of quality for the recreational driving experience, and (3) explore differences between recreational driving and more conventional transportation-oriented driving.

Concepts of Quality

The Highway Capacity Manual (HCM) is a widely used reference for roadway planning that defines transportation quality according to six "levels of service" (LOS), labeled A through F (Transportation Research Board 2000).

This chapter is an edited version of the following paper: Jeffrey Hallo and Robert Manning, "Transportation and Recreation: A Case Study of Visitors Driving for Pleasure at Acadia National Park, *Journal of Transport Geography* (forthcoming).

The conventional concept of quality in the field of transportation planning is determined predominantly by measures of travel efficiency. For example, LOS A is characterized by completely unimpeded traffic flows and LOS F is described by conditions where traffic ceases to flow (i.e., gridlock). This is measured in the HCM on a two-lane scenic or recreational road by the percent of time a vehicle spends following another vehicle. For example, LOS A is characterized by less than 40 percent of time spent following another vehicle, and LOS E occurs when a vehicle spends greater than 85 percent of time following another vehicle. LOS F occurs when traffic flows are greater than a road's capacity and vehicle travel ceases.

The HCM and its LOS framework provide an intuitive and useful approach for addressing the concept of quality in transportation. However, is the HCM's LOS framework appropriate for roads planned and managed for recreational driving? Is quality on recreational roads best represented by efficiency-oriented variables like percent of time spent following another vehicle?

Answers to these questions might be informed by the concept of quality as considered in contemporary park and outdoor recreation planning and management frameworks such as Visitor Experience and Resource Protection (VERP). As described in the introduction, these frameworks rely on indicators and standards that are formulated to define the level of resource and experiential quality that should be maintained in the context of parks and outdoor recreation.

Study Area

As described in chapter 1, the Park Loop Road is a principal attraction at Acadia. The Ocean Drive section of the Park Loop Road starts immediately after the park entrance station and closely follows the coastline for 1.5 miles. Like many high-use, landmark roads in national parks, Ocean Drive is intended to provide a recreational experience for visitors. Several of the park's most popular sites—Thunder Hole (an unusual geological feature), Sand Beach, and trailheads for the Beehive and Gorham Mountain Trails—are located along Ocean Drive. Moreover, the road itself was designed in the 1920s by the famous landscape architect, Fredrick Law Olmsted, Jr., to provide visitors classic scenic views of the rocky, picturesque Maine coast. Ocean Drive is now managed as a one-way road. The road has two lanes, and visitors are allowed to park in the right-hand lane. Parking lots along

Ocean Drive and much of the right-hand lane become filled with vehicles during the peak-use season (July and August). Ocean Drive is used by personal vehicles, recreational vehicles (RVs), tour buses, and a park-sponsored bus system called the Island Explorer.

STUDY METHODS

Interviews and surveys were used to gather data to study the experiential aspects of driving for pleasure on Ocean Drive.

Qualitative Interviews

Qualitative, semi-structured interviews were conducted with Ocean Drive private vehicle users (both drivers and passengers). These interviews asked respondents a core set of questions, but the interviewer was permitted to ask additional clarifying or exploratory questions. The first vehicle user encountered nearing the exit of Ocean Drive was asked to participate in the study. At the end of the interview (or if a vehicle user refused to be interviewed), the next most proximate vehicle user was asked to participate in the study. All interviews were recorded using a microcassette player and later transcribed.

A content analysis of transcripts was performed. This analytical method involves searching transcribed text for recurring words or themes that make up its primary meaning (Patton 2002). Transcripts from interviews of Ocean Drive vehicle users were coded based on established procedures in the literature (Patton 2002; Miles and Huberman 1994). Coding is the process of segmenting data into simpler, general categories that may be used to expand and tease out new questions and levels of interpretation (Coffey and Atkinson 1996). All codes were developed inductively—as they emerged from the text of the transcripts—but the core questions were used as an organizing framework. Transcribed text was coded only once, as it pertained to the most relevant question. However, multiple codes could be assigned to a single respondent's reply to a question. The frequencies of codes were calculated for each question.

Visitor Survey

A representative sample of Ocean Drive private vehicle users was selected and asked to complete a questionnaire as they exited the road. This survey applied methods adapted from a study that measured quality of service and customer satisfaction for urban road users (SAIC 2003). Survey respondents were asked to (1) identify the ten most important features from a list of features found on many national park scenic roads, and (2) rank the top five features of those identified that they consider the most important on a national park scenic road. Features provided to respondents replicated all those listed in the original study of urban road users, but it also included "scenery," "access to important park sites and attractions," and "opportunities to drive for pleasure" as additional features. These features were added to provide a more comprehensive list of items that might be important to park road users.

STUDY FINDINGS

Qualitative Interviews

A total of forty interviews were conducted. Data saturation, the point at which little new information emerged, was used to help determine an appropriate number of interviews to conduct (Marshall 1996). Respondents were intercepted at Thunder Hole, near the end of Ocean Drive. Interviews lasted approximately twenty minutes, and over three hundred pages of transcribed text were produced from the forty interviews. Codes resulting from key questions are shown in table 5.1 and are discussed below.

Respondents were asked two questions to gather information on the experiential importance of Ocean Drive. First, respondents were asked why they were driving on Ocean Drive. The most frequently occurring code associated with this question indicates that respondents were using the road to "see or get to specific sites." For example, Respondent 30 indicated that she was using the road solely for transportation.

> *Respondent 30*: We wanted to come here to see Thunder Hole and Sand Beach.

> *Interviewer*: So, is it part of the experience to drive on the road or is it just that the road's the way you get to Sand Beach and Thunder Hole?

> *Respondent 30*: The road's just the way you get to Sand Beach and Thunder Hole.

TABLE 5.1 Codes assigned for responses to key questions.

Question	Code	Frequency
"Why are you driving on Ocean Drive today?"		
	To see or get to specific sites	19
	To see beautiful scenery	6
	To begin exploring the park	4
	To see the park with others	3
	To go on a leisurely drive	1
"Can you describe the role that Ocean Drive plays in your overall visit to Acadia National Park? In other words, how important or unimportant is driving on Ocean Drive to your experience at Acadia National Park?" Important because it . . .		
	Allows access to and enjoyment of scenery/ocean	19
	Provides access to places of interest	15
	It's the "opening act" or "main act" for the park	8
	Not much different from other parts of the Park Loop Road	2
"What are the three things you enjoyed most about your visit on Ocean Drive?"		
	Seeing scenery	27
	One-way nature of road	14
	Accessing/seeing particular locations	13
	Parking and pull-offs to see scenery	8
	A tranquil, relaxing atmosphere	5
	Not too much traffic	4
	Cleanliness and maintenance of the road	2
	Ease of wayfinding because of signs	2
	Safety of the road	1
	Sharing it with family and friends	1
	Driving on the road	1
	Using the Island Explorer	1
"What are the three things you enjoyed least about your visit on Ocean Drive?"		
	Traffic and crowds	14
	Lack of parking	5
	Parking in the right lane	2
	Dangerous driving conditions (e.g., pedestrians, bicyclists, narrow)	2
	Fees or fee structure	2
	Vistas obscured by vegetation	1
	The one-way road	1
	Tour busses	1
	Others speeding	1
	Lack of signs	1

continued

TABLE 5.1 *Continued*

Question	Code	Frequency
"What things make for a good day while driving on Ocean Drive?"		
	Good weather	2
	Little traffic or crowds	15
	Beautiful scenery	4
	Friendly and courteous people	2
	A well-maintained road	2
	Easy access or places to park	2
	People obeying regulations	1

In other responses associated with this code, there is some suggestion that the road is contributing to the experience of visiting the park. This was seen in the response by Respondent 29.

Respondent 29: [We're on the road] to see Thunder Hole and to go on some of the trails.

Interviewer: Okay. Is the road just a way to get to these places or is the road part of the experience as well?

Respondent 29: This time it was just to get to the place, to the particular places. In the past, it's been to experience, you know, the whole thing.

Other codes for this question indicate that some Ocean Drive visitors use the road for more experiential reasons such as to "see beautiful scenery," "begin exploring the park," "see the park with others," or "go on a leisurely drive." For example, Respondent 1 stated that she was using Ocean Drive "because of the beautiful scenery [and] we have some visitors from out of state and we want to show them the area." Similarly, Respondent 36 said, "We're just driving through to stop here and there and just take a leisurely drive. We've been here before, but we enjoy it."

The second question focusing on the experiential importance of Ocean Drive was "Can you describe the role that Ocean Drive plays in your overall visit to Acadia National Park? In other words, how important or unimportant is driving on Ocean Drive to your experience at Acadia National Park?" Most codes associated with this question indicate the importance of Ocean Drive. Respondent 20 said that Ocean Drive was "very important. It's scenery that you can't see from other parts. I mean it's, to me, it's a great drive, a beautiful scenic drive." This quote characterizes many responses described by the code "Ocean Drive is important because it allows access to and enjoyment of the scenery." Other respondents, like Respondent 31, suggested that driving on Ocean Drive was a primary component—"an opening act" or "main act"—of their visit to Acadia.

Respondent 31: It's a very important section of the whole thing.

Interviewer: Can you describe why?

Respondent 31: Partly because it is in such a beautiful section. That's why I think it's the most visited also. This is just one minor attraction in a number of attractions here. Ocean Drive leads you right up to this part of the ocean, this part of the park. Without it, you'd be missing half the experience. That's why everybody else is here.

Interviewer: So, literally half the experience for you is coming down this road?

Respondent 31: Absolutely. It's a wonderful part of the experience.

Respondents were asked several questions intended to help understand the variables that add to or detract from a quality recreational driving experience on Ocean Drive. Respondents were asked to describe three things they enjoyed most about their visit on Ocean Drive. Many responses to this question were described by predominantly experiential codes such as "seeing scenery," "parking and pulloffs to see scenery," "tranquil, relaxing atmosphere," or "not too much traffic." For example, Respondent 40 said, "It's not a lot of traffic, you know, not like it is out in Bar Harbor and it's a good road and you can see a lot, it's scenic." Other codes mention the importance of conventional transportation concepts (e.g., parking, traveling/access, one-way nature of the road, directional signs), but these concepts were often expressed in a manner related to the recreational experience of visiting the park. For example, Respondent 17 reported that the one-way nature of the road allowed visitors to see the scenery better.

Respondent 17: I think the fact that it's one-way is very good. That way you . . . don't have to worry about oncoming traffic, so if you're in the left lane, you can enjoy the scenery as a driver and you know, just keeping an eye on the right hand, but you're not worrying about oncoming traffic or something like that. It makes it a lot easier.

Respondents were next asked what three things they enjoyed least about their visit on Ocean Drive. Responses to this question are represented by several codes. Respondent 11 replied by saying "The least [enjoyable]? The crowds, the lack of parking, just basically having to do with that I think is too many cars are allowed here." This response represents the two most frequently occurring codes to this question, "traffic and crowds" and "lack of parking." Respondent 2 indicated that traffic and crowding were not enjoyable, but he also did not enjoy the dangerous driving conditions created by the level of vehicle use on the road.

Respondent 2: It's too crowded with the traffic and stuff and there's a lot of people that are parking you know on the shoulder and then . . . it's kind of dangerous with a lot of bicycles riding around. I mean I saw some kids on bikes. I wouldn't let, you know, let my kids [on the road], that's besides the point, but yeah basically it's a little too crowded and the roads are a little small.

Several other codes that were assigned only once or twice emerged in response to this question. These codes include "parking in the right lane," "fees or fee structure," "vistas obscured by vegetation," "the one-way road," "tour buses," and "lack of signs." For example, Respondent 20 said "It's one-way and once you go there, you can't get back [and] the parking in the right lane is annoying at times, when there's a lot of traffic."

Respondents were asked what makes for a good day when driving on Ocean Drive. "Good weather" was the most frequent response code. Other response codes to this question are more manageable variables and therefore more useful. "Little traffic or crowds" was the next most frequently occurring code. Respondent 34 indicated that both weather and traffic levels were important variables.

Respondent 34: Weather is the first thing, I think.

Interviewer: Anything else?

Respondent 34: Oh, it depends on the number of people who are on there . . . the more, the less fun.

Other response codes associated with this question included "beautiful scenery," "friendly and courteous people," "a well-maintained road," "ease of access or places to park," and "people obeying regulations." For example, in response to this question Respondent 21 said, "Well, the road is, appears to be maintained well, which is important. If it was a bad road, then it would be less enjoyable."

Survey Findings

A total of 262 Ocean Drive users were approached and asked to complete a questionnaire. Of those approached, 128 agreed to participate, representing a response rate of 48.9 percent.

The survey of Ocean Drive visitors produced results showing the percentage of respondents who rated a list of road features as being important on a national park scenic road (table 5.2). The greatest number of visitors— more than two-thirds of respondents—reported that scenery (81 percent), access to park sites or attractions (72 percent), and traffic volume (67 percent) were important on national park scenic roads. Additionally, a majority of respondents reported that pavement quality (59 percent), visibility of signs or traffic signals (58 percent), speed limit (56 percent), traffic flow (52 percent), and opportunities to drive for pleasure (52 percent) were important on national park scenic roads. Conversely, less than 10 percent of respondents reported signalized intersections or signals (8 percent), merging traffic (7 percent), unsignalized cross-streets or driveways (5 percent), and traffic signal timing (5 percent) as being important on national park scenic roads.

These results differed to some extent from those of a similar survey of service quality on urban roads (table 5.2; SAIC 2003). More than two-thirds of respondents to the survey of service quality on urban roads reported that visibility of signs/signals (77 percent), traffic flow (77 percent), pavement quality (77 percent), and left-turn-only lanes at intersections (73 percent) were important. Also, on urban roads, a majority of respondents reported that traffic volume (55 percent), ability to maneuver (55 percent), and aggressive drivers (50 percent) were important. Speed limit (9 percent) was the only factor on urban roads selected as being important by less than 10 percent of respondents.

Results from this survey suggest the most important features on each

TABLE 5.2 Percentage of respondents identifying the most important features on national park scenic roads compared to urban roads.

Features	National park scenic road	Urban roads
Scenery	81	—
Access to important park sites and attractions	72	—
Traffic volume (amount of traffic on roadway)	67	55
Pavement quality	59	77
Visibility of signs and/or traffic signals	58	77
Speed limit	56	9
Rate of traffic flow (smoothness, pace, continuity, etc.)	52	77
Opportunities to drive for pleasure	52	—
Spacing of moving vehicles (density of traffic)	47	32
Trees	46	27
Sidewalks	44	23
Ability to maneuver vehicle (change lanes, merge into traffic, etc.)	43	55
Roadway width (overall roadway width)	40	32
Pedestrians or bicyclists	37	14
Consistency of speed	26	14
Number of lanes on roadway	25	36
Aggressive drivers	23	50
A divided roadway (with a center median or barrier)	17	41
Left-turn-only lanes at intersections	16	73
Consistency/reliability of travel time to destination	15	36
Interaction between vehicles	14	32
Overall travel time to destination	13	41
Truck and/or bus traffic	12	27
Right-turn-only lanes at intersections	10	41
Two-way center left-turn lane	10	18
Signalized intersections (or number of signals)	8	41
Frequency of merging traffic	7	27
Frequency of unsignalized cross-streets and driveway entrances	5	18
Timing of traffic signals (length of red/green for each movement)	5	41

type of road (table 5.3). The five most important features (on average and in rank order) for a national park scenic road were scenery, access to park sites/ attractions, opportunities to drive for pleasure, visibility of signs/signals, and speed limit. In comparison, the most important features on urban roads were visibility of signs/signals, timing of traffic signals, ability to maneuver, left-turn-only lanes, rate of traffic flow, and traffic volume (the latter three items were tied in their overall average ranking).

TABLE 5.3 Comparison of results from a question asking respondents to rank the five most important features on national park scenic roads and urban roads.

Features	National park scenic road	Urban roads
Scenery	1	—
Access to important park sites and attractions	2	—
Opportunities to drive for pleasure	3	—
Visibility of signs and/or traffic signals	4	1
Speed limit	5	Not ranked in top 5
Timing of traffic signals (length of red/green for each movement)	Not ranked in top 5	2
Ability to maneuver vehicle (change lanes, merge into traffic, etc.)	Not ranked in top 5	3
Traffic volume (amount of traffic on roadway)	Not ranked in top 5	4, tied
Rate of traffic flow (smoothness, pace, continuity, etc.)	Not ranked in top 5	4, tied
Left-turn-only lanes at intersections	Not ranked in top 5	4, tied

DISCUSSION

Importance of Ocean Drive to the Visitor Experience

Results from this study support the idea that Ocean Drive provides both a form of transportation and a means of experiencing Acadia. Some interview response codes (such as the code indicating that visitors are driving the road to "get to or see specific sites") suggest an interest by some visitors in the road for more conventional transportation purposes. However, even within the text associated with these more transportation-focused codes, some references connote experiential aspects of the road. For other visitors, the road seems more useful as a means for experiencing the park. Codes (and associated text) related to enjoying scenery, exploring the park, leisurely driving, and experiencing the park with others indicate that the primary intended purpose of the road for some visitors is experiential, not transportation-oriented. However, it may be that transportation aspects of the road are assumed by visitors who focused their responses on experiential uses of the road.

Ocean Drive seems to play a distinct role in many visitors' overall experience at Acadia. Most interview response codes indicate that it is a principal part of the experience at Acadia because it provides either access to and enjoyment of scenery, access to places of interest, or an "opening or main act" for a visit to the park. Again, these codes (and associated text) suggest a dual role for Ocean Drive in the visitor experience. It provides access through transportation, but it also allows people to see a scenic portion of the park with some of the park's primary attractions.

Indicators of the Recreational Driving Experience

Interview results suggest several potential indicators of driving for pleasure on Ocean Drive. First, vehicle use levels and related perceptions of vehicle congestion or crowding may be a primary indicator. Crowding/congestion was the most frequent code to emerge from a question asking visitors what they enjoyed least about Ocean Drive. It also emerged in codes for questions about what visitors enjoyed most (e.g., "not too much traffic") and what constitutes an ideal experience. Furthermore, other codes in these questions may be related closely to use levels on the road. For example, the tranquil, relaxing atmosphere cited by respondents as being enjoyable is likely to be at least partially related to the number of vehicles that use the road at any one time. Also, variables such as parking availability, safety of driving along the road, and the cleanliness and maintenance condition of Ocean Drive may be related closely to vehicle use levels on the road.

A second potential indicator is scenic value; "seeing scenery" was the most frequent code for what people enjoyed along Ocean Drive. But, how can scenic value be measured and managed? Other codes emerging from the interviews provide possible answers to this question. Respondents suggested that maintenance of roadway vistas and litter may be important variables in the park experience along Ocean Drive. These variables might be used as proxies to measure and manage scenic value along the road. For example, litter detracts from Ocean Drive's scenic value. Litter could be monitored along the road and managed to ensure that levels do not reach a point where they are considered unacceptable by park visitors. Moreover, key viewing points along the road could be kept clear of vegetation or other visual obstructions to enjoying the park's scenery.

Third, codes assigned to interview responses related to parking availability, speed of travel, the one-way nature of the road, wayfinding and signage, and driving conditions suggest that freedom, convenience, and safety of travel represent other possible indicators. These codes also provide potential ways in which freedom, convenience, and safety of travel might be measured and managed. For example, the percent of time that parking lots are at their capacity or number of opportunities for drivers to slow down or stop along the road might be measured directly or through a survey of visitors. (The issue of parking lot capacity is described more fully in chapter 20.) Similarly, safety of travel might be measured through a count of safety incidents (e.g., speeding violations or accidents) or by measuring perceptions of safety among visitors.

Comparing Recreational and "Transportation-Oriented" Driving

Survey results allow some general comparison of important variables for driving for pleasure and "transportation-oriented" driving. Several similarities appear in the top ten most important features on national park scenic roads and urban roads. Survey responses indicate that traffic volume, pavement quality, visibility of signs and traffic signals, and rate of traffic flow are variables that are important to a majority of users of both national park scenic roads and urban roads. Likewise, frequency of unsignalized cross-streets or driveway entrances and two-way center left-turn lanes were variables that were important to less than 20 percent of users of both road types.

Some differences were seen in variables selected as among the ten most important features on each type of road. Roadway features that had the largest absolute difference in percent of respondents who selected that feature are left-turn-only lanes at intersections, speed limit, timing of traffic signals, signalized intersections, right-turn-only lanes at intersections, and overall travel time to destinations. For example, speed limit was rated as being important by most national park scenic road survey respondents, but in the study of urban road users it was rated as important by only a small percentage of respondents. These differences seem to suggest that facilities or features found to a greater extent on urban roads are not viewed as important on national park scenic roads. However, the infrequency of these facilities or features on experiential roads might contribute to this finding.

Rankings for the five most important features on national park scenic roads suggest that Ocean Drive users value experiential aspects of the road as much, or more, than more conventional transportation-oriented aspects. For example, respondents rated scenery as the most important feature. The next two most important features—access to park sites/attractions and opportunities to drive for pleasure—also imply an experiential role for this type of road. However, transportation-oriented aspects of the road, such as being able to find and get to specific sites, are also evident in the ranking of the top five most important features on national park scenic roads. The only feature that is common in the rankings between national park scenic roads and urban roads is the visibility of signs/traffic signals.

Unfortunately, a statistical comparison of important variables on national park scenic roads and urban roads cannot be made from the survey results. The Acadia survey included scenery, access to important park sites and attractions, and opportunities to drive for pleasure as potential features. This was done to allow for a more complete (and arguably more accurate) examination of the most important roadway features on a national park scenic road. These features were not listed as options for selection in the comparison study of urban roads (SAIC 2003). Because of this discrepancy, a direct comparison of the percentage of respondents choosing each feature is inappropriate. However, results in this study may be used with reasonable reliability (as done above) to explore differences between national park scenic roads and urban roads by examining features appearing on both surveys. The above interpretation of survey results can be corroborated largely by triangulation with results from the qualitative portion of this study. As it is used here, triangulation is a process that can be used to judge and enhance the reliability of research findings by seeking a convergence of results using multiple methods, investigators, data sources, or theoretical lenses (Denzin 1970; Green, Caracelli, and Graham 1989; Tashakkori and Teddlie 1998). For example, vehicle crowding/congestion, signage, and the freedom and convenience of travel emerged as influential variables in results from both qualitative interviews and the quantitative survey.

Quality in Driving for Pleasure

The importance of traditional transportation concepts of travel efficiency and safety appear to be fully applicable to national park scenic roads. Potential indicators found in the qualitative component of this study such as speed of travel, parking, and wayfinding support this premise. Furthermore, comparison of the most important features on these roads and transportation-oriented urban roads indicates the importance of more traditional transportation concepts. For example, traffic volume, pavement quality, and visibility of traffic signs/signals all were rated as important by a majority of Ocean Drive users.

Potential indicators of quality suggested by study findings may serve as a basis for beginning to understand and manage the concept of quality of transportation in parks and other experiential contexts. Traditional transportation concepts are common indicators of quality to both experiential roads and transportation-oriented roads, but they may be manifested in very different ways. For example, traffic volumes (and associated perceptions of crowding or congestion) and traffic flow appear to influence the quality of both experiential and transportation-oriented roads. In the latter context, few examples exist for when high traffic volumes or low rates of traffic flow enhance quality. However, national park visitors driving for pleasure may want to slow down or stop frequently on more "experiential" roads. Visitors may slow down or stop to better appreciate scenery, to observe wildlife, or to enjoy a more leisurely driving experience. However, based on the results from this study, some use levels or use characteristics eventually may detract from the visitor experience. This indicates that traditional transportation indicators of quality need to be reregistered when applied in the context of a national park scenic road. For example, acceptable use levels for crowding or congestion on experiential roads might be lower than on urban roads.

Results of this study suggest that additional variables may need to be considered when planning and managing transportation quality on park roads. For example, opportunities to appreciate scenery—perhaps facilitated by providing stopping areas, maintaining roadway vistas, or through road designs focused on driving pleasure—should be considered in addition to traditional transportation variables. Also, speed limits were rated as important by a majority of respondents on experiential roads. This was not true for users of transportation-oriented urban roads. Speed limits on experiential roads may be more important to their users because they permit visitors to slow down or stop safely to appreciate the scenic beauty of a park.

Based on results from this study, other variables may need to be de-emphasized in planning and management of experiential roads as compared to transportation-oriented roads. These variables include turn lanes at intersections, traffic signal timing, and overall travel time to destinations. Little support was found for the importance of these variables in either the qualitative interviews or survey responses. Another factor that may need to be de-emphasized or reexamined is the percent of time spent following another vehicle, which is used in the HCM as a primary measure of quality on recreational or experiential roads (Transportation Research Board 2000). This measure did not emerge in the study of Ocean Drive. However, management of Ocean Drive as a two-lane, one-way road where parking is allowed on the road is not considered in the HCM, which makes a direct examination of this variable difficult. In the study of Ocean Drive, the number of vehicles within sight appeared to be important to respondents' experiences. This seems to be a more intuitive expression of an indicator for vehicle crowding or congestion given the scenic importance of Ocean Drive. Other findings, such as the lack of importance of travel times to a destination and the desire for a leisurely driving experience, support the idea that being delayed behind another vehicle is not of high importance to users of national park scenic roads. However, further research to examine more specifically the importance of this potential indicator to users of experiential roads may be warranted.

CONCLUSIONS

The study described in this chapter explored interrelationships between concepts of transportation and recreation in a national park. Ocean Drive, like many similar roads in the national park system, is a principal contributor to many visitors' overall "park experience." Most visitors to Acadia travel on the road. But Ocean Drive also was designed to provide an experience, and based on the findings from this study, it fulfills its intended purpose. At Acadia, transportation and recreation are inseparable companions in the visitor experience. This is most likely the case in many national parks and related areas.

The presence of scenic, experiential roads in most national parks suggests a need to understand more fully the experience of visitors who drive for pleasure on these roads. Moreover, management of transportation in parks should deliberately and thoughtfully address concerns about the quality of this experience. Indicators of quality may serve as a conceptual basis for such management. On Ocean Drive, the quality of the visitor experience can be managed using indicators of quality related to vehicle crowding and congestion; scenic value; and freedom, convenience, and safety of travel.

6 Research to Guide Trail Management at Acadia National Park

Acadia includes approximately 120 miles of trails, and hiking is one of the most popular recreation activities in the park (Littlejohn 1999). The popularity of the trail system presents a challenge to park staff in their efforts to protect trails from unacceptable visitor impacts, such as soil compaction and erosion, trampling of vegetation, trail widening, and creation of social or visitor-caused trails (Hammitt and Cole 1998). Trail use also must be managed to maintain the quality of visitor experience with regard to the social impacts of visitor use, including crowding and unacceptable trail management practices (Manning 1999).

Management of trails can be guided by indicators and standards of quality as suggested in the National Park Service Visitor Experience and Resource Protection (NPS VERP) framework. This study was designed to support formulation of trail-related indicators and standards of quality and addressed the resource, social/experiential, and management components of park management.

STUDY METHODS

The first phase of research focused on identifying potential indicators of quality. A visitor survey incorporated a series of open- and close-ended questions. Open-ended questions asked visitors what they enjoyed most and least about hiking in Acadia, and close-ended questions asked visitors to rate the importance of several trail-related issues. The survey was admin-

This chapter is an edited version of the following publication: Kelly Goonan, Robert Manning, and William Valliere, "Research to Guide Trail Management at Acadia National Park," *Proceedings of the 2008 Northeastern Recreation Research Symposium,* USDA Forest Service General Technical Report NRS-P-42, 266–74, 2009.

istered to a representative sample of hikers throughout the trail system yielding 249 completed questionnaires.

The second phase of research focused on identifying potential standards of quality for selected indicator variables. A visitor survey incorporated a series of questions that asked respondents to judge the acceptability of range of impacts to resource, social/experiential, and managerial conditions of trails. These questions adopted normative theory and methods (Manning 1985; Shelby and Vaske 1991; Vaske et al. 1986; Vaske and Whittaker 2004), and used narrative/numerical, visual, and long and short question formats, and several evaluative dimensions, including "preference," "acceptability," "management action," and "displacement" (Manning et al. 1999; Manning and Freimund 2004). (These theoretical and methodological issues are described in chapters 10, 12, and 13.) Three indicators were addressed: resource conditions, crowding, and type and intensity of management practices. The survey was administered to a representative sample of hikers throughout the trail system yielding 287 completed questionnaires.

STUDY FINDINGS

Indicators of Quality

Respondents were asked several questions to determine potential indicators of quality of the recreation experience afforded by Acadia's trail system. Questions addressed topics such as what visitors enjoyed most/least about their visit; the most desirable qualities of the park; and evaluation of problems or issues within the park. The results of this phase of research identified trail impacts (such as soil erosion and trail widening) and crowding as important indicators of quality. Level of trail development and management also was considered a potentially important indicator of quality, as trail impacts often are addressed through a range of development practices such as signage and trail surfacing.

Standards of Quality

Respondents were asked a series of questions to help identify standards of quality for each of the three indicator variables identified above. The first section of the survey addressed trail impacts. First, respondents were asked to evaluate the acceptability of five computer-generated photographs depicting increasing levels of visitor-caused soil and vegetation impact (figure 6.1). Acceptability was measured using a nine-point Likert-type scale rang-

Photo 1

Photo 2

Photo 3

Photo 4

Figure 6.1 *Trail impact study photographs.*

Photo 5

ing from −4 ("Very Unacceptable") to +4 ("Very Acceptable"). The second question asked respondents to indicate which photograph showed the amount of trail impact they would prefer to see. The next question addressed visitor displacement, and asked respondents to report the photograph that showed the level of trail impact that is so unacceptable that they would no longer hike on park trails. Respondents were given the opportunity to report that, "none of the photographs are so unacceptable that I would no longer hike on the trails I hiked today." The fourth question asked

TABLE 6.1 Summary of respondent assessments of trail impact levels, acceptability for the eight trail-management approaches, and use level.

	Trail impacts	Trail management	Number of other hikers	
	(mean photo number)	(mean acceptability rating)	Mean	Median
Acceptability	2.5		37.5	—
Preference	1.2		15.4	12.0
Displacement	4.3		54.2	44.0
Management action	2.8		84.5	50.0
Typically seen	1.7		18.8	15.0
Photo 1: No management		3.0		
Photo 2: Occasional rock borders		2.8		
Photo 3: Continuous rock borders		0.9		
Photo 4: "Stay on Trail" sign		2.5		
Photo 5: Stone paving		0.7		
Photo 6: Wooden planking		1.4		
Photo 7: Brushed social trail		2.1		
Photo 8: Brushed and signed social trail		2.1		

respondents to report which photograph showed the highest level of trail impact that the NPS should allow before restricting visitor use. Respondents were given the opportunity to report that, "none of the photographs show a high enough level of environmental impact to restrict people from hiking on these trails" or that, "the number of people hiking on these trails should not be restricted." The final question asked respondents to indicate the photograph that looked most like the amount of environmental impact that they typically saw on the trails they hiked.

A summary of visitor responses to this battery of questions referring to trail impacts is shown in table 6.1. Study findings suggest that increasing levels of trail impacts are found to be increasingly unacceptable. This is shown graphically by the social norm curve in figure 6.2. Mean acceptability rating falls out of the acceptable range and into the unacceptable range between photographs 2 and 3. Respondents prefer to see very low levels of trail impact, with a mean photo preference of 1.2. Visitors reported a displacement level corresponding to an average photograph number of 4.3, but this is substantially underestimated because 43 percent of respondents re-

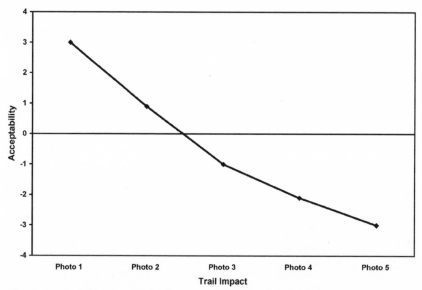

Figure 6.2 *Social norm curve for the acceptability of trail impacts.*

ported that none of the photographs showed a level of trail impact that was so unacceptable that they would be displaced from the area. Visitors felt that the NPS should allow trail impacts corresponding to an average photograph number of 2.8 before restricting people from using the trails. However, this is also underestimated because 17 percent of respondents reported that none of the photographs showed a level of impact sufficient to restrict use, and 5 percent felt that visitor use should not be restricted under any circumstances. Finally, visitors reported that they saw trail impacts corresponding to a mean photograph number of 1.7 on the day they were contacted for the study.

The second section of the survey explored visitor attitudes toward alternative trail-management practices used to encourage visitors to stay on the designated trail thereby limiting environmental impacts. Respondents were presented with a series of eight computer-generated photographs depicting alternative trail-management practices and asked to evaluate the acceptability of each according to the same response scale described above (figure 6.3). A summary of findings is presented in table 6.1. Visitors found "no management" and "occasional rock borders" to be the most acceptable trail-management practices, and "continuous rock borders" and "stone pav-

Photo 1: No management

Photo 5: Stone paving

Photo 2: Occasional rock border

Photo 6: Wooden planking

Photo 3: Continuous rock border

Photo 7: Brushed social trail

Photo 4: "Stay on Trail" sign

Photo 8: Brushed and signed social trail

Figure 6.3 *Trail management study photographs.*

ing" to be the least acceptable. However, none of the management practices received a mean negative acceptability rating.

The final section of the survey addressed crowding levels on trails through the number of encounters with other hikers. Respondents were first presented with a range of encounters with other hikers (from no other hikers up to more than one hundred other hikers). Scenarios were presented in a narrative/numeric format, and respondents were asked to evaluate the acceptability of each encounter level using the same nine-point response scale as the previous questions. After evaluating each encounter level, respondents were asked to indicate the number of other hikers they would prefer to see on the trails per day. The third question addressed displacement by asking respondents to indicate the maximum number of other hikers seen per day before they would no longer hike these trails. Respondents were given the option to report that they "would continue to hike these trails regardless of the number of other hikers seen." The fourth question asked respondents to indicate the maximum number of other hikers seen per day that the NPS should allow on trails before restricting hikers. Respondents were given the option to report that, "the number of hikers on these trails should not be restricted." The fifth question asked the approximate number of other hikers the respondent saw while hiking on the day they were administered the survey. Next, respondents were asked how much time (in minutes) they had spent hiking on the day of the survey. Finally, respondents were asked to rate how crowded they felt on the trails they hiked. The rating was based on a scale of 1 ("Not at all crowded") to 9 ("Extremely crowded").

A summary of visitor responses to the battery of questions addressing crowding is shown in table 6.1. Study findings suggest that encountering increasing numbers of other hikers on trails is increasingly unacceptable. This is presented graphically in the social norm curve shown in figure 6.4. The mean acceptability rating falls out of the acceptable range into the unacceptable range at an encounter rate of about 37 other hikers per day. Respondents prefer to see a mean of about 15 other hikers per day on trails in Acadia. Visitors reported that they would be displaced from the trails if they encountered more than about 54 other hikers per day, but this is an underestimate because approximately 25 percent of respondents reported that they would continue hiking the trails regardless of the number of other hikers they saw. Visitors felt that the NPS should allow an encounter level of

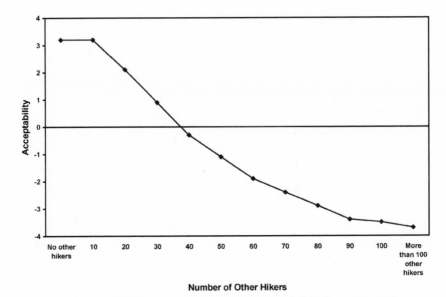

Figure 6.4 *Social norm curve for the acceptability of encountering other hikers.*

about 85 hikers per day before restricting use on the trails, but this is also an underestimate because approximately 52 percent of respondents felt that visitor use should not be restricted. Finally, visitors reported seeing an average of about 18 other hikers, and perceived that crowding levels were low. About 54 percent of visitors reported that they felt "not at all crowded" while hiking on the day they were contacted for this study.

A Comparison of High- and Low-Use Trails

Acadia's trails receive varying amounts of use. Trails sampled in phase 2 of the study were divided into "high-use" and "low-use" categories based on a census of the park's hiking trails. Trails that received 100 hikers or fewer per day were designated as "low-use," and trails receiving more than 100 hikers were designated as "high-use." Survey responses from these two classes of trails were compared and tested to see if normative standards of hikers varied significantly based on trail use level.

Little difference was observed regarding trail impacts between visitors on high- and low-use trails. An independent samples test found no significant differences of the acceptability of the range of trail impacts depicted in the study photographs. Of the other questions addressing trail impacts, the only variable showing a statistically significant difference between high-

and low-use trails is the level of impact that respondents reported seeing ($t = -4.675$; $p \leq 0.001$).

As with perceptions of trail impacts, very little difference was measured between high- and low-use trails with regard to the acceptability of photographs showing different trail-management practices. Responses to Photo 6 were the only ones to show a statistically significant difference between use levels ($t = -3.171$; $p = 0.002$). Respondents hiking on low-use trails gave the use of wooden planking a higher acceptability rating than respondents hiking on high-use trails (mean acceptability ratings of 1.87 and 0.93, respectively).

No significant differences were observed in responses to the range of encounter levels with other hikers. However, differences were observed in the approximate number of other hikers seen, the length of time spent hiking, and respondents' perceived level of crowding. Visitors hiking on high-use trails reported seeing a significantly higher number of other hikers than did visitors hiking on low-use trails ($t = 3.334$; $p = 0.001$). Visitors hiking on high-use trails also reported feeling significantly more crowded than hikers on low-use trails ($t = 4.212$; $p \leq 0.001$). On average, visitors on high-use trails also spent less time hiking than visitors on low-use trails ($t = -5.471$; $p \leq 0.001$).

CONCLUSION

Findings reported in this study suggest that visitors hiking in Acadia are receiving a relatively high-quality recreation experience. Visitors generally are encountering trail impacts that are much lower than the minimum acceptable condition they report and that are very close to the conditions they would prefer to see. Although visitors reported having seen a higher number of other hikers than they would prefer to see, the difference is very small and far below their minimum acceptable condition. Visitors typically rated no trail management or "light-handed" management as being more acceptable than "heavier-handed" forms of management and trail hardening. However, none of the trail-management practices depicted in the study received an average negative (unacceptable) rating, suggesting that visitors are willing to accept a variety of trail-management practices that are deemed necessary to protect trails and the hiking experience.

Relatively few significant differences were found between responses given by visitors hiking on high- and low-use trails. Differences that were observed tended to relate mostly to what visitors saw, such as environmental impacts on trails and the number of other hikers. For example, visitors hiking on high-use trails reported more encounters with other people than visitors hiking on low-use trails. Consequently, hikers on high-use trails reported feeling more crowded than hikers on low-use trails. Overall, it appears as though hikers on high-use trails are equally as accepting of management actions as hikers on low-use trails, and both groups display very similar norms relating to environmental and social conditions on park trails.

Study findings help provide an empirical basis for formulating indicators and standards of quality for the resource, social/experiential, and managerial components of trail management at Acadia. The range of potential standards of quality identified in the study provide a basis for designing and maintaining a diverse system of trail conditions and hiking opportunities across the park.

7

Indicators and Standards of Quality across Space and Time

Acadia includes several iconic attractions, including Cadillac Mountain, Sand Beach, and Thunder Hole, that attract thousands of visitors on peak-season days. Also within the park are several lesser-known and less-visited sites, such as Acadia Mountain and Little Hunter's Beach. During peak season, these alternate sites provide opportunities for lower-use recreation. Visitors to these alternate sites may be seeking a different recreation experience than those visiting more popular areas of the park. Visitation at popular sites also fluctuates throughout the day, providing an opportunity to consider how individuals visiting during nonpeak hours (i.e., early in the morning or late in the afternoon) may differ from those visiting during peak daytime hours.

The purpose of this study was to compare indicators and standards of quality of visitors based on their spatial and temporal distribution within the park. The three objectives of the study were to: (1) identify indicators and standards of quality of visitors at several locations throughout Acadia, (2) compare indicators for visitors to high-use and low-use sites, and (3) compare indicators and standards for visitors to high-use sites at peak and nonpeak times.

STUDY METHODS

Data for this analysis were collected by means of visitor surveys conducted during the summer use season at seventeen sites within Acadia (table 7.1). Questionnaires were self-administered, and included open- and close-ended

This chapter is an edited version of the following paper: Laura Anderson, Robert Manning, and William Valliere, "Indicators and Standards of Quality Across Space and Time," *Proceedings of the 2008 Northeastern Recreation Research Symposium*, USDA Forest Service General Technical Report NRS-P-42, 170–76, 2009.

TABLE 7.1 Acadia National Park survey locations and response rates.

High-use sites	Low-use sites	Peak-time sites	Nonpeak-time sites
Bass Harbor	Acadia Mountain	Sand Beach	Sand Beach
Cadillac Mountain	Compass Harbor	Ocean Drive	Ocean Drive
Echo Lake	Hunter's Beach	Thunder Hole	Thunder Hole
Jordan Pond	Little Hunter's Beach		
Ocean Drive	Loop Drive		
Precipice Trail	Seawall		
Sand Beach	Valley Cove		
Sieur de Monts			
Thunder Hole			
Wildwood Stables			
$N = 1{,}197$	$N = 759$	$N = 387$	$N = 298$
Response rate 72.7%	Response rate 84.7%	Response rate 68.4%	Response rate 72.1%

questions about indicators and standards of quality at each location. Based on discussions with park staff, ten of the seventeen sites were identified as "high-use" locations while the remaining seven sites were identified as "low-use" locations. Visitors to each location were surveyed between 9 a.m. and 4 p.m. on sample days. At high-use locations, every nth visitor was approached and asked to complete the survey, while at low-use locations a member of each group encountered was asked to participate. Three high-use locations—Ocean Drive, Sand Beach, and Thunder Hole—also were surveyed between 7 a.m. and 9 a.m. and 5 p.m. and 7 p.m. Visitors surveyed during early morning and evening hours were classified as "nonpeak time" respondents; individuals surveyed during the middle of the day were classified as "peak time" respondents.

A total of 1,197 questionnaires (72.7 percent response rate) were completed at the ten high-use locations and 759 (84.7 percent response rate) were completed at the seven low-use locations. At the three high-use locations where visitors were surveyed during different times of day, 387 questionnaires (68.4 percent response rate) were completed during peak hours and 298 (72.1 percent response rate) surveys were completed during nonpeak hours.

STUDY FINDINGS

Indicators of Quality

Visitors to the seventeen sites were asked about the characteristics of their group, their perceptions of crowding and other issues specific to their location, and their opinions about issues in Acadia in general. Respondents visited Acadia with an average of one to two other people. While no differences in group size emerged between those visiting at peak and nonpeak times, respondents at high-use locations came with slightly larger groups than those at low-use sites. Similarly, there were no differences in the amount of time that peak and nonpeak time visitors spent at the three high-use sites. However, visitors to low-use sites stayed at those locations for a longer time than those visiting high-use sites. Visitors to low-use sites reported that they had visited Acadia more times in the past than visitors to high-use sites. In the case of peak and nonpeak time visitors, the opposite finding emerged. On average, those visiting the three high-use sites during nonpeak times reported fewer previous visits to the park than those visiting at peak times.

Respondents were asked to rate how crowded they felt at their location on a nine-point scale, with 1 representing "not at all crowded" and 9 representing "extremely crowded." Overall, visitor perceptions of crowding at their locations were low, with average response scale scores ranging from 2.12 to 3.5. However, significant differences emerged in both the time and location comparisons. Visitors to high-use sites felt more crowded than visitors to low-use sites. Similarly, those visiting during peak times felt more crowded than those visiting during nonpeak times.

Survey respondents were presented with a list of potential issues at their location and asked to indicate the extent to which they perceived that these were problems. While several potential problems were listed for each individual site, only three were common across the seventeen locations considered in this analysis: (1) difficulty finding a parking place, (2) cars parked illegally, and (3) too many people in this area of the park. Significant differences emerged in five of the six comparisons made. Visitors to high-use sites rated difficulty finding a parking place and too many people as larger problems than did their low-use counterparts. Similarly, those visiting during peak times of day perceived greater problems with finding parking, illegal parking, and presence of too many people than did those visiting at nonpeak times.

Visitors also were asked four crowding-related questions about Acadia in general. Significant differences emerged in three cases. Although the magnitude of differences were not great, visitors to low-use sites agreed more strongly than did visitors to high-use sites that the park was generally too crowded and that road and traffic conditions create a safety hazard. Respondents visiting at peak times agreed more strongly that the park was generally too crowded than did those visiting at nonpeak times.

Standards of Quality

Respondents at the three peak and nonpeak time sites (Sand Beach, Thunder Hole, and Ocean Drive) were presented with a series of six photographs in which the number of people or vehicles at their location were varied. Respondents were asked to rate the acceptability of each photograph on a nine-point scale ranging from -4 representing "Very Unacceptable" to $+4$ representing "Very Acceptable." Visitors were then asked to choose the photograph that showed the use level they (1) would prefer to see, (2) would find so unacceptable that they would no longer visit, (3) thought was the highest level of use that the NPS should allow, and (4) thought looked most like the level of use they saw during their visit.

The series of Sand Beach photographs included 0, 172, 344, 516, 688, and 860 people (figure 7.1). The social norm curve resulting from graphing mean acceptability ratings is shown in figure 7.2. For both peak and nonpeak time visitors, acceptability levels decreased as the number of people in the photographs increased. At the three lowest use levels, there were no significant differences in acceptability ratings between the two groups. At the three highest use levels, however, nonpeak time visitors reported significantly lower acceptability ratings than peak time visitors.

Nonpeak time visitors indicated that they typically saw fewer people during their visit (191) and generally preferred to see fewer people (204) than did peak time visitors (283 and 253, respectively). There were no differences between the two groups, however, in their perceptions of the point at which visitor use should be restricted. Both groups perceived that management action would be needed when visitation reached about 550 people. Similarly, both groups indicated that they would be displaced at a similar point (around 730 people).

Photographs of Thunder Hole showed 0, 9, 18, 27, 36, and 45 people (figure 7.3). The social norm curve resulting from graphing mean acceptability ratings is shown in figure 7.4. As for Sand Beach, peak and nonpeak time visitors assigned lower acceptability ratings to photographs with greater numbers of people. However, at all six use levels, there were no significant differences in acceptability ratings between the two groups.

0 people   516 people

172 people   688 people

344 people   860 people

Figure 7.1 *Study photographs showing different use levels at Sand Beach.*

As for Sand Beach, nonpeak time visitors indicated that they typically saw fewer people during their visit (18) than did peak time visitors (25). However, there were no differences in the two groups in their preference, management action, and displacement ratings. Both groups perceived that management action would be needed when visitation reached about 30 people and reported that they would be displaced when visitation reached about 40 people.

Zero, 4, 8, 12, 16, and 21 vehicles were shown in photographs of Ocean Drive (figure 7.5). The social norm curve resulting from graphing mean acceptability ratings is shown in figure 7.6. As for Sand Beach and Thunder Hole, peak and nonpeak time visitors assigned lower acceptability ratings to photographs showing higher levels of use. At all six use levels, there were no significant differences in acceptability ratings between the two groups.

As for Sand Beach and Thunder Hole, nonpeak time visitors to Ocean

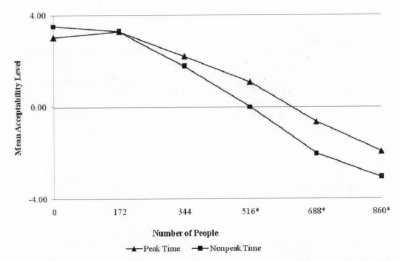

Figure 7.2 *Social norm curve for number of people at Sand Beach. *Indicates statistically significant difference between peak and non-peak times.*

Drive indicated that they typically saw lower use levels (5 vehicles at one time) during their visit than did peak time visitors (7 vehicles at one time). There were no differences in the two groups in their preference, management action, and displacement ratings. Both groups perceived that management action would be needed at 13 vehicles and perceived that they would be displaced when about 16 vehicles were present.

CONCLUSIONS

Comparisons by location and time were made for a number of indicator variables and related measures, including size of group, length of stay, number of previous visits, perceptions of crowding at the location, perceptions of problems, and opinions about Acadia as a whole. Significant differences were more prevalent in the high- and low-use site location comparisons than they were in the time comparisons, though similar patterns emerged in both cases.

Visitors to high-use sites belonged to slightly larger groups, stayed a shorter time, and reported fewer previous visits to Acadia than visitors to low-use sites. When asked about crowding-related issues specific to their location, high-use site visitors perceived greater crowding and felt that finding a parking place and too many people were bigger problems. When considering Acadia as a whole, however, the opposite pattern emerged. In this case,

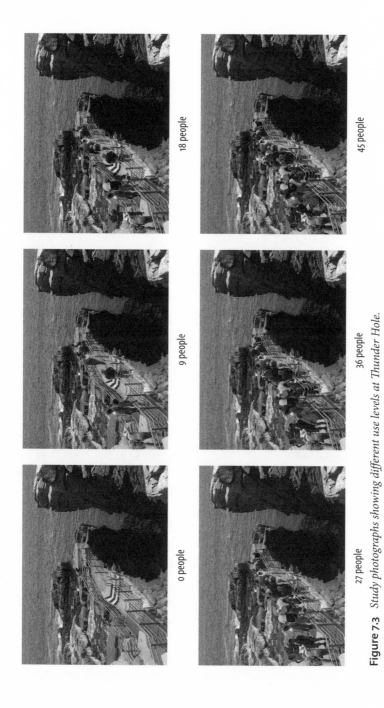

0 people

9 people

18 people

27 people

36 people

45 people

Figure 7.3 *Study photographs showing different use levels at Thunder Hole.*

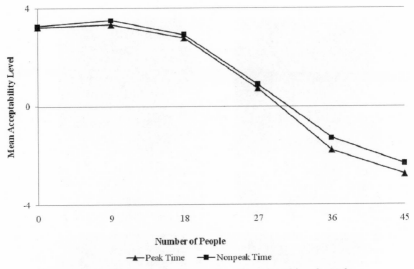

Figure 7.4 *Social norm curve for number of people at Thunder Hole.*

it was the low-use site visitors who felt more strongly that the park was too crowded and that road and traffic conditions created a safety hazard.

Similar to high-use site visitors, peak time visitors perceived greater crowding and felt that finding a parking place, people parking illegally, and too many people were bigger problems at their location than nonpeak time visitors. Unlike the location comparisons, peak time visitors reported more previous visits to Acadia than nonpeak time visitors. It should be noted, however, that median values for previous visitation were identical for the two groups. Also, when considering Acadia as a whole, peak time visitors felt the park was more crowded, a finding that seems to contradict the same comparison made by location.

The number of significant differences in the indicator variables suggests that recreationists to low-use sites and to high-use sites during nonpeak times have found different recreation experiences than their peak time, high-use site counterparts. These visitors perceived lower crowding and fewer problems at their location. The higher number of previous visits reported by low-use site visitors suggests that these may be "displaced" individuals who have sought out less popular recreation areas to cope with crowding. (The issues of displacement and coping are addressed more fully in chapter 11.) However, this cannot be confirmed, since no direct measure of displacement was included in the study.

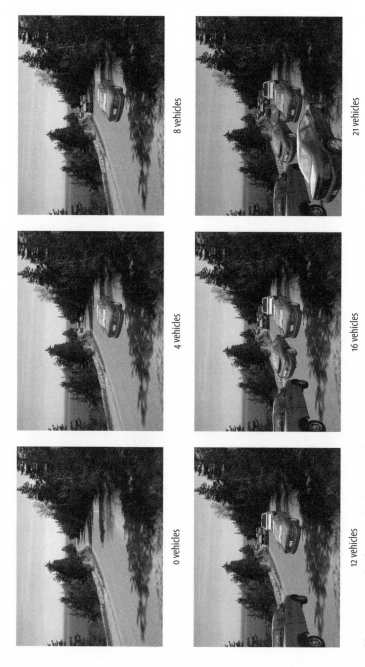

0 vehicles

4 vehicles

8 vehicles

12 vehicles

16 vehicles

21 vehicles

Figure 7.5 *Study photographs showing different use levels along Ocean Drive.*

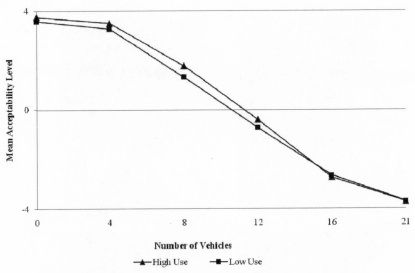

Figure 7.6 *Social norm curve for number of vehicles along Ocean Drive.*

Comparisons of crowding standards by time revealed few significant differences. As would be expected, nonpeak time visitors at all three locations reported seeing fewer other people or vehicles than did peak time visitors. However, with the exception of a marginally significant difference in encounter preferences at Sand Beach, there were no differences between the two groups in preference, management action, and displacement ratings. Furthermore, the social norm curves were nearly identical for both groups at all three locations, except at Sand Beach, where nonpeak time visitors reported higher unacceptability ratings at the three highest use levels.

Why did so few differences emerge in the peak and nonpeak time standards comparisons? Significant differences in the number of people seen indicates that peak and nonpeak time visitors had different recreation experiences. A comparison of previous visitation suggests that nonpeak time visitors may not be exhibiting displacement behavior. On average, peak time visitors reported that they had previously visited Acadia more times than nonpeak time visitors. Median comparisons suggest that the number of previous visits between the two time groups may not be all that different. Furthermore, peak time visitors agreed more strongly that Acadia as a whole was too crowded. If respondents were visiting at nonpeak times due to displacement, the opposite finding would be expected.

While the indicator comparisons in this study suggest that nonpeak time visitors were not displaced, the findings also suggest that low-use site visitors could be. If so, differences in standards may have emerged between the high- and low-use site groups, had they been measured. While it may not be appropriate to compare site-specific standards at two different locations, similar high- and low-use sites could be chosen. For example, a general set of beach photographs could be shown to visitors at Sand Beach and Little Hunter's Beach. While this would not serve to determine crowding-related standards at each specific location, it would provide a means for comparing standards for a general beach setting between the two groups.

Future research could examine the link between spatial displacement and standards of quality for crowding and other visitor-caused impacts. Studies should include a direct measure of displacement, and also consider the extent to which coping mechanisms influence indicators and standards of quality. Future research also could be expanded to include sampling during off-season time periods.

8 Do Parks Make Good Neighbors?
Community Residents' Perceptions of Acadia National Park

Many of America's national parks have become islands of nature in a sea of civilization. Development of land around parks has raised a variety of management issues, including air and water pollution that flow into the parks, limited range for wildlife, increasing demand for recreation opportunities, and incompatible development along park boundaries. These and related park-management issues—collectively termed "external threats"—have reached crisis proportions.

However, another side of this issue is beginning to emerge as well. Just as parks and park management can be affected by surrounding lands, so too can surrounding lands and their owners be affected by parks. Parks, wilderness, and related public lands often draw thousands or even millions of visitors annually, and public ownership of land can have important implications for local economies and community life. This study was designed to explore how the presence of a national park is perceived to affect private landowners and their communities.

STUDY METHODS

The study focused on Acadia where the park coexists on Mount Desert Island (MDI) with a number of small communities. The park boundary is highly irregular, resulting in a complex landownership pattern highlighted by substantial intermixture of public and private lands.

The principal objective of the study was to determine the effects of the park on surrounding areas as perceived by residents of MDI. A question-

---

This chapter is an edited version of the following paper: Robert Manning, "Do Parks Make Good Neighbors?" *Park Science* 11 (1990): 19–20.

naire was administered by mail to a 10 percent systematic random sample of residential property owners on the island. Sampling was conducted using the property tax records of all communities on MDI. Using a five-point response scale, residents were asked to rate the degree to which the park positively or negatively affected thirty-three issues related to personal and community life. A response rate of 83 percent was attained, yielding 542 completed questionnaires.

STUDY FINDINGS

Study findings are summarized in figure 8.1 which reports mean responses for the thirty-three study items. Several conclusions may be drawn. First, respondents feel that the park does affect them in a multitude of ways. For only two of the thirty-three items included in the questionnaire did a majority of respondents feel the park had "no effect."

Second, it is clear that the park is perceived by residents as having both positive and negative effects. Using the mean responses shown in figure 8.1, it can be concluded that respondents felt the park had a slightly to moderately negative effect for twelve of the thirty-three items explored. The most clearly negative items were property tax rate, cost of land and housing, and traffic congestion. Most residents apparently believe that property tax rates are abnormally high due to the presence of the park. This situation may be due to the fact that land in public ownership generates little or no property tax revenue for local governments, placing what is perceived to be an undue burden on private property owners.

Another contributing factor may be an abnormally high rate of appreciation of private land values because the supply of private land is reduced and the market price may be bid up quite steeply. (Demand for commercial tourist development and vacation homes is spawned by the presence of the park.) Most residents also believe the park has a negative effect on the cost of land and housing; that is, the presence of the park has caused land and housing costs to rise abnormally high. Finally, respondents clearly believe that the high level of visitation to the park causes traffic congestion with which local residents must contend.

The majority of items explored were perceived to be slightly to strongly positively affected by the park. The most clearly positive were availability of recreational and cultural opportunities, opportunities for jobs, income of

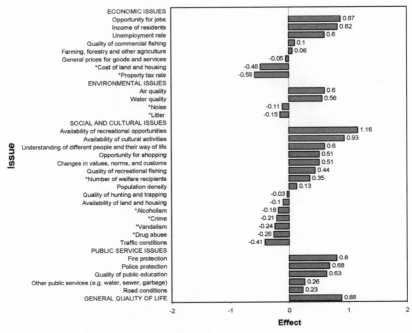

Figure 8.1 *Average responses for the thirty-three study items.*

residents, and fire protection. Respondents apparently recognize that the large number of visitors attracted to the park makes possible the provision of opportunities for recreation, shopping, and culture that otherwise could not be supported on the island. They also appreciate the economic benefits brought about by a large infusion of park visitors and understand that these expenditures create jobs and income in local communities. There is also an apparent belief that the presence of a major unit of the national park system can enhance traditionally local government services such as fire and police protection.

Finally, a summary item, "general quality of life," was included in the questionnaire. The vast majority of respondents felt the park had an overall positive effect on their lives and on their communities.

CONCLUSIONS

Findings from this study indicate that, for the most part, parks indeed can be good neighbors. However, two notes of caution are in order. First, it should be emphasized that these findings relate to perceived effects of the park. These perceptions may or may not be related to real effects, at least for some items. Nevertheless, perceptions of local residents are important unless they can be proven wrong empirically. Second, although most items explored in the questionnaire were perceived as positively affected by the park, the attention of park managers should be drawn to the issues perceived as negatively affected. Negative perceptions should be corrected where they are believed to be in error, and action should be taken to ameliorate negative effects where possible.

Over the past decade, it has become clear that parks are tied inextricably to lands outside their boundaries. This issue has been framed primarily in terms of the effects of these surrounding lands on park management. This study illustrates that there is another side of this issue as well. Parks clearly are perceived to affect surrounding lands and communities. As the interconnectedness of public and private lands is recognized more widely, it will be necessary for park managers to reach out beyond the borders of their areas to deal successfully with "external threats." They are likely to be more effective in this process if they are aware of and sensitive to effects they in turn have on surrounding communities.

Study findings also can contribute to formulation of indicators and standards of quality to help guide park management. For example, like visitors (as reported in chapter 1 and elsewhere in this book), many MDI residents feel that traffic congestion is an important problem related to park use, and that some measure of traffic congestion should be considered as an indicator of quality for the park and surrounding areas. People who live in and around parks can constitute an important stakeholder group that should be engaged in park planning and management.

9 Design and Assessment of Transportation Systems on Mount Desert Island

This chapter explores transportation issues at Acadia and Mount Desert Island (MDI) from the standpoint of managers of businesses in the gateway communities of Acadia. The research was based on an evaluation of a field operational test (FOT) of intelligent transportation systems (ITS) on MDI. Spending by visitors to Acadia is a mainstay of the local economy, and many business managers have a vital stake in the performance of the MDI transportation system. A brief background on the FOT is provided, followed by a discussion of the study methods and findings of the research.

Background on the ITS Field Operational Test

Acadia was selected by the U.S. Departments of Transportation and Interior to test the effectiveness of ITS in dealing with transportation problems in national parks. ITS has provided effective tools for dealing with problems of traffic congestion in other settings, and it was believed that testing the application of ITS in a national park was warranted. In addition to the federal agencies, the FOT included several stakeholders, such as the Maine Department of Transportation (DOT), the nonprofit Friends of Acadia, the Maine Office of Tourism, and local groups, including representatives of MDI towns and businesses. Together, they planned a suite of ITS components to support the region's needs for public transportation management, traffic management, and traveler information.

The results reported in this chapter are part of a larger study that as-

This chapter is an edited version of the following paper: Carole Zimmerman, John Daigle, and James Pol, "Tourism Business and Intelligent Transportation Systems: Acadia National Park, Maine," *Transportation Research Record: Journal of the Transportation Research Board* 1895 (2004): 182–187.

sessed the benefits of ITS across all the deployed technologies and from the points of view of visitors, stakeholders, and the business community (Zimmerman, Coleman, and Daigle 2003). This chapter focuses on the perspectives of the managers of businesses on MDI. The evaluation sought to determine if ITS had a noticeable impact on the local tourism-based economy.

STUDY METHODS

The primary study method was a survey of businesses on MDI. The Total-Design Method, a standardized methodology consisting of questionnaire construction and survey administration, was utilized as a guide for the mail survey (Dillman 1978). The survey gathered information on business manager perceptions of the Island Explorer bus system, and awareness, use, and benefits associated with the ITS technologies. Using mailing lists supplied by the local chambers of commerce, questionnaires were mailed to 454 businesses; 257 completed questionnaires were returned for a response rate of 60 percent.

The survey questions were formulated based on in-person interviews with business managers. These interviews were helpful in identifying the range of issues of interest to managers on the topics of transportation, tourism, the Island Explorer, and Acadia. Information collected was used to develop the closed-end questions that were suitable for the mail-back survey.

STUDY FINDINGS

Business Manager Characteristics and Views about Tourism

With 74 percent of managers classifying their main business as lodging, retail, restaurant, or tour guide, tourism clearly dominates the local economy. The greatest clusters of businesses are in the villages of Bar Harbor (37 percent) and Southwest Harbor (18 percent), and many businesses are highly seasonal (43 percent open six months or less). Managers tend to be year-round residents of MDI (86 percent) who have lived in the area a decade or more (70 percent) and have operated their business five or more years (77 percent).

Business managers generally held a positive view of tourism in the area. Respondents tended to report strong levels of agreement with statements about the positive impacts of tourism and either neutrality or disagreement with negative impacts. For example, managers strongly agreed that tourism would continue to have a major economic role in the community and that they personally support this role of tourism. On the other hand, the data reveal a more neutral or less strong view on whether additional tourists beyond current levels would be a positive thing.

When asked about Acadia, business managers believed that the park contributed to the local economy. A majority of managers agreed or strongly agreed that Acadia contributed to job creation (52 percent), the stability of the economy (59 percent) and to attraction of tourism dollars (83 percent).

Business Managers' Views of Transportation Issues

Transportation was one area that drew negative views from business managers. Business managers were concerned about summer travel on MDI and in Acadia in several ways. Their greatest concern was with parking problems and congestion. Parking and congestion both within and outside the park were rated as a "big" or "moderate" problem by 72 and 70 percent of respondents, respectively.

Concern about the economic effect of parking and congestion can be discerned from managers' views on visitor access. Visitors' ability to fully access desired attractions outside the park (such as restaurants and shops) was seen as a moderate or big problem to 57 percent of mangers. However, access was seen as more of a problem outside than inside of the park. Business managers generally did not believe that travel and traffic information was insufficient to help visitors plan trips in the park, as only 20 percent rated it as a moderate or big problem.

Business Managers' Attitudes toward the Island Explorer

The Island Explorer, the free shuttle bus service that runs throughout the park and three of the largest towns on the island, is readily available to the vast majority of local businesses. It stops in front of 21 percent of businesses and is within a five-minute walk of an additional 58 percent. Sixty-nine percent of the businesses distributed schedule and other information related to the bus. It is no surprise, therefore, that 64 percent of managers reported that their customers use the bus. Moreover, at least one employee of 21 percent of businesses uses the bus to get to work.

Business managers were asked to rate the potential benefits of the bus to tourists and residents. Bus usage and strength of perceived benefits clearly are correlated in the minds of respondents. For all but two of the potential benefits included in the questionnaire, business managers who reported use of the bus system by customers and/or employees rated those benefits higher than those who either didn't use or weren't sure about use of the bus. The differences between the two groups were statistically significant for six of the fourteen benefits. The biggest benefit reported by both groups was that the Island Explorer bus created less worry about driving and parking for tourists along busy roads. In terms of economic impact, both groups of managers believed that the bus is helping to create a new tourist segment that doesn't need to have their own vehicle and that it improves access to businesses in the villages.

When asked about the Island Explorer's direct impact on their businesses, managers tended to be more neutral in their views. They didn't necessarily agree that more customers were patronizing their business because parking was less of a problem or that the Island Explorer would cause visitors to stay longer. On the other hand, managers who did not report usage of the bus by their customers or employees tended to report that businesses closer to a bus stop than their own did benefit.

Awareness and Usage of ITS Technologies

Business manages were asked if they were aware of any of the four ITS technologies for delivering traveler information: parking information signs, parking information on the park website, automated annunciators onboard the Island Explorer, and electronic bus-departure signs. The majority of business managers (61 percent) reported being unaware of the ITS-based traveler information technologies. Of those business managers who reported being aware of at least one of the traveler information sources (n=48), electronic signs that displayed real-time departures of the next Island Explorer bus were the most frequently known.

Almost half of the ninety-eight ITS-aware business managers used at least one of the traveler information sources (n=48). Use was much lower for information on parking conditions as compared to the Island Explorer traveler information. A possible explanation is that managers who have lived in the area a long time are likely to know the daily parking patterns at park attraction sites such as Sand Beach and Jordan Pond House. Moreover, they would have been less likely to frequent the park campgrounds and the Visitor Center where the parking information signs were deployed.

When asked about their customers' use of ITS technologies, only 29 percent of business managers reported their customers had used one or more of the traveler information sources. Of the twenty-eight business managers who reported customers using different sources of traveler information, a high proportion of managers (67 percent) reported customers using the electronic signs that displayed real-time departures of the next Island Explorer bus and 33 percent reported customers using the audio announcement of the next Island Explorer bus stop. As with the business managers themselves, their customers' use of the parking availability information was lower compared to the Island Explorer traveler information.

Business Managers' Perception of Benefits of ITS Technologies

To assess the potential impact of ITS, business managers were asked about the benefits to their business and to tourists, who form the base of the region's economy. Findings suggest that there is some uncertainty among business managers (48 percent) that real-time parking availability would be helpful to their business. However, there were generally high levels of agreement on the benefits that tourists likely would derive from using the parking availability information. Business managers believed that parking information would help tourists increase the likelihood of using the Island Explorer bus (86 percent), avoid parking problems in the park (84 percent), avoid traffic congestion in the park (81 percent), plan the time of day for visiting destinations in the park (81 percent), get around more easily (78 percent), and avoid large crowds in the park (70 percent).

Business managers were asked to assess the benefits of the electronic bus-departure signs and the automatic next-stop announcements on the Island Explorer buses. In contrast to the parking information, a majority of business managers (56 percent) thought that the Island Explorer bus traveler information would be helpful to their own businesses. This might be a reflection of the use of the bus by themselves or their employees; or it might be because buses stop near their business, thereby increasing its availability to customers.

Business managers view the ITS enhancements to the bus system more positively in terms of benefits to tourists. Managers believe that the electronic bus-departure signs and the automatic next-stop announcements will help tourists get around more easily (95 percent), increase the likelihood of using the Island Explorer bus (93 percent), relieve uncertainty about when the bus will arrive at the bus stop (90 percent), improve the travel experience overall (90 percent), relieve uncertainty about when to exit the bus (85 percent), and utilize their time more efficiently, such as visiting shops before a bus arrives (87 percent).

CONCLUSIONS

The majority of business managers recognize the importance of tourism and the benefits to their business or community from being situated near Acadia. However, they are concerned about problems of summer travel on MDI and in the park, including parking and congestion as well as related concerns about air quality and safety. Many business managers believe that the Island Explorer bus system helps to address some of their concerns about summer travel, and most reported that they provide information to visitors about the Island Explorer bus. Managers also perceived many benefits associated with ITS, such as making it easier for tourists to get around; avoiding parking problems, traffic congestion, and crowds in the park; relieving uncertainty for users about when the bus would arrive at bus stops and where to exit the bus; and improving the travel experience in and around Acadia.

The business community is an important stakeholder in Acadia and should be integrated into park planning and management to the degree possible. Like visitors and community residents, as reported in chapters 1 and 8, respectively, many business operators are concerned about traffic congestion and lack of parking in Acadia and surrounding communities and these issues should receive strong consideration as potential indicators of quality for Acadia and MDI more broadly.

10 Crowding in Parks and Outdoor Recreation

Crowding is a perennial issue in parks and other outdoor recreation locations. Research at Acadia suggests that visitors and residents of surrounding communities are concerned about crowding in the form of traffic congestion, lack of parking, and encounters with other groups on trails and the carriage roads. The purpose of this chapter is to examine crowding from theoretical, empirical, and managerial perspectives to deepen our understanding and enhance our ability to manage this issue. First, a review of the theoretical literature on crowding is presented. Normative theory is used to define crowding and to construct a conceptual model of the primary variables affecting judgments of crowding in parks and outdoor recreation. Second, an empirical study of crowding in Acadia is used to illustrate this theoretical foundation. Data from this study illustrate the ways in which crowding is influenced by the characteristics of visitors, characteristics of those encountered, and situational variables. Third, a managerial analysis of crowding is presented by exploring the management implications of this theoretical and empirical work.

THEORETICAL ANALYSIS OF CROWDING

Normative theory has proven useful in analyzing and understanding crowding in parks and outdoor recreation. Developed in the fields of sociology and social-psychology, normative theory offers two important insights into

This chapter is an edited version of the following paper: Robert Manning, William Valliere, Ben Minteer, Ben Wang, and Charles Jacobi, "Crowding in Parks and Outdoor Recreation: A Theoretical, Empirical and Managerial Analysis," *Journal of Park and Recreation Administration* 18, no. 4 (2000):57–72.

crowding. First, normative theory distinguishes between the concepts of use level and crowding (Stokols 1972a, 1972b; Heberlein 1977). Use level is a physical concept relating number of people per unit of space; it is "neutral" and suggests no psychological or experiential evaluation or interpretation. Crowding, on the other hand, has a psychological meaning; it is a subjective and negative evaluation of a use level. Thus, use level may increase to a point where it is perceived to interfere with one's activities or intentions, but only at this point does crowding occur. Social-psychological studies indicate that crowding judgments are influenced both by the activities being pursued and by the settings in which they occur (e.g., Desor 1972; Cohen, Sladen, and Bennett 1975). Therefore, crowding appears to be a normative concept, dependent upon a variety of circumstances.

Second, people may have normative standards about appropriate use levels in a variety of situations, including parks and outdoor recreation areas (Donnelly, Vaske, and Shelby 1992; Shelby and Vaske 1991; Vaske et al. 1986; Vaske and Whittaker 2004; Manning 1999, 2007). Moreover, to the extent there is agreement about such norms across social groups, data on crowding norms can be used to help manage crowding in parks and outdoor recreation.

Findings from studies of crowding in parks and outdoor recreation can be synthesized and interpreted within the framework of normative theory. A variety of factors have been found to influence normative judgments of crowding in parks and outdoor recreation. These factors can be grouped into three basic categories: characteristics of visitors, characteristics of those encountered, and situational variables.

Characteristics of Visitors

A variety of characteristics of visitors have been found to influence crowding norms. These include the recreation activity engaged in, motivations for outdoor recreation, preferences and expectations for use level, experience level, and attitudes toward management.

For example, a survey of recreationists on the Buffalo National River in Arkansas found wide diversity in perceived crowding among the sample of river floaters, and motivations for the trip were found to be related significantly to perceived crowding (Ditton, Fedler, and Graefe 1983). Not surprisingly, respondents who felt crowded reported significantly higher ratings on the motivation "to get away from other people," while those whose enjoyment was enhanced by contacts reported significantly higher ratings on the motivations "to be part of the group," "to have thrills and excitement," and "to share what I have learned with others." The survey also included questions on expected and preferred number of contacts with others. Respondents who felt crowded were more likely to report having seen more people than expected. The same results were obtained for preferred contacts: Those who felt crowded were distinguished from others by the fact that they tended to report experiencing more contacts than they preferred.

Characteristics of Those Encountered

There is considerable evidence that the characteristics of those encountered also affect crowding norms. Factors found important include type and size of group, behavior, and the degree to which groups are perceived to be alike.

For example, an early study of the Boundary Waters Canoe Area in Minnesota found that paddling canoeists distinguished sharply among the three types of area users when asked their reactions to meeting other groups (Lucas 1964a, 1964b). They disliked encountering motorboats, were less resentful of encountering motorized canoes, and were relatively tolerant of encountering at least some other paddled canoes. Motor canoeists made similar distinctions, though not as sharply. Thus, canoeists felt crowded at much lower levels of use where motorboats were present. These differential crowding effects have been found to persist over time (Adelman, Heberlein, and Bonnickson 1982).

Situational Variables

The context in which encounters occur can influence the way in which those encounters are perceived and evaluated. Important variables include the type of recreation area, location within an area, and environmental quality and design. For example, heightened sensitivity to encounters has been found in the "interior" of recreation areas as opposed to the "periphery." Given the choice, 68 percent of wilderness visitors expressed a preference for encounters to occur within the first few miles from the road rather than interior zones (Stankey 1973). An analogous study of boaters found that respondents were more sensitive to crowding on the lake than at access points (Graefe and Drogin 1989).

EMPIRICAL ANALYSIS OF CROWDING

Theoretical understanding of crowding as outlined in the previous section allows for more systematic and comprehensive empirical study. This approach was taken in a recent series of studies on the carriage roads at Acadia. (Research on indicators and standards of quality for the carriage roads is described more fully in chapter 2.) Initial research included administration of open- and close-ended questions to a representative sample of 900 carriage road visitors (Manning, Negra, et al. 1996). Study findings confirmed that crowding, or seeing too many other visitors along the carriage roads, was an issue of concern to many respondents.

A second study sought to quantify crowding using the theoretical framework described above. A survey was designed to measure the normative standards for crowding of carriage road visitors, including the ways in which such standards are influenced by type of respondent, type of visitor encountered, and situational variables. The survey was administered to a representative sample of 511 carriage road visitors (Manning et al. 1997). The survey incorporated a visual approach to measuring crowding norms, whereby a series of computer-generated photographs was prepared illustrating a range of use levels and types along a typical 100-meter section of the carriage roads. (Use of visual research methods to measure standards of quality is described more fully in chapter 12.) The series of photographs contained nineteen images that showed a range from 0 to 30 visitors and included equal and unequal mixes of bicyclists and walkers, the primary types of users. The study design is illustrated in figure 10.1, and representative photographs are shown in figure 2.1 (in chapter 2). The nineteen photographs were presented to respondents in random order, and respondents were asked to rate the acceptability of each photograph on a scale from +4 ("Very Acceptable") to −4 ("Very Unacceptable").

Study findings are shown in figure 10.2. It's clear from all the graphs in this figure that acceptability declines as use level increases. However, the graphs also illustrate the ways in which normative judgments of crowding are influenced by type of respondent and type of visitor encountered. All graphs plot average acceptability ratings of respondents. However, figure 10.2A includes only data from respondents who were walkers, and includes their acceptability ratings of photographs that included walkers only. The point at which aggregate ratings fall out of the acceptable range and into the unac-

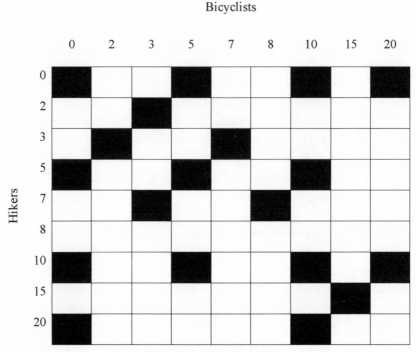

Figure 10.1 *Study design for photographs of carriage road use. Blackened cells represent the combinations of hikers and bicyclists in the nineteen study photographs.*

ceptable range (the "0" point on the acceptability scale) is approximately 16 persons per viewscape (16 PPV). However, Figure 10.2B plots walkers' acceptability ratings of photographs that include only bicyclists, and illustrates the effect of type of visitor encountered: Walkers find a maximum of only about 10 PPV to be acceptable when other visitors are bicyclists. Figures 10.2C and D present similar data for respondents who were bicyclists. Taken together, these graphs empirically illustrate the ways and extent to which type of respondent (defined in this case as mode of activity—walking or bicycling) and type of visitor encountered (again defined as mode of activity) influence normative judgments of crowding.

Finally, an analysis was also conducted illustrating the effect of situational variables, or context, on normative judgments of crowding. In this case, respondents were administered a "short form" of the normative crowding question in which they were asked to report the photograph (among the nineteen study photographs) that showed the highest level of use acceptable

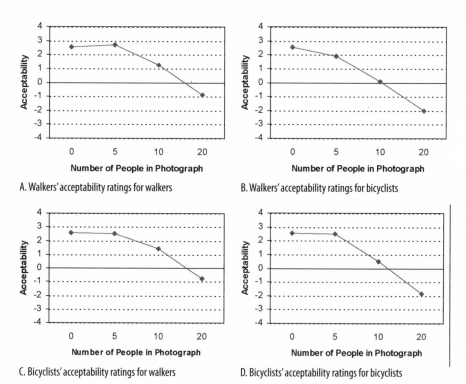

A. Walkers' acceptability ratings for walkers

B. Walkers' acceptability ratings for bicyclists

C. Bicyclists' acceptability ratings for walkers

D. Bicyclists' acceptability ratings for bicyclists

Figure 10.2 *Alternative crowding norms for the carriage roads.*

(rather than rating the acceptability of all study photographs). (The issue of question format and wording is addressed in chapter 13.) Respondents who visited less heavily used portions of the carriage road system (areas away from the heavily used Eagle Lake section) were less tolerant of seeing other visitors, to a statistically significant extent, than were visitors to more heavily used portions of the carriage roads.

Managerial Analysis of Crowding

Theoretical and empirical analysis of crowding enhances understanding of this perennial and increasingly important issue in outdoor recreation. This enhanced understanding, in turn, suggests a number of management implications. First, the distinction between use level and crowding inherent in normative theory suggests that increasing use of parks and other outdoor recreation areas is not necessarily a problem. Indeed, there are good reasons to celebrate the increasing popularity of parks and related outdoor recreation areas, as this suggests the contribution of such areas to the quality of life and may contribute to broadened public support for parks and outdoor recreation areas. However, at some point (defined by type of visitor, type of visitor encountered, and situational variables), increasing use levels may be judged as crowding, and this will diminish the quality of the visitor experience. At this point, crowding is a problem that warrants management attention.

Second, an increasing number of studies suggest that normative judgments of crowding can be measured to help determine the point at which crowding is unacceptable. The data outlined above in the study of visitors to the carriage roads of Acadia provide an empirically informed basis for formulating crowding-related standards of quality, and for managing this area to avoid unacceptable levels of crowding. Incorporating the research outlined in this paper, a management plan for the carriage roads of Acadia has been formulated and implemented (Jacobi and Manning 1997). A number of studies conducted in a variety of parks and outdoor recreation areas have experimented with related research approaches to measuring visitor judgments of crowding as it is manifested in a variety of forms as compiled in recent books (Manning 1999, 2007).

Third, crowding-related studies have led to development of frameworks designed to manage crowding and other impacts of visitor use. Development of VERP by the NPS is a good example, and this framework was used to guide development of the carriage road management plan at Acadia. These frameworks require formulation of standards of quality for crowding and other elements of the recreation experience, and management action to ensure that such standards are maintained. These frameworks can be especially useful in developing rational, thoughtful, traceable, and defensible management policies applied to crowding and other potential impacts of recreation.

Fourth, it is clear that crowding can be influenced by both the type of recreation visitor and the type of visitor encountered. Thus crowding can include a strong behavioral component, often characterized as conflict. The behavioral component of crowding introduces several important considerations. When normative judgments of crowding are influenced by behavioral conflict, management action is imperative. Study findings from Acadia demonstrate that walkers are more sensitive to crowding than bicyclists, and that the presence of bicyclists disturbs walkers more than the presence of walkers disturbs bicyclists. Heightened sensitivity of some types of visitors, and asymmetric antipathy of recreation conflict, are common findings in the outdoor recreation literature (Manning 1999). If this situation is not managed, then some types of visitors are likely to be dissatisfied or, ultimately, displaced.

Two basic strategies can be used to manage behaviorally based crowding. The first is zoning or separation of conflicting uses. The second strategy is managing the behavior of visitors to minimize conflicts. Study findings at Acadia indicated that most visitors—both walkers and bicyclists—did not want to be responsible for displacing other visitors, and were committed to sharing the carriage roads with other types of visitors (Jacobi and Manning 1997; Manning et al. 1997). Thus, the NPS chose not to zone or restrict use of the carriage roads to only walkers or bicyclists, but rather chose to manage the behavior of all visitors. Study findings indicated that certain "problem behaviors" were at the root of much of the conflict between walkers and bicyclists. For example, walkers objected that some bicyclists rode too fast, creating a safety hazard, and that they often were startled by bicyclists who passed from behind without warning. Bicyclists objected to groups that walked abreast impeding passing, and to walkers who had dogs off-leash. The park instituted a vigorous information and education program to curb these problem behaviors. This program included formulating and posting a set of "rules-of-the-road" for all carriage road visitors, a video that is shown at local bicycle rental shops, courtesy patrols of the carriage roads by rangers and volunteers, and self-policing by recreation user groups. Monitoring of the carriage roads indicates that incidences of all problem behaviors have dropped substantially (Jacobi 1997).

Finally, crowding also can be influenced by situational variables or context. It may be wise to establish and manage for a diversity of outdoor recreation opportunities to the extent feasible, and use level may be an important consideration in this process. As noted earlier, visitors to less-used sections of the carriage roads were less tolerant of seeing other visitors than were visitors to more heavily used sections of the carriage roads. Based on this and related information, the NPS decided to "zone" the carriage roads by use level. This zoning was done in both spatial and temporal dimensions. Two standards of quality for maximum allowable use level were established for the carriage roads. The first, a more lenient standard, was established for peak use areas and times. The second, a more restrictive standard, was set for non-peak areas and times. This zoning system creates a continuum of recreation opportunities designed to meet differing sensitivities to crowding among carriage road visitors.

CONCLUSION

Crowding is a long-standing and challenging issue in parks and outdoor recreation. However, theoretical and empirical research on crowding has enhanced understanding of this issue, and has suggested several important management implications. Crowding can be understood through normative theory, and this suggests that (1) crowding judgments are influenced by a variety of factors, including type of visitor, type of visitor encountered, and situational variables; and (2) visitors may have normative standards for appropriate use levels in parks and outdoor recreation. A study of crowding on the carriage roads of Acadia empirically illustrates the application of normative theory. Respondents were able to report normative standards for crowding on the carriage roads. Moreover, respondent judgments of crowding were found to be influenced by (1) the type of respondent (whether the respondent was a walker or bicyclist), (2) the type of visitor encountered (whether the visitor was a walker or bicyclist), and (3) the location of encounters (whether it was a heavily or lightly used area). A number of studies have measured normative standards for crowding in a variety of park and outdoor recreation contexts, and frameworks have been developed to help incorporate such data into park and outdoor recreation management plans.

Research suggests that crowding in parks and outdoor recreation can be a function of both use level and visitor behavior. To the extent to which crowding is driven by use levels, restrictions on public use may have to be imposed. In this case, normative crowding standards of visitors can be useful in informing managers about appropriate use levels. To the extent to which crowding is driven by visitor behavior and resulting conflict, zoning to separate conflicting uses and educational programs designed to modify visitor behavior are potentially effective management strategies. Finally, where feasible, it may be wise to manage for a diversity of outdoor recreation opportunities based on varying visitor sensitivities to crowding and conflict.

11 Crowding, Conflict, and Coping in Outdoor Recreation

As noted in the previous chapter, crowding and conflict are long-standing and challenging issues in outdoor recreation. As the number and diversity of visitors to parks and outdoor recreation areas has risen over the past several decades, so has concern over the potential effects of these trends on the quality of outdoor recreation experiences. Research on crowding and conflict suggests the complex nature of these topics. In particular, empirical research has often found that visitor satisfaction may remain relatively high even when use levels of a park or related area increase (Manning 1999). A possible explanation of these findings suggests that some recreationists may adopt one of several coping mechanisms in response to crowding and conflict. For example, if some visitors "cope" with crowding and conflict through the process of "displacement" (that is, they don't go to that park as often, or stop going altogether), then those visitors may not be present to register their dissatisfaction. Moreover, such visitors ultimately may be replaced (or "displaced") by visitors who are not as sensitive to increased use levels. In this way, use levels may continue to increase, and visitor satisfaction (at least as it is commonly measured through on-site surveys) may continue to be high.

Coping is a widely used concept in psychology and generally is defined as "any behavior, whether deliberate or not, that reduces stress and enables a person to deal with a situation without excessive stress" (Sutherland 1996). A number of coping mechanisms have been identified in the general crowding literature (Altman 1975). The classic work of Milgram (1970), for instance,

This chapter is an edited version of the following paper: Robert Manning and William Valliere, "Coping in Outdoor Recreation: Causes and Consequences of Crowding and Conflict among Community Residents," *Journal of Leisure Research* 33 (2001):410–26.

has illustrated the ways in which urban residents cope with excessive population density—brusque conversations, unlisted telephones, and disregard of strangers, even when they may be in need. The literature on outdoor recreation has identified a number of coping mechanisms that might be used by recreationists to deal with crowding and conflict, including shifting use to other locations and/or times and redefining appropriate outdoor recreation experiences.

The purpose of this chapter is to explore further the use of coping mechanisms in outdoor recreation. More specifically, the objectives of the study are to (1) measure perceived changes in the amount and type of recreation use that has occurred on the carriage roads at Acadia, (2) measure the extent to which a variety of coping mechanisms have been adopted by visitors to that area, and (3) analyze the relationships among perceived changes in recreation use and adoption of selected coping mechanisms to explore how perceived changes in the amount and type of recreation use may influence the adoption of selected coping mechanisms. The study is applied to residents of communities in and around the park.

Coping in Outdoor Recreation

The literature on coping in outdoor recreation suggests that outdoor recreationists may utilize three primary coping mechanisms: displacement, rationalization, and product shift (Manning 1999). While most conceptual and empirical studies have focused attention on coping mechanisms within the context of crowding, recent research has suggested that recreation visitors also may adopt coping strategies to deal with problems of conflict (Schneider and Hammitt 1995). Displacement is a behavioral coping mechanism in that it involves spatial or temporal changes in use patterns in response to crowding or conflict. Rationalization and product shift are cognitive coping mechanisms involving changes in the ways visitors think about recreation experiences and opportunities.

Displacement. A number of studies have suggested that as use levels increase, some recreationists may become dissatisfied and alter their patterns of recreation activity to avoid crowding, perhaps ultimately moving on to less-used areas (Anderson and Brown 1984; Shelby, Bregenzer, and Johnson 1988; Hammitt and Patterson, 1991; Robertson and Regula, 1994; Nielson and Shelby, 1977; Stankey, 1980; Kuentzel and Heberlein, 1992; Nielson and

Endo, 1977; Wohlwill and Heft, 1977; Vaske, Donnelly, and Heberlein 1980; Becker, 1981; Becker, Niemann, and Gates 1981; West, 1981; Hammitt and Hughes 1984). In this manner, they are "displaced" by recreationists more tolerant of higher use levels. This suggests that the reason for a lack of relationship between use levels and satisfaction is that people who are sensitive to existing use levels at each recreation site have been displaced from these sites. It is important to note that displacement does not have to involve a shift from one recreation area to another (intersite displacement) but can involve shifts within a recreation area (intrasite displacement) and shifts from one time period to another (temporal displacement). The concept of displacement was suggested as early as 1971 when it was described as a process of "invasion and succession" (Clark, Hendee, and Campbell 1971).

Rationalization. A second coping behavior suggested in outdoor recreation involves a process of rationalization. Since recreation activities are selected voluntarily and sometimes involve a substantial investment of time, money, and effort, some people may rationalize their experience and report high levels of satisfaction, regardless of conditions. This hypothesis is rooted in the theory of cognitive dissonance developed by Festinger (1957) and others, and suggests that people tend to order their thoughts in ways that reduce inconsistencies and associated stress. Therefore, to reduce internal conflict, people may be inclined to rate their recreation experience highly regardless of actual conditions. This, then, may explain why reported satisfaction is often not related to use levels.

This hypothesis appears reasonable when applied, as it originally was, to rafters on the Colorado River in Grand Canyon National Park in Arizona (Heberlein and Shelby 1977). For most people, this trip is a substantial undertaking: Trips are long, normally requiring at least a week; commercial passengers pay high fees; and private trips may have to wait years to receive a permit. Under these conditions, many people might refuse to be easily disappointed. The hypothesis loses some of its appeal, however, when applied to less extraordinary circumstances. Little support for this hypothesis, for example, was found in a study of river use in Vermont (Manning and Ciali 1980). Most visitors were in-state day users. With such a relatively small investment in their trip, it seems more likely that they would have reported that they had had an unsatisfactory experience because of crowding or for any other reason. Indeed, many respondents were not hesitant to express dissatisfaction, with reported satisfaction ratings ranging throughout the response scale.

Product Shift. The third coping mechanism suggested in outdoor recreation involves the cognitive behavior of product shift (Herberlein and Shelby 1977; Stankey and McCool 1984; Shelby and Heberlein 1986; Stankey 1989; Hendee, Stankey, and Lucas 1990; Moore, Schockey, and Brickler 1990; Shindler and Shelby 1995; Kuentzel and Heberlein 1992). This hypothesis suggests that visitors who experience higher use levels than expected or preferred may alter their definition of the recreation opportunity in congruence with the condition experienced.

Several studies have addressed this issue empirically. Studies of users of the Rogue River in Oregon suggest that product shift is a relatively common coping strategy (Shelby, Bregenzer, and Johnson 1988). When users were asked how they would react to encountering more visitors on the river than expected, 34 percent responded that they would change the way they thought about the river, deciding it was less remote than initially believed. A follow-up survey conducted seven years later compared these two samples with respect to the type of recreation opportunity provided by the river. Over this time period, the river experienced a 45 percent increase in use. In the initial survey, 20 percent of respondents reported that the river provided a "wilderness" experience, 66 percent a "semi-wilderness" experience, and 14 percent an "undeveloped recreation" experience. In the follow-up survey, these percentages had changed to 4, 59, and 37 respectively, suggesting substantial product shift.

STUDY METHODS

The study reported in this chapter was conducted on the carriage roads of Acadia and was applied to residents of the four communities in and around the park. Local residents comprise an especially interesting population for a study of coping in outdoor recreation because they are likely to use their local park often for recreation and they are likely to have used the park over a relatively long period of time. In fact, the study found that nearly all respondents (93.1 percent) had used the carriage roads, that most residents have used the carriage roads for nearly twenty years, and that current users use the carriage roads about ten times per year.

Community residents were studied by means of a mail survey. A systematic random sample of 939 community residents, stratified by the four towns in and around the park, was developed from telephone directories. The survey was conducted using procedures recommended by Dillman (1978). An initial mailing consisted of a questionnaire and cover letter explaining the study. The back cover of the questionnaire was pre-addressed and postage was prepaid. A week after the initial mailing, a postcard reminder was sent to all members of the sample. A second questionnaire with cover letter was sent to nonrespondents three weeks after the initial mailing. One hundred and seventy-eight questionnaires were undeliverable. Three hundred and seventy-seven completed questionnaires were returned, yielding a response rate of 49.5 percent.

Two batteries of questions dealt specifically with coping and related matters. The first battery of questions was designed to measure perceived changes in the amount and type of visitor use on the carriage roads over time. Respondents were presented with a series of statements describing possible changes in recreation use of the carriage roads, and respondents were asked to indicate the degree to which they agreed or disagreed with each statement. These statements dealt with the overall use level on the carriage roads, the use levels of selected recreation activities, and levels of selected "problem behaviors" on the carriage roads. The possible changes in carriage road use addressed in these statements were developed from a series of open- and close-ended questions administered in a previous phase of research on the carriage roads (Manning et al. 1996). Statements are shown in table 11.1. The second battery of questions was designed to measure coping mechanisms adopted in response to perceived changes in carriage road use. Respondents were asked if and how their "use of the carriage roads has changed over the past several years." The items contained in this battery of questions included a variety of potential coping mechanisms designed to test for spatial and temporal displacement, rationalization, and product shift. These coping mechanisms, and statements designed to measure them, were adapted from previous studies of coping in outdoor recreation (Hammitt and Patterson 1991; Robertson and Regula 1994). Statements are shown in table 11.2.

Analysis of study data was conducted on both descriptive and analytical levels. Descriptive findings from the two batteries of questions indicate perceived changes in the amount and type of carriage road use, and the level

TABLE 11.1 Perceived changes in carriage road use.

| | Level of agreement | | | |
| | Strongly agree | Agree | Disagree | Strongly disagree |
Statement		(Percentage of responses)		
A. The number of people using the carriage roads has increased	59.9	36.7	2.5	0.9
B. The number of walkers/hikers using the carriage roads has increased	35.6	53.3	9.1	1.9
C. The number of bikers using the carriage roads has increased	72.0	24.8	2.2	0.9
D. The number of runners using the carriage roads has increased	18.5	58.4	21.5	1.7
E. The number of horses/carriages using the carriage roads has increased	5.6	32.9	54.9	6.6
F. The number of bicycles startling you by passing from behind without warning has increased	34.4	41.2	22.4	1.9
G. The number of bicycles traveling at excessive speeds has increased	37.3	34.7	27.0	1.0
H. The number of dogs off-leash has increased	16.7	33.1	43.9	6.3
I. The number of people obstructing or blocking the carriage roads has increased	21.0	40.7	34.9	3.4

and type of coping mechanisms adopted by respondents. These two data sets were then related using linear and logistic regression analysis to determine the extent to which adoption of coping mechanisms is statistically related to perceived changes in carriage road use.

STUDY FINDINGS

Study findings are presented in three sections corresponding to the three study objectives. The first two sections outline descriptive findings to the two batteries of questions described above. The final section describes findings from a series of analyses designed to explore the relationships between findings from these two batteries of questions, or the degree to which selected types of perceived changes in carriage road use (e.g., overall use level, use level of certain types of recreation activities, or incidences of certain types of problem behaviors) are related statistically to adoption of selected types of coping mechanisms (e.g., displacement, rationalization, or product shift).

TABLE 11.2 Adoption of coping mechanisms.

Statement	Response Yes	No
	(Percentage of responses)	
A. My use of the carriage roads has not changed much over the years	59.6	40.4
B. I use the carriage roads more now than I used to	31.1	68.9
C. I use the carriage roads less often because of the changes in use that have occurred on them	25.0	75.0
D. I no longer use the carriage roads because I don't like the changes in use that have occurred on them	7.4	92.6
E. I use the carriage roads more in the off-season to avoid the changes in use that have occurred on them	64.6	35.4
F. I use the carriage roads more on weekdays rather than weekends to avoid the changes in use that have occurred on them	44.8	55.2
G. I use the carriage roads during the early and/or later times of the day to avoid the changes in use that have occurred on them	41.5	58.5
H. I use different sections of the carriage roads to avoid the changes in use that have occurred on them	46.0	54.0
I. My use of the carriage roads has not changed much over the years, but the type of experience provided by the carriage roads has changed because of the changes in use that have occurred on them	49.8	50.2
J. My use of the carriage roads has not changed much over the years, but I am not as satisfied with my experience on the carriage roads because of the changes in use that have occurred on them	35.4	64.6

Perceived Changes in Carriage Road Use

Responses to the first battery of questions are shown in table 11.1. It is clear from these findings that most respondents believe that most recreation activities and problem behaviors have increased "over the past several years." This applies to the overall number of people using the carriage roads (item A) (96.6 percent agree or strongly agree); the number of people participating in biking (item C) (96.8 percent agree or strongly agree), walking/hiking (item B) (88.9 percent agree or strongly agree), and running (item D) (76.9 percent agree or strongly agree); and the number of incidences of three problem behaviors, including the number of bicycles startling you by passing from behind without warning (item F) (75.6 percent agree or strongly agree), the number of bicycles traveling at excessive speed (item G) (72 percent agree or strongly agree), and the number of people obstructing or blocking the carriage roads (item I) (61.7 percent agree or strongly agree). Only a minority of respondents indicated (38.5 percent agree or strongly agree) that the number of horses or carriages using the carriage roads has increased (item E) or that the number of incidences of dogs off-leash has increased (item H) (49.8 percent agree or strongly agree).

Adoption of Coping Mechanisms

Responses to the second battery of questions are shown in table 11.2. These data are more complex. Responses to statements A through D paint a broad picture of how the study population generally has responded to changes in carriage road use. Most respondents (59.6 percent) reported that their use of the carriage roads "has not changed much over the years" (item A). A substantial minority (31.1 percent) reported that they use the carriage roads "more now than [they] used to" (item B). A smaller minority (25.0 percent) reported that they use the carriage roads "less often than [they] used to because of changes in use that have occurred on them" (item C). Only a small minority (7.4 percent) reported that they "no longer use the carriage roads because [they] don't like the changes in use that have occurred on them"(item D). At an individual level, only a very small percentage of community residents have adopted this most extreme coping mechanism of intersite displacement. Most community residents have continued to use the carriage roads at about the same level they have in the past, while nearly a third have increased their use, and a quarter have decreased their use. Given these findings, residential use of the carriage roads at an aggregate level probably has not changed much over time. However, the composition of residential users may be changing incrementally.

Responses to statements C through H describe use of the coping mechanism of displacement. As suggested in the literature reviewed earlier in this chapter, displacement can take many forms, including temporal and spatial. Substantial percentages of respondents—nearly half or more—reported adopting both temporal and spatial displacement behaviors. Temporal displacement behaviors included shifting use to the off-season (item E; 64.6 percent), shifting use to weekdays (item F; 44.8 percent), and shifting use to earlier and/or later hours of the day (item G; 41.5 percent). Spatial displacement behaviors included shifting use to other sections of the carriage roads (item H; 46.0 percent), no longer using the carriage roads (item D; 7.4 percent), and using the carriage roads less often (item C; 25.0 percent).

Responses to statements I and J describe use of the cognitive coping mechanisms of product shift and rationalization. Nearly half of respondents

(49.8 percent) engage the mechanism of product shift in that their use of the carriage roads has not changed much over the years, but they believe the type of experience provided by the carriage roads has changed (item I). Findings regarding rationalization are not as clear. Over a third of respondents (35.4 percent) reported that their use of the carriage roads has not changed much, but they are not as satisfied with their experiences (item J). This compares with 59.6 percent of respondents who reported that their use of the carriage roads has not changed much over the years (item A; as reported above). The latter group minus the former group leaves 24.2 percent of the sample that could be hypothesized as adopting the cognitive coping mechanism of rationalization. That is, these respondents continue to use the carriage roads as in the past, but report being just as satisfied despite increasing levels and diversity of use. Another and perhaps more technically accurate way to calculate this subsample is to find all respondents who answered "Yes" to item A and "No" to item J. This procedure yielded a subsample of 112 respondents, or 29.7 percent of the sample. These estimates regarding rationalization are clearly conjectural, and may more accurately represent the upper bounds of the percentage of respondents using rationalization. It is certainly possible that the satisfaction of some respondents is truly unaffected—possibly even increased—by perceived increases in levels and diversity of carriage road use.

Another way to examine these data is the cumulative number of coping mechanisms used by respondents, as shown in table 11.3. These data show that use of coping mechanisms is pervasive across the sample—only 6 percent of respondents did not use any of the coping mechanisms included in the study. Many respondents used more than one coping mechanism, up to a maximum of seven.

Relating Perceived Changes to Adoption of Coping Mechanisms

To explore relationships among perceived changes in carriage road use and adoption of coping mechanisms, a series of linear and logistic regressions were computed. The first regression analysis explored perceived changes in carriage road use and an overall, cumulative (additive) index of seven of the eight coping mechanisms (items C through I in table 11.2; the measure of the cognitive coping mechanism of rationalization was not included in this overall index because of the uncertainties surrounding measurement of this variable). Responses to the seven coping mechanism questionnaire

TABLE 11.3   Cumulative number of coping mechanisms adopted.

Number of coping mechanisms adopted	Percent	Cumulative percent
0	6.0	6.0
1	16.7	22.7
2	17.4	40.1
3	19.5	59.6
4	13.8	73.4
5	18.4	91.8
6	6.4	98.2
7	1.8	100.0

items were coded so that the higher the index score, the more coping mechanisms adopted by respondents. The resulting linear regression equation was statistically significant and perceived changes in carriage road use explained 27 percent of the variation in adoption of coping mechanisms. Three perceived changes in carriage road use entered the equation. The perceived number of bicyclists traveling at excessive speeds was most strongly and positively related to adoption of coping mechanisms ($B = 0.79$): The more this change in carriage road use was perceived, the more likely respondents were to adopt coping mechanisms. Other perceived changes in carriage road use positively related to adoption of coping mechanisms were increasing number of people using the carriage roads ($B = 0.32$) and increasing number of people obstructing or blocking the carriage roads ($B = 0.46$).

Remaining analyses examined the relationships among perceived changes in carriage road use and adoption of selected subsets of coping mechanisms: overall displacement behaviors (items C through H), temporal displacement behaviors (items E through G), spatial displacement behaviors (items C, D, and H), the cognitive coping mechanisms of product shift (item I), and rationalization (item J). Linear regression was used with analysis of all displacement behaviors because they contained multiple-item dependent variables, and logistic regression was used with both cognitive coping mechanisms because they used single-item dependent variables.

Results from these additional analyses were generally consistent with the findings described above. Perceived changes in carriage road use explained between 16 and 23 percent of the variance in adoption of the three subsets of displacement behaviors. Perceived changes in carriage road use allowed correct prediction of whether or not respondents adopted the two cognitive coping mechanisms in 68 to 72 percent of the cases. For the three subsets of displacement behaviors, perceived increases in problem behaviors (specifically, bicycles traveling at excessive speeds and people obstructing or blocking the carriage roads) were more powerful predictors of adoption of displacement behaviors than were increases in use level. However, for the two cognitive coping mechanisms, perceived increases in either the number of people using the carriage roads or the number of people participating in selected recreation activities was as important or more important in predicting adoption of these coping mechanisms, as were selected problem behaviors.

CONCLUSIONS

Study findings suggest that coping mechanisms are used widely by the study population. Adoption of the eight individual coping mechanisms studied ranged from about 24 to nearly 65 percent of the sample. Even more impressively, 94 percent of respondents use at least one coping mechanism to avoid or otherwise reconcile perceived undesirable changes in use that have occurred on the carriage roads. These findings, together with previous research, suggest that coping may be pervasive in outdoor recreation.

Study findings also generally corroborate previous research by suggesting that recreationists employ a variety of coping mechanisms. Respondents reported using both behavioral and cognitive coping mechanisms, employ at least two and perhaps all three types of coping mechanisms hypothesized in the literature—displacement, product shift, and rationalization—and utilize both spatial and temporal displacement strategies. Coping is not a monolithic response to changing recreation conditions, and is clearly more complex than intersite displacement as initially conceived and described as the phenomenon of "invasion and succession."

Is coping a "productive" response to perceived changes in outdoor recreation? And how much coping is "too much"? Study findings cannot answer these and related questions definitively. However, they may be suggestive. At the level of the individual, coping can be a normal, healthy response to adverse stimuli. A need for extreme levels of coping, however, may indicate important problems in outdoor recreation, and may not be in the best interest of either the individual or society at large. For example, the coping mechanisms of some crowded, urban populations identified by Milgram

(1970), described earlier, may represent levels and types of coping that are unhealthy and ultimately dysfunctional. In the context of outdoor recreation, too much coping may be excessively stressful at the individual level. The 7.4 percent of the sample that reported intersite displacement from the carriage roads represents an extreme response: These local residents report no longer using this significant recreation resource that is an important part of the national park in their "backyard," and this change in use of the carriage roads is attributed by respondents to the fact that they "don't like the changes in use that have occurred on them."

Study findings may be more troubling at a societal level. The degree of coping reported in this study (and other, related studies) may result in diminished diversity of outdoor recreation opportunities. As visitors sensitive to crowding and conflict adjust their behavior and thinking, recreation opportunities characterized by relatively low-use levels and relatively low potential for conflict become more scarce. Low-density recreation opportunities characterized by relatively similar recreation activities are not inherently "better" than high-density, more diverse opportunities. However, a very large percentage (94 percent) of respondents in this study are taking behavioral and cognitive action to seek the former and avoid the latter. This suggests that it may be wise for park managers to deliberately design and maintain recreation opportunities on the carriage roads, and elsewhere, that serve the needs of a variety of visitors. Ironically, the displacement-related coping mechanisms used by such large percentages of the sample population, in fact, may be exacerbating the situation. As displaced carriage road visitors shift their use to previously low-use times and places, these times and places are no longer as "low-use." In this way, changes in recreation use patterns and experiences can "ripple through" the societal spectrum of recreation opportunities, systematically reducing opportunities for selected types of recreation experiences.

Study findings illustrate the potential for multiple causes for adoption of coping mechanisms, including increasing total use, increasing diversity of recreation activities, and increasing incidences of problem behaviors. All three of these types of changes in carriage road use were statistically significant predictors of behavioral and cognitive coping mechanisms, although their importance varied by type of coping mechanism adopted. This suggests that, when warranted, the need for adoption of coping mechanisms can be minimized by managing any or all of these causative factors.

This research represents the first coping-related study focusing on people who live in or around a park or outdoor recreation area. Do local residents differ from other, more traditional visitors? Local residents may find it easier than other visitors to adopt temporal and intrasite displacement mechanisms because they are probably more knowledgeable about the park and have more opportunities to shift their temporal use patterns. Therefore, the relatively high rate of adoption of these coping mechanisms among the study population may not be representative of other, more traditional visitors. However, because of the high potential for "place attachment" between local residents and their "hometown" park, adoption of intersite displacement as a coping mechanism may be a relatively extreme response among this group, and therefore underestimated in this study compared to other, more traditional visitors. Despite these potential differences between resident and nonresident visitors, findings from this study generally corroborate previous research and the substantive level of coping in outdoor recreation. The relatively high level of coping found in this study suggests the importance of involving local populations, as well as other interest groups, in outdoor recreation planning, management, and research.

This and other coping-related research suggests the inherent complexity of monitoring and managing outdoor recreation. Measures of overall visitor "satisfaction" may be too simplistic to evaluate management of outdoor recreation adequately. To the extent to which recreation visitors adopt behavioral and cognitive mechanisms to cope with undesirable changes in recreation use and users, "satisfaction" may be a superficial and even misleading measure of quality in outdoor recreation. Even though visitor surveys may find high levels of visitor satisfaction, park use and users may be changing in important and potentially undesirable ways. At the level of the individual, behavioral and cognitive coping mechanisms represent stressful adaptations to perceived undesirable changes in outdoor recreation. At the level of society, adoption of coping mechanisms may indicate incremental and unintended changes in the spectrum of outdoor recreation opportunities. This issue is magnified by the fact that this and other studies suggest that coping mechanisms in outdoor recreation may be pervasive.

12 Use of Visual Research Methods to Measure Standards of Quality for Parks and Outdoor Recreation

Visual research methods offer a potentially important research approach to measuring normative standards of quality in parks and outdoor recreation, and they offer several potential advantages over narrative and numerical descriptions of park and outdoor recreation conditions that have been used conventionally in recreation research. Visual research methods can help "standardize" such research by presenting a series of nearly constant images for all respondents. For example, in visual studies of crowding, all respondents see not only the same number of visitors encountered, but also potentially important characteristics of those encountered, including recreation activity engaged in, mode of travel, and group size. In more conventional narrative/numerical approaches in which respondents are asked to judge the acceptability of seeing or encountering a range of other visitors as described in numerical terms, respondents may have to make assumptions about such characteristics, and these assumptions are likely to vary among respondents.

Similarly, visual research methods can focus directly and exclusively on the variables under study. For example, in visual studies of crowding, the number and type of visitors encountered is the only "treatment" allowed to vary, with all other variables held constant. Visual research methods can be especially useful in studying standards of quality for indicator variables that are difficult or awkward to describe in narrative or numerical terms. For example, visual images of trail and campsite impacts may represent a more powerful and elegant means of communication with respondents than detailed and technical narrative descriptions. Finally, visual images can be ed-

This chapter is an edited version of the following paper: Robert Manning and Wayne Freimund, "Use of Visual Research Methods to Measure Standards of Quality for Parks and Outdoor Recreation," *Journal of Leisure Research* 36, no. 4 (2004):557–79.

ited to present conditions that are difficult to find in the field or that do not currently exist. For example, visual studies of crowding have incorporated images of use densities that do not now exist, but that will occur in the future as a function of historical use trends.

Recent research has used computer-generated photographs to measure visitor-based standards of quality for selected components of parks and outdoor recreation areas and experiences. For example, initial research at Arches National Park in Utah found that the number of visitors at attraction sites such as Delicate Arch was important in determining the quality of the recreation experience (Manning et al. 1995; Manning et al. 1993). A second phase of research was designed to measure visitor-based standards of quality for the maximum acceptable number of visitors at such sites (Hof et al. 1994; Manning, Lime, et al. 1996; Manning, Lime, and Hof 1996). A series of sixteen computer-generated photographs was prepared showing a range of visitor use levels at Delicate Arch. A representative sample of visitors who had just completed their hike to Delicate Arch was asked to examine the photographs in random order and rate the acceptability of each on a scale of −4 ("Very Unacceptable") to +4 ("Very Acceptable") with a neutral point of 0. Individual acceptability ratings were aggregated into a social norm curve (a line tracing mean acceptability ratings for each of the study photographs) and provided an empirical foundation for helping to formulate a density-related standard of quality for this site.

Visual research methods have been expanded to address other social and resource components of park and outdoor recreation areas and experiences. For example, outdoor recreation research suggests that perceived crowding may be influenced by visitor behavior, including recreation activities, as well as by density of use. Visual research methods have been used to assess the influence of visitor behavior on crowding-related standards of quality. A study of crowding on the carriage roads at Acadia used a series of nineteen photographs illustrating a range of use levels as well as alternative mixes of hikers and bicyclists, the two principal user groups (Manning et al. 1999; Manning et al. 2000). (Components of this study are described in chapters 2 and 10.) Representative photographs are shown in figure 2.1 of chapter 2. Study findings estimated crowding-related standards of quality for the carriage roads and the influence of type of user group on such standards. Alternative crowding-related standards of quality were found depending on the mix of recreation activities.

Visual research methods also have been applied to selected resource-related impacts of outdoor recreation (Manning, Bacon, et al. 2004; Martin, McCool, and Lucas 1989; Shelby and Shindler 1992). For example, an initial visitor survey at the Isle au Haut and Schoodic Peninsula sections of Acadia identified several potential indicators of quality of the recreation experience, including trail erosion and social trails (informal or visitor-caused trails) (Manning, Bacon, et al. 2004). (The study at the Schoodic Peninsula section of the park is described more fully in chapter 3.) To measure standards of quality, two series of five computer-generated photographs were developed for these indicator variables illustrating a range of impact levels. (The photographs for the Schoodic Peninsula study are shown in figure 3.4 in chapter 3.) These photographs were incorporated into a second visitor survey, and respondents were asked to rate the acceptability of each photograph. Social norm curves derived from these data provide an empirical basis for helping to formulate standards of quality for resource conditions (at least their aesthetic dimensions) at this area.

Technological innovations in visual research methods continue to expand, including digital photography, desktop digital editing software, and development of videotapes, compact disks (CDs), and digital video disks (DVDs). Moreover, adoption of home computers and Internet access is also growing. These trends suggest an increasing variety of media that might be adopted in visual research methods designed to measure standards of quality in parks and outdoor recreation. For example, a recent study incorporated computer-edited images of a range of social and resource conditions at Gwaii Haanas National Park Reserve, British Columbia, onto a videotape that was sent to a representative sample of park visitors (Freimund et al. 2002). The videotape included survey instructions. More than 75 percent of respondents reported that the images on the videotape served as useful reminders of their visit and helped them articulate their normative standards for recreation-related impacts.

THEORETICAL AND METHODOLOGICAL ISSUES

Use of visual research methods in measuring standards of quality in parks and outdoor recreation has raised a number of theoretical and methodological issues. These issues include the contexts in which visual research methods may be most appropriate, comparison of standards of quality derived from visual research methods and more-conventional narrative/ numerical methods, validity of visual research methods, and methodological cal issues in applying visual research methods.

Application to Frontcountry and Other High-Density Contexts

Much of the research on crowding-related standards of quality in outdoor recreation has focused on wilderness or backcountry areas. By definition, use levels in these areas are relatively low. In this context, a narrative/ numerical approach to measurement of standards of quality is probably appropriate. Standards-related questions usually take one of two such forms: Respondents are asked to rate the acceptability of encountering various numbers of other visitors or groups of visitors, or respondents are simply asked to report the maximum acceptable number of encounters.

However, in frontcountry and other relatively high-use contexts, this measurement approach may be less appropriate. In such high-use areas, it may be unrealistic to expect respondents to judge or report accurately the maximum acceptable number of visitors or groups of visitors. The research literature is suggestive of this issue. First, several studies have found that respondents are less likely to be able to report a discrete maximum acceptable number of encounters in relatively high-use areas as compared to relatively low-use areas (Roggenbuck et al. 1991; Shelby and Vaske 1991; Vaske et al. 1986). Second, there tends to be less consensus about such crowding-related standards in relatively high-use areas, and this may be due at least in part to measurement error (Manning 1999). Third, there is evidence that self-reports of encounters by visitors in relatively high-use areas are not accurate. A study of river use found that floaters who experienced fewer than six encounters per day with other river users generally were able to report them accurately (by comparison with actual encounters as counted by a trained observer; Shelby and Colvin 1982). But at higher levels of encounters, most visitors reported only about half as many encounters as actually occurred.

Thus, in frontcountry or other high-use density contexts, visual research methods may be more appropriate than conventional narrative or numerical methods because they do not require visitors to keep track of and report accurately discrete numbers of other visitors or groups of visitors encountered (or that are acceptable). For this and other reasons (as outlined in the following section), visual research methods may offer more valid estimates of crowding-related standards of quality, especially in high-density settings.

However, it should be noted that in some high-use areas, the absolute number of other visitors encountered (along trails or at attraction sites) may not be an especially salient indicator variable. Crowding can be manifested in potentially many ways, including waiting times to access visitor attractions (Budruk and Manning 2003). In such cases, narrative/numerical question formats to elicit visitor-based standards of quality may be appropriate and effective.

Comparison of Visual and Narrative/Numerical Research Methods

A related issue concerns comparison of crowding-related standards derived from visual and narrative/numerical research methods. A test of this relationship was conducted as part of the research at Arches National Park described earlier (Manning, Lime, et al. 1996). A social norm curve derived from respondent ratings of the acceptability of the sixteen photographs illustrating a range of visitors at Delicate Arch estimated a crowding-related standard of quality of approximately 28 visitors at one time (the point at which aggregate acceptability ratings fell out of the acceptable range and into the unacceptable range). Using a narrative/numerical approach, respondents also were asked to report a discrete maximum number of visitors at one time acceptable at this site. The average number of visitors reported was just under 17, suggesting a substantially lower crowding-related standard of quality than that derived from the visual research method.

The literature may help to explain why the crowding standards derived from visual research methods are substantially higher than those derived from conventional narrative/numerical methods, and why the former may be a more valid or realistic estimate. Studies of crowding in outdoor recreation indicate that perceived crowding may be a function of several categories of variables, including the characteristics of respondents, the characteristics of visitors encountered, and situational or environmental variables (Manning 1985, 1999). (This issue is addressed more fully in chapter 10.) The second category of variables—the characteristics of visitors encountered—may be of particular interest when comparing visual and narrative/numerical research methods. Considerable evidence in the literature indicates that the characteristics of visitors encountered can affect crowding-related standards of quality. Factors found important include the type and size of group, visitor behavior, and the degree to which groups are perceived to be alike. For example, several studies have found differential crowding effects based on nonmotorized versus motorized boats (Lucas 1964b), hikers and horseback riders (Stankey 1973, 1980), and small versus large groups (Lime 1972; Stankey 1973). In all of these cases, encounters with one type of visitor (the latter type in the above cases) has greater impact on perceived crowding than encounters with the other type of visitor.

Similarly, inappropriate behavior (e.g., noncompliance with rules and regulations, boisterous behavior) can contribute in important ways to perceived crowding. In fact, several studies indicate that such behavior can have a greater impact on perceived crowding than sheer number of encounters (Driver and Bassett 1975; Titre and Mills 1982; West 1982).

The studies and ideas described above may suggest why crowding-related standards of quality developed from the traditional narrative/numerical approach might be interpreted most appropriately as the lower bounds of acceptability. The crowding literature illustrates that all contacts do not contribute equally to perceived crowding. However, studies that query respondents directly about appropriate encounter levels (i.e., narrative/numerical studies) contain an implied assumption that all encounters are similar. Moreover, such studies by their very nature focus on encounters that require full and explicit attention by the respondent. In other words, they present the worst case. Encounters between groups that are similar and thus may require and receive little conscious attention, and may have relatively little effect on perceived crowding, are left unconsidered. Crowding-related standards of quality based on narrative/numerical research methods might be increased to the extent that groups are compatible in mode of travel, size, behavior, and other factors that contribute to perceptions of alikeness.

Based on this reasoning, visual research methods may represent a more realistic approach to measuring crowding-related standards of quality. Respondents are able to examine a visual portrayal of use conditions, including at least some relevant characteristics of those encountered (e.g., recreation activity, mode of travel, size of group). It is likely that some of the visitors portrayed in these scenes may not consciously register in the minds of respondents. The differences in crowding-related standards of quality found in studies comparing visual and narrative/numerical research methods tend to support this idea empirically.

Validity of Visual Research Methods

As visual research methods are applied increasingly to measure standards of quality in parks and outdoor recreation, it is important that the validity of this approach be assessed. However, the issue of validity is complex and can be assessed in multiple ways (Carmines and Zeller 1979; Nunnally 1978). In its most generic sense, the concept of validity refers to the degree to which an instrument does what it is intended to do or measures what it purports to measure. To what degree do visual research methods for measuring standards of quality provide valid estimates of the minimum acceptable conditions of parks and related areas? Several approaches to measuring validity may be appropriate to answering this question.

"Face" validity is a conventional approach to assessing validity, and refers to the extent to which an instrument "looks like" it measures what it is intended to measure. Studies incorporating visual research methods in measuring standards of quality for parks and outdoor recreation might contribute to assessing face validity in two ways. First, several studies conducted in national parks have adapted and applied a "verbal protocol analysis" (Schkade and Payne 1994) designed to assist respondents in assessing the degree to which they understood study questions and the extent to which they are confident in their answers (Manning et al. 2001). In these studies, a series of statements was presented to respondents at the conclusion of visitor surveys employing visual research methods to measure standards of quality, and respondents were asked to indicate the extent to which they agreed or disagreed with these statements. Statements included "I understood the questions that were asked," "The photographs realistically represent different levels of use at this area," "I was confused by the questions that asked me to choose between the photographs," "It was very difficult to rate the acceptability of the photographs," "The answers I gave to these questions accurately represent my feelings about acceptable use levels on the trails I hiked," and "The National Park Service should manage visitor use levels based on the kind of information collected in studies like these." In almost all cases, study findings indicated that most respondents had confidence in the visual research methods used.

A second way of assessing face validity concerns the logic and consistency of study findings derived from visual research approaches. Three approaches might be used to explore this issue. First, the social norm curve shown in figure 12.1 is a representative example of those derived from visual research methods. Data used to derive the figure are from a study employing six photographs illustrating a range of use densities at Sand Beach, a popular attraction site at Acadia. (Study photographs are shown in figure

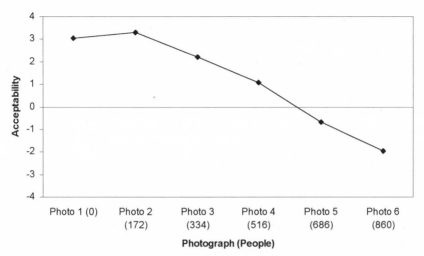

Figure 12.1 *Social norm curve for Sand Beach.*

7.1, chapter 7.) The points defining the social norm curve are mean acceptability ratings for the six photographs. As would be expected, average acceptability ratings decline with increasing use levels, and a strong statistical relationship exists between these variables, with the number of visitors in the photographs explaining 40 percent of the variance in acceptability scores.

A second approach to examining the logic and consistency of study findings from visual research concerns the use of alternative "evaluative dimensions." (This issue is described in more detail in chapter 13.) Visually based studies at several popular attraction sites at Acadia (Sand Beach, Thunder Hole, Ocean Drive) incorporated four evaluative dimensions in measuring visitor-based standards of quality: "preference" (the condition respondents preferred), "acceptability" (the maximum level of impact respondents judged acceptable), "management action" (the maximum level of impact respondents felt the NPS should allow before limiting visitor use), and "displacement" (the level of impact that would keep respondents from visiting the park again) (Manning et al. 1999; Manning 2001). Logic suggests that crowding-related standards of quality estimated from these alternative evaluative dimensions would be ordered, with the lowest standards associated with the preference dimension, the highest standards associated with the displacement dimension, and the acceptability and management action related standards near the midpoint of the range. This pattern of findings was consistent across all sample sites.

Another approach to assessing validity concerns the concept of "predictive" or "criterion" validity. This approach examines the correlation between findings derived from a study instrument and some important form of behavior that is external to the instrument, the latter referred to as the criterion. The concept of congruence offers a test of criterion validity. Congruence refers to the extent to which visitors behave in relation to their stated standards (Manning 1999; Shelby and Heberlein 1986). Data from the study of visitors to Delicate Arch reported earlier in this paper offer a test of congruence (Manning, Lime, et al. 1996). Three variables were used to test congruence: (1) the visitor-based standard of quality for the maximum acceptable number of visitors at Delicate Arch, (2) the number of visitors in the photograph that respondents reported as best representing the density condition when they visited Delicate Arch, and (3) a measure of perceived crowding at Delicate Arch. It was hypothesized that if respondents experienced more visitors at Delicate Arch than the visitor-based standard of quality, they would rate the experience as at least "slightly crowded." Likewise, if they experienced fewer visitors than the standard of quality, they would rate the experience as "not at all crowded." Study findings showed that 74 percent of respondents fell into one of these two categories of congruence.

A fourth conventional approach to assessing validity applies the concept of "construct" validity. This approach to validity examines the degree to which multiple variables that comprise a theoretical construct are represented in instruments designed to measure that construct. Measures of crowding-related standards of quality are ultimately aimed at the theoretical construct of crowding. As noted earlier in this chapter, normative interpretation of crowding in outdoor recreation generally has recognized three broad types of variables as mediating perceived crowding: (1) characteristics of respondents (e.g., recreation activity in which the respondent is engaged), (2) characteristics of those encountered (e.g., recreation activity in which those encountered are engaged), and (3) situational variables (e.g., location in which encounters occur) (Manning 1985, 1999). (This issue is described more fully in chapter 10.) Visual research methods applied to measuring standards of quality have begun to incorporate all three types of these variables. For example, the study of carriage road use at Acadia described earlier in this chapter used a visual research approach to measure crowding-related standards of quality for two types of respondents/trail users (hikers and bicyclists), for encountering two types of trail users (hikers and bicyclists), and for two types of trails (high- and low-use trails) (Manning et al. 2000). Inclusion of multiple variables or dimensions of the theoretical construct of crowding into visually based measures of crowding-related standards of quality can be seen to enhance the power and resolution of such measures as well as contributing to their construct validity.

The concept of validity is complex, and might be described most appropriately as an objective to which research should aspire rather than an end to be reached. In the words of Nunnally, "validity is usually a matter of degree rather than an all or none property, and validation is an unending process" (1978, 87). Validity can be assessed through theoretical, empirical, and common sense approaches. Findings from visual research approaches described above tend to support the validity of visual research methods applied to measurement of standards of quality in parks and outdoor recreation.

Methodological Issues

As application of visual research methods to measuring standards of quality proceeds, methodological issues have arisen. For example, in other environmental applications of visual research methods, the landscape perspective of photographs may influence assessments of environmental conditions reported by respondents (Brown et al. 1989; Daniel and Boster 1976; Hollenhorst et al. 1993). This issue was explored in the context of measuring crowding-related standards of quality in parks (Manning et al. 2002). As part of a study at Grand Canyon National Park described earlier in this chapter, two sets of photographs were prepared to illustrate a range of visitor use levels on the Bright Angel Trail, the principal trail that connects the South Rim of the canyon with the Colorado River. Both sets of photographs showed the same range of visitor use levels along the same 50-meter section of trail. However, one set of photographs was taken looking up the trail (showing a characteristically "closed-in" view) while the other set of photographs was taken looking down the trail (showing a characteristically "open" view). Half the sample of 310 hikers viewed the former set of photographs and half viewed the latter. Study data indicate virtually no differences in the crowding-related standards reported by respondents.

"Starting point bias" represents another potential methodological issue associated with visual research methods (as well as more conventional narrative/numerical methods). Research on willingness to pay for environmental amenities suggests that the initial monetary values presented to respondents may influence the ultimate value derived from the research (Desvousges et al. 1983; Rowe et al. 1986; Thayer 1981). To explore this issue in the context of using visual research methods in measuring park and outdoor recreation standards, respondents to one site in the Grand Canyon National Park study described above were split into two subsamples. The first group of respondents was shown the six study photographs of a range of visitor use levels in increasing order of use density, while the other group of respondents saw the photographs in decreasing order. Study data indicate no substantive differences in the crowding-related standards reported by the two groups of respondents.

While many methodological issues are likely to be inherent in visual research methods as they are applied to measuring standards of quality in parks and other outdoor recreation areas, initial research suggests that these methods may be relatively robust. That is, careful applications do not appear to be influenced heavily by methodological variations.

CONCLUSIONS

Visual research methods have played an important role in environmental research and management for several decades. More recently, these methods have been adapted for use in measuring standards of quality in parks and outdoor recreation. Study findings suggest that visual research methods may have some advantages over more-conventional narrative/numerical research approaches, and that visual research methods may be particularly appropriate in selected park and outdoor recreation contexts such as frontcountry and other high-use areas and for resource-related impacts that are difficult to describe in narrative and numerical formats. Moreover, in certain contexts (e.g., high-use areas) visual research methods may result in more realistic estimates of visitor-based standards of quality. Findings from studies employing visual research methods generally meet conventional tests of research validity. Finally, tests of selected methodological issues inherent in visual research approaches suggest that these methods may be relatively robust in that resulting data do not appear to be greatly influenced by methodological alternatives. Visual research methods increasingly are being adopted into studies of park and outdoor recreation standards, and have received strong endorsement in the literature. For example, a recent analysis by Hall and Roggenbuck concluded that "the short phrases used in normative questions (such as 'number of encounters per day') cannot capture the true complexity and nature of a recreation experience and respondents must inevitably fill in background assumptions and conditions . . . Thus, we feel that . . . visual approaches are superior to the traditional . . . form of numerically based question[s]" (2002, 334).

Although visual research methods are promising as an approach to measuring standards of quality in parks and outdoor recreation, several issues warrant attention and may limit their usefulness. A photograph can portray a more realistic description of a recreation setting than can a number or short narrative statement, but there are limitations to what a photograph can present. It is unrealistic to expect that photographs can display all relevant characteristics of visitor use and users. Moreover, still-photographs are static, only account for visual stimuli, and by definition may not be well suited to representing the inherent dynamics of a recreation experience. Video photography and other dynamic media may represent at least a partial solution to this issue. For example, videotape has been used to portray interactions between customers and service personnel (Bateson and Hui 1992), and nonvisual variables, such as sound and smell, have been found to affect perceived crowding (Eroglu and Harrell 1986; Rohrmann and Bishop 2002). Given the pace of technological advancement, the possibilities for edited digital video, virtual reality, and other ways of representing realty may emerge as viable research tools much sooner than might be expected. When they do, this review suggests that these visual media will further facilitate effective communication between researchers and respondents and our understanding of the acceptability of social and ecological conditions in parks and outdoor recreation.

13 Alternative Measurement Approaches for Normative Standards of Crowding in Parks and Outdoor Recreation

As research on normative standards for crowding and other impacts of outdoor recreation has proceeded, several approaches to measuring norms have evolved. Moreover, several issues surrounding norm measurement and application also have arisen. The purposes of the study described in this chapter were to apply and compare alternative approaches to measuring crowding norms and to identify and explore several issues surrounding measurement and application of crowding norms.

Traditionally, crowding norms have been measured using a "numerical" approach. For example, respondents are asked to evaluate a range of encounters (0, 5, 10, 15, etc.) with other groups per day along trails. The personal norms derived are aggregated and graphed to construct a "norm curve" from which social norms can be identified (as illustrated throughout the book). This numerical approach is often shortened to reduce respondent burden by simply asking respondents in an open-ended format to report the maximum acceptable number of encounters with other groups per day. These two approaches might be called the "long" and "short" versions of this measurement technique.

More recently, visual approaches to measuring crowding and other recreation-related norms have been developed whereby a range of visitor use levels are portrayed through a series of computer-generated photographs. (This issue is described more fully in chapter 12.) As with the numerical approach described above, long and short versions of this measurement technique can be used. The long version asks respondents to evaluate each

This chapter is an edited version of the following paper: Robert Manning, William Valliere, Ben Wang, and Charles Jacobi, "Crowding Norms: Alternative Measurement Approaches," *Leisure Sciences* 21, no. 2 (1999): 97–115.

photograph in a series of photographs. The short version asks respondents to select the photograph that illustrates the highest use or impact level acceptable.

An issue implicit in all of these measurement approaches concerns the evaluative dimension used in these questions. When respondents have been asked to evaluate a range of use levels and related impacts, the response scale has included terminology specifying a number of evaluative dimensions, such as "preference," "acceptability," and "tolerance." These alternative evaluative dimensions may have substantially different meanings to respondents and may result in significantly different personal and social norms.

A related issue concerns the normative nature of evaluation measures. Researchers applying normative theory and techniques to outdoor recreation have noted several important elements of norms as they traditionally are defined (Heywood 1993a, 1993b, 1996a, 1996b; Noe 1992; Roggenbuck et al. 1991; Shelby and Vaske 1991; Shelby, Vaske, and Donnelly 1996; Williams, Roggenbuck, and Bange 1991). One of these elements suggests that social norms usually are interpreted as being applied externally. That is, individuals tailor and conform their behavior to what they believe is expected of them by social groups or society at large. This suggests that norms might be measured by asking respondents about what recreation conditions or impacts they believe other visitors feel are appropriate or acceptable. A second element of social norms as traditionally defined suggests that norms have a strong obligatory nature. That is, norms define what "should" be. This suggests that norms might be measured by asking respondents about what recreation conditions or level of impacts they feel managers should maintain.

STUDY METHODS

The norm measurement approaches and issues identified here were incorporated in a series of studies of crowding on the carriage roads of Acadia. The studies included two surveys of carriage road users and a survey of residents of communities in surrounding towns. The norm measurement approaches and issues described above were incorporated into these studies in the following ways:

1. Visual Approach

A visual approach to norm measurement was used by producing a series of nineteen photographs of a generic 100-meter section of carriage roads showing varying levels and types of use. This measure is called persons-per-viewscape" (PPV). Types of use were restricted to hikers and bikers because these are the predominant uses. Sample photographs are shown in figure 2.1 (chapter 2). A "long" version of the visual approach to measuring crowding norms was used by asking respondents to rate the acceptability of each of the nineteen photographs using a scale from -4 ("Very Unacceptable") to $+4$ ("Very Acceptable"). [The survey of community residents used a subset of six of the nineteen photographs used in the survey of carriage road visitors. This was done to minimize the materials and associated costs of including a large number of photographs in a mailed questionnaire. However, both sets of photographs covered the same range (0 to 30) of visitors.] Several "short" versions of the visual approach also were used, employing the evaluative dimensions as described in items 3 through 6 below.

2. Numerical Approach

A short version of the numerical approach to measuring crowding norms was used by asking respondents, "What do you think is the maximum number of visitors that would be acceptable to see at any one time on the section of the carriage roads shown in the photographs?" Respondents were asked to answer this question for three mixes of use: (1) all visitors are hikers, (2) all visitors are bikers, and (3) half of visitors are hikers and half are bikers. Respondents were given the option of indicating that the number of visitors seen did not matter, or that the number of visitors seen mattered but they could not report a maximum acceptable number.

3. Preference and Acceptability

Using the photographs, respondents were asked two questions employing the commonly used evaluative dimensions of preference and acceptability. These questions were, "Which photograph shows the highest pattern of visitor use that you would prefer to see along this section of the carriage roads?" and "Which photograph shows the highest pattern of visitor use that you think would be acceptable to see on this section of the carriage roads?" For the latter question, respondents were given the option of indicating that all of the photographs were acceptable.

4. Displacement

Using the photographs, respondents were asked, "Which photograph shows the pattern of visitor use that is so unacceptable that you would no longer use the carriage roads or would shift your use of the carriage roads to a different location or time?" Respondents were given the option of indicating that none of the photographs represented this condition. This question was designed to explore the relationship between the two commonly used evaluative dimensions noted previously and a third dimension that might be called "displacement."

5. Management Action

Using the photographs, respondents were asked, "Which photograph shows the highest pattern of visitor use that the National Park Service should allow on this section of the carriage roads? In other words, at what point should visitors be restricted from using the carriage roads?" Respondents were given the option of indicating that visitor use should not be restricted at any point represented in the photographs. This question was designed to explore the effect on crowding norms of a more explicitly obligatory or prescriptive evaluative dimension that might be called "management action."

6. Acceptability to Others

Using the photographs, respondents were asked, "Which photograph shows the highest pattern of visitor use that you think most other visitors would find acceptable to see on this section of the carriage roads?" Respondents were given the option of indicating that most visitors would find all of the photographs acceptable. This question was designed to explore the effect on crowding norms of a more externally imposed evaluative dimension that might be called "acceptability to others."

Table 13.1 outlines the application of each of the norm-measurement approaches within the three study surveys described at the beginning of this section. The first column of the table lists alternative measurement approaches. The measurement approaches of greatest concern to this study are designated with letters A through G. Measurement approach A repre-

TABLE 13.1 Social norms derived from alternative measurement approaches

Measurement approach	First visitor survey				Second visitor survey				Community survey			
	Mean	SD	CV	Statistical test[a]	Mean	SD	CV	Statistical test[a]	Mean	SD	CV	Statistical test[a]
Visual approach												
Long form												
All hikers	11.6	4.5	0.38									
All bikers	10.0	4.0	0.40									
Equal distribution (A)	12.7	5.1	0.39	(C)					12.6	5.2	0.41	(C, E)
Short form												
Preference (B)					5.4	5.0	0.93	(C, D, E, F)	7.0	5.8	0.83	(C, D, E, F)
Acceptability[b] (C)	10.7	5.1	0.48	(A, D, E, F, G)	9.7	4.3	0.44	(B, D, E, F)	10.1	5.3	0.52	(A, B, C, D, E, F, G)
Acceptability to others[c] (D)	14.8	7.9	0.53	(C, E, F)	11.4	4.7	0.41	(B, C, E, F)	11.3	5.1	0.45	(B, C, E, F)
Management action[d] (E)	17.8	8.5	0.48	(C, D, E)	17.5	5.9	0.34	(B, C, D, F)	15.6	5.8	0.37	(B, C, D, F)
Displacement[e] (F)	25.2	7.1	0.28	(C, D, E)	20.9	6.6	0.32	(B, C, D, F)	19.1	6.7	0.35	(B, C, D, E)
Numerical approach												
All hikers	17.6	39.0	2.23						10.1	11.8	1.17	
All bikers	12.8	31.6	2.47						6.1	7.0	0.86	
Equal distribution (G)	16.4	45.6	2.78	(C)					8.1	7.0	0.86	(C)

[a]Statistical tests consisted of t-tests of difference of means using an alpha level of 0.05.

[b]Number of respondents who checked the response option "all of the photographs would be acceptable." First visitor survey = 40; Second visitor survey = 14; Community survey = 25.

[c]Number of respondents who checked the response option "all of the photographs would be acceptable to most visitors." First visitors survey = 34; Second visitor survey = 15; Community survey = 31.

[d]Number of respondents who checked the response option "visitor use should not be restricted." First visitor survey = 184; Second visitor survey 115; Community survey = 91.

[e]Number of respondents who checked the response option "none of the photographs represent this condition." First visitor survey = 29; Second visitor survey = 39; Community survey = 38.

Note: SD = standard deviation. CV = coefficient of variation.

A = Long form of visual approach; acceptability. B = Short form of visual approach; preference. C = Short form of visual approach; acceptability. D = Short form of visual approach; acceptability to others.
E = Short form of visual approach; management action. F = Short form of visual approach; displacement. G = Short form of numerical approach; acceptability.

sents the long form of the visual approach as described in item 1 above. This measurement approach incorporates the commonly used evaluative dimension of acceptability. Measurement approaches B, C, D, E, and F represent short forms of the visual approach, also described in item 1. However, they incorporate the alternative evaluative dimensions as described in items 3 through 6. Measurement approach G represents the short version of the numerical approach as described in item 2.

STUDY FINDINGS

Study findings are summarized in table 13.1. The table includes mean values for social norms as derived from all of the measurement approaches described above. Standard deviations and coefficients of variation also are included as measures of the degree of consensus regarding these social norms. Standard deviations commonly are used in normative research as measures of consensus. However, coefficients of variation, which are calculated by dividing the standard deviation by the mean, standardize measures of variance across the alternative measures of crowding norms.

In keeping with the emphasis of this paper, comparisons within this table are focused on visual versus numerical measures, long versus short question format, and alternative evaluative dimensions. Statistical analysis consisted of t-tests of differences of means using an alpha level of 0.05. Comparison of visual and numerical norm-measurement approaches uses the measures signified by the letters C and G. Comparison of long and short norm-measurement question formats uses the measures signified by the letters A and C. Comparison of the alternative norm measurement evaluative dimensions uses the measures signified by the letters B, C, D, E, and F. Letter designations in the statistical test columns of table 13.1 indicate statistically significant differences among the alternative measures. For example, the letter C in the third row of the first statistical test column indicates that the norm of 12.7 PPV derived from the long form of the visual measurement approach used in the first visitor survey is significantly different from the norm of 10.7 PPV derived from the short version of the visual measurement approach used in this same survey.

It is clear from the table that social norms can vary widely depending upon the measurement approach used. PPV-related norms vary across the studies and range from 5.4 (for the preference-based norm using the short question format for the second visitor survey) to 25.2 (for the displacement-based norm using the short question format for the first visitor survey). In fact, these differences are even greater than they appear, as several visually based measures of social norms are underestimated—sometimes substantially—because some respondents reported that none of the levels of use shown in study photographs reached their personal norm or that visitor user should not be restricted at any level.

Measures of variance also show substantial variation across the measurement approaches. Variance tends to be relatively high for the numerically derived measures compared with the visually derived measures. However, much more consistency exists across the studies with regard to individual measurement approaches, at least for those that are visually based. For example, mean social norms derived from the short form of the visual approach using the evaluative dimension of acceptability range only from 9.7 to 10.7 across the three studies.

Study findings and their implications are discussed in the following section. This discussion is organized according to the issues that are the focus of this paper: numerical versus visual approaches, long versus short question formats, and evaluative dimensions. A final discussion point draws on several aspects of study findings to suggest that traditional norm research may lead to crowding-related standards of quality that are overly conservative.

DISCUSSION

Numerical Versus Visual Approach

Findings indicate that statistically significant differences exist between crowding norms derived from the visual and numerical measurement approaches. It seems most appropriate to compare findings from the short question format for both of these measurement approaches, using the evaluative dimension of acceptability for the visual approach. These measures are most directly comparable. The first visitor survey resulted in a higher mean acceptable PPV norm of 16.4 for the numerical approach than the comparable mean acceptable PPV norm of 10.7 for the visual approach. However, for the community survey, the difference was in the opposite direction: The mean acceptable PPV norm for the numerical approach was 8.1 compared with 10.1 for the visual approach. The community survey may present the more rigorous test, as the visual approach used six photographs, all depicting equal distribution of hikers and bikers. The first visitor survey used a larger number of photographs that depicted both equal and unequal distribution of hikers and bikers, although the total set of photographs was balanced among those that depicted an equal distribution of hikers and bikers, a majority of hikers, and a majority of bikers.

These findings are obviously confounding but might be explained or interpreted in light of the variance associated with these measures. As noted previously, the variance associated with the numerical measures is relatively high, especially for the first visitor survey. The differences in variance for the numerical measures between the two surveys might be explained by the experience level of the two populations. Community residents report that they use the carriage roads an average of ten times per year, whereas over 30 percent of respondents in the first visitor survey reported that they were first-time users of the carriage roads. Previous research suggests that more-experienced and involved visitors are more likely to be able to report a crowding-related norm, and that such norms tend to be more highly crystallized (Shelby, Vaske, and Donnelly 1996; Young, Williams, and Roggenbuck 1991). This suggests once again that the community survey might be a more appropriate test of differences between the numerical and visual approaches. Although the numerically and visually based norms differed to a statistically significant degree in the community survey, the difference was substantively small.

Findings regarding variance also suggest potential advantages of the visually based measurement approach. The high variances associated with the numerically based approach, especially in the case of the visitor surveys, indicate that less consensus or crystallization is associated with this measurement technique, and this diminishes its potential value. However, it also should be noted that the lower variance associated with the visual approach may be contrived, at least to some degree. With this measurement approach, respondents choose from a limited range of use levels and, by definition, this may reduce resulting variance compared with the numerical approach. The number of visitors who reported some form of the response that none of the photographs represented the condition addressed in the questions concerning alternative evaluative dimensions is suggestive of the extent to which this was an issue in this study. With the exception of "management action," less than 10 percent of respondents chose this option.

This issue suggests that it is important that studies using the visual approach include photographs depicting a wide range of use levels.

If findings from the community survey are considered the more appropriate and rigorous comparison of the numerical and visual measurement approaches, then study findings are consistent with the only other such test (Manning, Lime, et al. 1996). In that study, norms for the number of people at one time at an attraction site (Delicate Arch in Arches National Park, Utah) were found to be nearly twice as high using the visual approach compared with the numerical approach. That study reasoned that numerically based measurement approaches may underestimate crowding-related norms because such questions, by definition, call the explicit attention of respondents to all other visitors encountered. Crowding research suggests that not all encounters are equivalent and that encounters with some types of visitors—those engaged in similar activities, with similar group size, and those engaged in appropriate behaviors (that is, those visitors perceived to be generally "like" respondents)—may contribute little to perceived crowding (Manning 1985, 1986). Visually based studies are more likely to allow for such considerations to be included in judgments about crowding norms and therefore may provide more "realistic" estimates of crowding norms.

The magnitude of the differences between this study and that of Delicate Arch (Manning, Lime, et al. 1996) may be a function of the use levels studied. In the latter study, use levels and crowding norms were much higher than in the study described here. Research suggests that visitors tend to substantially underreport encounters if use levels are relatively high (Shelby and Colvin 1982). This suggests that differences between the numerical and visual approaches are likely to be magnified under conditions of relatively high-use, and that the visual approach may be especially applicable in such situations. If use levels are relatively low, numerical and visual approaches may yield crowding-related norms that are more comparable.

Long Versus Short Format

Findings indicate that a statistically significant, but relatively small, difference exists between crowding norms derived from the long and short question formats. The long format resulted in higher crowding norms for both studies in which both question formats were used. The first visitor survey resulted in mean acceptable PPV norms of 12.7 and 10.7 for the long and short question formats, respectively. The community survey resulted in comparable norms of 12.6 and 10.1 PPV for the long and short question formats, respectively.

The reason for these differences is not certain. However, it may be that the long question format provides an estimate of the absolute lowest level of acceptability that results, in turn, in a higher crowding norm. Crowding norms for the long question format are determined by the point at which the norm curve crossed the neutral point on the acceptability scale. By definition, this is the point at which acceptability falls out of the acceptable range and into the unacceptable range.

By contrast, the short question format is less definitive. Respondents are asked to report the highest level of use that is acceptable, and they may tend to report a level of use that is somewhat lower than "absolute lowest" acceptability. This issue may be magnified with the visual approach, in which respondents report the highest use level acceptable by selecting one of a series of photographs. If none of the photographs precisely shows the highest level of use acceptable, respondents must select a photograph that shows a level of use that is close to highest level of use acceptable. Respondents may tend to select a photograph that shows a lower level of use rather than a higher level of use to ensure that the use level they report is indeed acceptable.

There is little to indicate whether the long or short question format is "best" or more "valid." However, if respondent burden allows, the long question format may be preferred, as it provides more information than the short format (it estimates a range of norms from most to least acceptable) and may provide more precise estimates of the highest level of use acceptable.

Evaluative Dimensions

Findings related to the issue of evaluative dimension are the clearest and have the most obvious research and management implications. The five evaluative dimensions tested differed from one another significantly and often substantively. A clear hierarchy of crowding norms among these dimensions resulted that appears to be intuitively meaningful. Norms range from a low associated with preference to a high associated with displacement. Acceptability, the most commonly used evaluative dimension, is closest to preference but is substantially lower than the more obligatory or prescriptive measure of management action. This may reflect the fact that respondents are more willing to accept higher use levels if they are made more explicitly aware of the tradeoffs associated with public access. Finally, acceptability to other visitors falls in the middle of the range and is closest to acceptability of respondents. Most respondents apparently feel that they are at least a little more discriminating (or more sensitive) than most other visitors.

These findings are generally consistent with previous research, although they offer a more extended treatment of this issue than has been possible to date. For example, studies consistently have found preferred norms to be substantially lower than acceptable or displacement norms, often less than half (Hammitt and Rutlin 1995; Martinson and Shelby 1992; Tarrant et al., 1997; Watson 1995; Young et al., 1991). A similar pattern is evident in findings from this study. Findings from studies using the long question format also are suggestive of these relationships. The norm curves constructed from such data often identify a range of norms that are above the neutral point on the evaluative scale and therefore all are judged to be at least minimally acceptable. This range of acceptable norms generally is anchored at the highest point on the norm curve (which is generally equivalent to preference) and the point on the norm curve that crosses the neutral point of the evaluation scale (which is generally equivalent to acceptability).

These findings suggest several research and management implications. First, the evaluative dimension of norm measurement should receive careful attention, as it substantially influences the norms derived. Researchers should give thoughtful consideration to the evaluative dimensions selected for inclusion in norm research and should encourage managers to interpret and apply study findings with caution. The norm for displacement was more than four times the preference-based norm for carriage road visitors and more than three times as high for local residents.

Second, there is little to suggest which of these evaluative dimensions is "best" or most "valid." Each has potential advantages and disadvantages. For example, standards of quality based on preference-related norms may result in very high-quality recreation experiences but would restrict access to a relatively low number of visitors. In contrast, standards of quality based on acceptability, management action, or displacement allow access to greater numbers of visitors but may result in recreation experiences of lesser quality. Findings that offer insights into multiple evaluative dimensions provide the richest base of information and may lead to formulation of the most thoughtful and informed standards of quality. Such data allow more explicit understanding of the potential trade offs between use level and quality of the recreation experience.

Third, alternative norm-measurement approaches can be used to provide insight into multiple evaluative dimensions for norms. One approach would adopt the short question format but would present the question using several evaluative dimensions. A second approach would adopt the long question format using a single evaluative dimension. The evaluative dimension of acceptability might be recommended because it results in the norms that are not at the extremes of the range and because it is used commonly, allowing comparisons across areas and study populations. This long question format results in a norm curve suggesting a range of norms from preference to displacement.

Fourth, it is important that researchers explicitly specify what evaluative dimensions have been used in norm-related studies. It is particularly important to specify whether or not respondents have been asked explicitly to consider potential tradeoffs between crowding and public access, as is the case with the management-action evaluative dimension used in this study. As noted previously, this information needs to be considered carefully by managers. This information is also important to other researchers who may wish to compare recreation-related norms across studies, areas, and time.

A final observation concerns the variance associated with the five alternative evaluative dimensions. A relatively consistent pattern can be observed across the three surveys used in this study. Variance is consistently lowest for the "highest impact" evaluative dimensions, while variance is consistently higher for preference-based norms.

Norms and Standards of Quality

A final point of discussion is based on several study findings and their implications. Consideration of findings from this study and others suggests that recent research on crowding and related norms may lead to standards of quality that are overly conservative and, therefore may limit public access unnecessarily. This is suggested most strongly by findings related to alternative evaluative dimensions. First, most studies to date have used acceptability, preference, or another evaluative dimension that is in the lower range of potential norms. If other evaluative dimensions were used, they probably would suggest higher crowding-related standards of quality.

Second, the management-action evaluative dimension explored in this study may have special appeal for formulating standards of quality. As noted previously, it incorporates the more strictly obligatory or prescriptive element of norms as they traditionally are defined. It also might be interpreted as a more informed judgment on the part of respondents because it implies the management implications of their responses. The question is phrased in such a way that respondents are informed that their answers will be used to help set standards of quality and that such standards of quality ultimately may restrict public access to the recreation area under study. In this context, respondents have an opportunity to process internally the inherent trade-offs between the quality of the recreation experience and public accessibility. This may result in a more informed judgment on the part of respondents than a more isolated and independent measure of preference, pleasantness, or another evaluative dimension. To the extent to which this reasoning is valid, it is magnified by the very substantive differences among preference, acceptability, and management action found in this study. Moreover, it should be remembered that the management action–based norms found in this study are substantially underestimated by virtue of the fact that approximately one-third of visitors and community residents responded that "use of the carriage roads should not be restricted," at least not at any levels of use represented in the study photographs.

Findings regarding numerical and visual approaches to measuring crowding-related norms also suggest that standards of quality may be overly conservative using traditional measures. However, this issue is less clear. Numerical measures may underestimate crowding-related norms by calling explicit and conscious attention to all encounters. Visual measures, on the other hand, allow some encounters to be "processed" more implicitly and subconsciously, and this may lead to a more realistic assessment of crowding-related norms. This issue may be more important in relatively high-use conditions.

Finally, findings regarding the long versus short question format also suggest that commonly used measures of crowding norms may lead to standards of quality that are overly conservative. In this study, crowding norms (using the visual approach and the evaluative dimension of acceptability) for both visitors and residents were lower using the short question format than the long question format. Although the reasons for these findings are uncertain, the long question format may be a more realistic estimate of crowding norms. Regardless of reason, study findings suggest that the long question format provides a more liberal estimate of crowding norms than does the short question format. However, in an effort to reduce respondent burden, an increasing number of studies have adopted the short question format.

CONCLUSION

Alternative measurement approaches can result in significantly and substantially different estimates of crowding norms. Each measurement approach may have advantages and disadvantages that recommend its application in a variety of contexts. For example, a visual approach may be especially applicable in situations in which use levels are high. The short question format may be appropriate if norm measurement is part of a longer survey and respondent burden is high. The evaluative dimension of management action may be appropriate if study data are likely to be used in setting limits on public use. And the visual approach and the evaluative dimensions of displacement and management action result in the lowest variance, suggesting that there is more agreement or consensus with regard to these measurement approaches. However, regardless of these potential advantages and disadvantages, researchers should be explicit in specifying the types of measurement approaches used and their potential implications. Findings from this and other studies of crowding norms begin to clarify such implications.

Because of the potential advantages and disadvantages of alternative norm measures, multiple measures may be warranted and desirable if possible. For example, use of several evaluative dimensions such as preference, acceptability, and management action provides a relatively rich source of information about how visitors or other interested parties feel about alternative use levels. Such information facilitates more informed decision making by managers about appropriate standards of quality.

Finally, study findings suggest that commonly used norm-measurement approaches may provide relatively conservative estimates of crowding norms. Many, perhaps most studies of crowding norms have employed a numerical approach, use the short question format, and use the evaluative dimension of acceptability. Study findings indicate that a visual approach, the long question format, and the evaluative dimensions of acceptability to others, management action, and displacement yield higher crowding norms. The wide differences in public use levels associated with standards of quality based on these alternative crowding norms underscore the importance of this issue.

14

What's Behind the Numbers?
Qualitative Insights into Normative
Research in Outdoor Recreation

Conventional studies of normative standards of quality in outdoor recreation rely on quantitative research methods as described in previous chapters. While these studies derive measures of acceptability (or other evaluative dimensions), they may not inform researchers or managers of potentially important elements of the cognitive process respondents use to derive and report such numbers. These cognitive insights may be important in informing researchers of the normative character of such judgments and in allowing managers to assess whether these judgments are rendered within a context of realistic consideration of the tradeoffs inherent in park and outdoor recreation management.

Qualitative research might be used to gain insights into the cognitive processes underlying normative research. The study described in this chapter uses both quantitative and qualitative research methods to measure and more fully understand crowding-related norms of visitors to Acadia. The specific objectives of the study were to assess (1) the extent to which respondents consciously considered the inherent tradeoffs between protecting the quality of park resources and the visitor experience, and maintaining reasonable public access for recreation; and (2) the effect of such consideration on the norms derived. Verbal protocol analysis, developed in psychology, was adopted as an appropriate qualitative method.

Tradeoffs in Outdoor Recreation

One of the most fundamental conflicts, tensions, or tradeoffs in park and outdoor recreation management is the amount of use that can be accom-

This chapter is an edited version of the following paper: Robert Manning, Jennifer Morrissey, and Steven Lawson, "What's Behind the Numbers? Qualitative Insights Into Normative Research in Outdoor Recreation," *Leisure Sciences* 27 (2005):205–24.

modated without causing unacceptable impacts to park resources and/or the quality of the visitor experience. Indeed, this tension is at the heart of the carrying capacity concept and its genesis lies in the dual mandate of most park and outdoor recreation agencies that requires them to protect significant natural resources and the quality of the visitor experience while also providing for public access (Manning 1999).

The dual mandate of park and outdoor recreation agencies suggests that normative research on recreation-related standards of quality should be informed by tradeoffs inherent in park and outdoor recreation management. A stronger emphasis on such tradeoffs would move normative research more in line with the "should" or "ought" dimension of norms as they traditionally were conceived, and also could incorporate the notion of sanctions often associated with the concept of norms—either formal sanctions on visitor use adopted by park management agencies or self-sanctions adopted by park visitors who choose not to visit parks under certain resource or social conditions (Heywood 1996a, 1996b; Roggenbuck et al. 1991; Shelby and Vaske 1991). It also would suggest that information derived in this way would be more thoughtful and considered, and might be more directly useful in formulating standards of quality. In fact, normative research has been subject to criticism that it may simply represent "unconstrained preferences" that may not be incorporated easily or directly into management decision making (Stewart and Cole 2003).

These issues raise the potentially important questions of the extent to which respondents to normative research are aware and conscious of the fundamental tradeoffs inherent in such issues, and how this knowledge might affect the responses that are forthcoming. As noted above, normative research in outdoor recreation conventionally is driven by quantitative methods and results in numerical estimates of respondents' norms for selected recreation-related impacts. However, as the title of this chapter suggests, it may be important to "look behind the numbers." What are respondents thinking as they read, consider, and answer such questions? More specifically, to what extent are respondents consciously considering tradeoffs inherent in park and outdoor recreation management? How do such considerations affect respondent norms? How might insights into these questions and issues help inform the design and administration of normative research and its eventual application in park and outdoor recreation management?

Verbal Protocol Analysis

To help answer these questions, this study used a qualitative research method known as verbal protocol analysis. The verbal protocol or "think aloud" research method was developed in psychology to trace the cognitive processes people use while completing a task, making a decision, or rendering a judgment. Respondents are asked to verbalize everything they are thinking while making a decision, and the verbalizations are recorded. Respondents' thought processes can be recorded while they are performing the assigned task (concurrent protocols), or after they have completed the task (retrospective protocols). Concurrent protocols require respondents to access and report the contents of their short-term or working memory, while retrospective protocols involve drawing upon respondents' longer-term memory (Ericsson and Simon 1993). The verbal protocols provide insight into the information, choices, and contingencies respondents consider during the decisionmaking process.

While verbal protocol analysis has been applied widely, some researchers have raised questions concerning the validity of verbal protocol data. First, there is concern that verbal protocols may influence the cognitive processes they are trying to trace, an issue referred to as "reactivity." Findings from a number of studies suggest that asking individuals to think aloud may slow down cognitive processes but does not change them fundamentally (Ericsson and Simon 1993). However, at least one study found that concurrent protocols can affect the cognitive processes and decisions of respondents (Russo, Johnson, and Stephens 1989). Second, the accuracy of verbal reports of cognitive processes has been called into question. Concurrent protocols may reflect individuals' cognitive processes accurately because the verbalizations are drawn from their short-term memory, which is relatively easily accessed (Ericsson and Simon 1993). Retrospective protocols, on the other hand, are more susceptible to recall errors due to their reliance on longer-term memory (van Someren, Barnard, and Sandberg 1994).

In this study, verbal protocols were used to examine the factors that respondents consider as they make normative decisions concerning the acceptability of park conditions. Concurrent protocols were used to capture cognitive processes as respondents rendered judgments concerning the acceptability of alternative park conditions. In addition, retrospective protocols were obtained immediately following the think-aloud session to provide respondents an opportunity to report factors that they considered but withheld during the concurrent protocols. Responses to the concurrent and retrospective protocols were combined for the analysis reported in this chapter. This study also explores the issue of reactivity by comparing the social norms for park conditions of respondents to the verbal protocol questionnaire to the norms of a second sample of respondents who were not asked to participate in the "think-aloud" procedure as they completed the questionnaire about acceptable park conditions.

STUDY METHODS

A visitor survey was administered on ten randomly selected days during the peak use season at the Schoodic Peninsula section of Acadia. (This study is described more fully in chapter 3.) The visitor survey used a visual approach to measuring crowding norms, where visitors were asked to evaluate the acceptability of alternative use levels as depicted by two sets of five computer-generated photographs. (The use of visual research methods is described more fully in chapter 12.) One set of photographs illustrated a range of people at one time (PAOT) at Schoodic Point, a major visitor attraction (see figure 3.2, chapter 3), and the other set of photographs illustrated a range of traffic levels on the one-way scenic drive through the park (see figure 3.1, chapter 3). The survey was administered to two subsamples of visitors as they exited the park. One subsample ($N = 640$) was administered the survey in a conventional manner (without the verbal protocol) and the other subsample ($N = 163$) was administered the survey with the verbal protocol. Respondents were assigned to the subsamples on a random basis. Two survey stations (one for the conventional quantitative survey and one for the verbal protocol) were established at a roadside pulloff near the park exit, and exiting cars were stopped and ushered into the first survey station that was available. The overall response rate to the survey was 70 percent and did not vary by type of survey.

The survey asked respondents to (1) rate the "acceptability" of each of the study photographs using a nine-point response scale anchored at "Very Acceptable" ($+4$) and "Very Unacceptable" (-4), and (2) report a norm (by indicating one of the study photographs) for two other dimensions of evaluation: "displacement," and "management action." The displacement question asked, "Which photograph shows the number of people [cars] that would be *so unacceptable that you would no longer visit Schoodic Point* [the Schoodic Peninsula section of Acadia National Park]?" The management action question asked "Which photograph shows the highest number of people [cars] you think *the National Park Service should allow*? In other words, at what point do you think people [cars] should be restricted from visiting Schoodic Point [entering the Schoodic Peninsula section of Acadia National Park]?"

The verbal protocol was administered by reading a brief instructional statement to respondents explaining the think-aloud procedure asking respondents to verbalize their thinking as they answered the survey questions. Respondents were asked to think aloud as they provided answers to two warm-up questions designed to make the respondent comfortable with the verbal protocol procedure. After completing the warm-up questions, respondents were instructed to continue thinking aloud as they responded to the remainder of the questionnaire (which focused on visitor norms). Following established procedures for obtaining verbal protocols (Ericsson and Simon 1993), the interviewer minimized interactions with the respondent, only prompting the respondent to keep talking if they stopped verbalizing for more than a few minutes. Retrospective protocols were collected at the end of each interview by asking respondents to report everything they remembered thinking about as they were answering the survey questions. All responses were recorded in their entirety on audiotape and later transcribed.

As is customary in verbal protocol studies, the coding scheme for the verbalizations was developed with the research question in mind (Ericsson and Simon 1993). That is, it was designed to identify responses that reflect concern for some aspect of the inherent tradeoffs between protection of park resources and experiences and maintaining reasonable public access. The coding scheme was developed based on an initial reading of the transcribed reponses to the verbal protocol and is shown in table 14.1. The codes that were developed represent identifiable alternative dimensions of the inherent tradeoffs between protection of park resources and experiences and maintaining reasonable public access, as reported by respondents. Two coders (graduate research assistants working on the study) independently assigned these codes to each respondent's verbal protocol responses, capturing the main thought processes or reasoning as related to the inherent tradeoffs under study. Since a respondent may have followed more than one train of thought in answering each question, the coders were allowed to assign multiple codes when appropriate (up to four codes per question). The coders initially agreed on 62 percent of their codings. The coders then resolved each difference by discussing them, and the resolved codings were used for analysis. The initial agreement level of 62 percent between coders may be considered relatively low (Denzen and Lincoln 1994; Kirk and Miller 1986), but may be due to the relatively large number of categories used and the sometimes subtle differences among them. For analysis purposes, many of the categories were collapsed into larger groups, which probably has the effect of increasing the initial level of agreement between coders.

STUDY FINDINGS

Descriptive Findings

The first type of descriptive findings concerns respondent comments derived from the verbal protocol. Respondent comments related to study objectives were classified into the nineteen categories as shown in table 14.1. (Some responses were not related to study objectives and are not discussed in this chapter. For example, some responses simply expounded on the scenic beauty of the park.) Response categories are listed in table 14.1 in descending order in accordance with the number of respondents who reported them. The first two columns of the table are the code number and label given to each category. The third column is a representative statement illustrating the meaning of each category. The fourth and fifth columns report the number of respondents who mentioned each response category and the total number of times each category was mentioned, respectively. (Many respondents mentioned more than one response category, and mentioned the same response category more than once as they proceeded through the questionnaire.) Most respondents (71.2 percent) mentioned at least one of the response categories, and the response categories were mentioned a total of 308 times.

Response categories were grouped in conceptually related ways by the researchers, as illustrated in figure 14.1. Thirteen response categories (code numbers 1, 5, 6, 8, 10, 11, 12, 13, 14, 15, 18, 19, 20) were classified as "protection-oriented": responses that illustrated concern about either the resource or social impacts of visitor use. An example of a response reflecting a resource-protection oriented concern is "I would never want to see that [a photo-

TABLE 14.1 Classification of verbal protocol responses.

Code number	Category	Sample statement	Number of respondents	Number of mentions
1	Solitude	"I don't want to see anyone and I don't want them to see me."	27	35
2	Parks are for people	"I don't think the park should be restricted from the people because it is their land."	26	35
3	Prefer to see some people	"I like to see a few people to chat with them."	22	25
4	Balancing personal preferences and democratic concerns	"Everybody ought to have access even though I don't like it and they're getting in my way."	20	23
5	Concern for resource protection, ecological health	"The more people you have in here, the more that you have impacts on the soil and vegetation."	18	20
6	Traffic detracting from park experience	"The more traffic the less time you have to see the scenery."	17	18
7	Preference not realistic	"Obviously I would prefer to see none, which is photo 1. But we're in the real world."	16	21
8	Need for public transportation	"I think they can alleviate a lot of this situation by using a bus transportation system."	15	19
9	Don't want to see people turned away, inconvenienced	"If I had driven all the way down to Schoodic Peninsula and then was told I couldn't go in, I would be undone, so I wouldn't recommend that."	14	15
10	Traffic a safety concern	"You are so worried about the traffic ahead of you that you are not able to look out and look for pull-off places and so on so that you can safely pull off the road."	11	12
11	Concern for potential parking shortage	"Where are these people going to park?"	11	16
12	Trash/litter	"When I look out and see how beautiful it is and I see a Mountain Dew bottle, it just destroys everything for me."	10	11
13	Difficulty taking photos	"If you're here to take pictures, and there are a lot of people, you can't take the pictures of people you're interested in."	10	10
14	People are okay, cars are not	"As long as it wasn't a traffic issue, we'd probably still come regardless of the number of people."	9	11

continued

TABLE 14.1 *Continued*

Code number	Category	Sample statement	Number of respondents	Number of mentions
15	Would go elsewhere	"I would probably just turn around and go into Winter Harbor and check out the antique stores or something."	8	9
16	Concern about being excluded	"I don't want it to be so nobody can go, because I'm one of those people."	8	8
17	Concern about park finances/need people to keep park going	"I know how the National Park Service is paid and the more people they can get in, the better off they are."	6	6
18	Values feeling of wildness	"I think the particular wild nature of the peninsula is an important factor in how many people should be allowed . . . the wildness of the site is important to try to sustain."	6	6
19	Concerned an increase in park visibility would affect resources	"As far as I'm concerned, if they never announce this place it would be fine with me."	4	4
20	Air pollution concern	"I would never want to see that. Think of the air pollution."	3	4

graph illustrating a relatively large number of cars along the park road]. Think of the air pollution." An example of a response reflecting an experience-protection oriented concern is [in response to a photograph illustrating a relatively large number of people at Schoodic Point], "I would probably just turn around and go into Winter Harbor and check out the antique stores or something." Protection-oriented response categories were mentioned by 87 respondents (53.4 percent of the sample) and were mentioned a total of 175 times (56.8 percent of all responses).

The thirteen protection-oriented responses noted above can be divided into two groups that represent resource-sensitive responses and crowding-sensitive responses. Resource-sensitive responses (code numbers 5, 12, 18, 19, 20) were mentioned by 35 respondents (21.5 percent of the sample) and were mentioned a total of 45 times (14.6 percent of all responses). Crowding-sensitive responses (code numbers 1, 6, 8, 10, 11, 13, 14, 15, 18) were mentioned by 74 respondents (45.4 percent of the sample) and were mentioned a total of 136 times (44.2 percent of all responses).

Crowding-sensitive responses can be divided further into people-sensitive

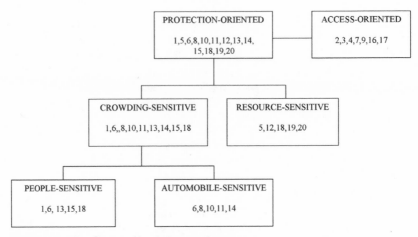

Figure 14.1 *Classification of verbal protocol responses.*

responses and automobile-sensitive responses. People-sensitive responses (code numbers 1, 6, 13, 15, 18) were mentioned by 54 respondents (33.1 percent of the sample) and were mentioned a total of 78 times (25.3 percent of all responses). Automobile-sensitive responses (code numbers 6, 8, 10, 11, 14) were mentioned by 45 respondents (27.6 percent of the sample) and were mentioned a total of 76 times (24.7 percent of all responses).

Finally, seven response categories were classified as "access-oriented": responses that illustrated concern for maintaining reasonable public access to the park. An example of a response reflecting an access-oriented concern is, "Everybody ought to have access even though I don't like it and they're getting in my way, everybody ought to have access." Access-oriented responses (code numbers 2, 3, 4, 7, 9, 16, 17) were mentioned by 78 respondents (47.9 percent of the sample) and were mentioned a total of 133 times (43.2 percent of all responses). Some respondents (48, representing 29.5 percent of all respondents) mentioned both protection- and access-oriented responses.

The second type of descriptive findings concerns the normative standards derived from the quantitative portion of the survey. The social norm curves for both subsamples (those visitors who received the verbal protocol and those who didn't) derived from respondent ratings of the acceptability of each of the study photographs were nearly identical; no substantive differences existed between the two subsamples.

Normative standards for the management action and displacement evaluative dimensions are shown in table 14.2. (The issue of alternative evalua-

TABLE 14.2 Tests of differences in norms for Schoodic Point and the scenic drive by response category.

Evaluative dimension	People-at-one-time at Schoodic Point					Vehicles-at-one-time on Park Road				
	Sample administered verbal protocol		Sample not administered verbal protocol		Test	Sample administered verbal protocol		Sample not administered verbal protocol		Test
	Mean	SD	Mean	SD		Mean	SD	Mean	SD	
Management action	81.4	30.6	71.2	28.6	$t = -2.9$; $p = 0.004$	8.6	3.7	8.5	3.4	$t = -0.27$; $p = 0.78$
Displacement	99.0	25.9	102.0	29.1	$t = 0.87$; $p = 0.38$	12.0	3.5	12.7	3.3	$t = -2.2$; $p = 0.03$

tive dimensions is described more fully in chapter 13.) Mean values for each subsample are shown, along with standard deviations. Standard deviations offer some indication of the relative consensus about norms (or "crystallization" of norms). While there is little absolute basis to judge whether the standard deviations are high or low, they are consistently less than half of the respective means, and this suggests at least some degree of consensus. Frequency distributions for these data were also plotted showing the percentage of respondents that chose each of the five study photographs in response to the evaluative dimensions of management action and displacement. These distributions generally suggest a relatively high level of agreement among the subsamples. For example, nearly 80 percent of respondents who received the verbal protocol selected either photographs 4 or 5 as the point at which they would be displaced from Schoodic Point.

Analytical Findings

Several analytical procedures were conducted to accomplish the study objectives. The first procedure tested for differences in reported crowding-related norms among respondents who mentioned the six categories of responses illustrated in figure 14.1. For example, the crowding-related norms of respondents who mentioned a people-sensitive response were compared to the crowding-related norms of respondents who did not mention a people-sensitive response for each evaluative dimension. Of the 24 such tests conducted, only one was statistically significant at the 0.05 level. Respondents who mentioned a resource-sensitive comment reported a lower management-action norm for PAOT at Schoodic Point than did respondents who did not mention a resource-sensitive comment, and this difference is in the expected direction.

The second procedure compared crowding-related norms between (1) respondents who mentioned *both* protection-oriented and access-oriented responses (i.e., respondents who consciously considered both sides of the inherent tradeoffs in carrying capacity) and (2) respondents who did not mention both protection-oriented and access-oriented responses (i.e., respondents who did not consciously consider both sides of the inherent tradeoffs in carrying capacity). None of the four statistical tests conducted found significant differences.

A third analytical procedure tested for differences in reported crowding-related norms between the sample of visitors who participated in the verbal protocol analysis and the separate sample of visitors who answered the normative questions, but were not asked to participate in the verbal protocol. As noted above, the norm curves for the two subsamples were nearly identical. Normative standards for the management-action and displacement evaluative dimensions also were tested between the two subsamples as shown in table 14.2. Of the four tests conducted, two were statistically significant, but only one of these (the difference between 81.4 and 71.2 PAOT at Schoodic Point for the management-action normative dimension) might be considered substantively important.

DISCUSSION

This study was designed to "look behind the numbers" that are derived from normative research in outdoor recreation, with special emphasis on the inherent tradeoffs associated with carrying capacity. Verbal protocol analysis has been used successfully in other research contexts, and was adopted in this study to explore the tradeoff-related issues considered by respondents when asked to make normative judgments about acceptable conditions in park and related environments. In particular, the study was designed to determine the extent to which respondents consciously consider various manifestations of the inherent tradeoffs between protecting the quality of park resources and recreation experiences and maintaining reasonable public access to parks and related areas, and the effect these considerations might have on resulting normative standards.

Study findings suggest that the research methods were generally successful in tapping into the cognitive processes of respondents, and that most respondents were thinking about some aspects of the inherent tradeoffs associated with the subject of carrying capacity. Most respondents were able to verbalize at least some of their thinking as they responded to study questions, and many respondents identified several issues of concern at multiple points in the study. While respondents identified a diverse set of issues, most of these issues dealt with some manifestation of the inherent tradeoffs associated specifically with carrying capacity and with park and outdoor recreation management more generally. It is interesting to note that roughly half of the sample (53.4 percent) administered the verbal protocol reported resource and/or experiential protection-oriented responses, while a nearly equal percentage (47.9 percent) reported access-oriented responses. However, only a minority of respondents (29.5 percent) reported *both* protection- and access-oriented responses. Moreover, of those who reported protection-oriented responses, over twice as many reported crowding-related responses as resource-related responses (45.4 and 21.5 percent, respectively). While the experimental stimulus administered in the study depicted a range of visitors and cars, these alternative use levels can cause both social and resource-related impacts. Finally, it should be noted that all of the absolute numbers and percentages derived from the verbal protocol are probably underestimated. It's likely that at least some issues considered by at least some respondents were not verbalized.

Analysis of study data found few differences in the norms reported among the various subsamples identified. These subsamples included (1) respondents who reported each of the six basic categories of responses (shown in figure 14.1) versus those who did not, (2) respondents who reported both protection- and access-oriented responses versus those who did not, and (3) respondents who were administered the verbal protocol versus those who were not.

The relatively high percentage of respondents who reported conscious consideration of selected manifestations of the tradeoffs inherent in carrying capacity, and in particular the lack of statistically significant differences in norms reported by various study subsamples, may be related to the intentional and deliberately normative nature of the management-action and displacement questions. These questions were designed to sensitize respondents at least subconsciously to the tradeoffs inherent in carrying capacity determination, to introduce the "should" or "ought" dimension of norms, and to incorporate the notion of sanctions often associated with norms. The management-action question asked respondents to consider the point at which visitor use should be restricted in order to protect the quality of park resources and the visitor experience, and in this way is suggestive of the inherent tradeoffs associated with carrying capacity. The displacement question asked respondents to consider the point at which the quality of park resources and/or the visitor experience has deteriorated so much that they would no longer visit the area in question, in effect, denying access to themselves. In this way, the question is also intended to sensitize respondents to both sides of the inherent tradeoff between quality and access.

The effect of the normative nature of these questions is supported empirically by other questions included in the study that asked respondents to indicate which of the study photographs they would "prefer" to experience. The evaluative dimension of preference has little or no normative connotation and does not suggest—either explicitly or implicitly—any consideration of tradeoffs. As the word preference suggests, it is the desired condition absent of any constraints. The effect of the six base categories of verbal protocol responses was tested on respondent preferences for PAOT at Schoodic Point and number of cars along the scenic drive, just as it was for the management-action and displacement questions. Of the twelve statistical tests performed, eight found significant differences based on whether or not a respondent had reported a category-specific response. Seven of the eight statistically significant differences were in the expected direction. For example, respondents who reported a people-sensitive response preferred a PAOT of 16.1 compared to a PAOT of 28.6 for respondents who did not report a people-sensitive response. It also should be noted that the standard deviations of the preference-based data were relatively high (approximating the means), at least compared to data derived from the management-action and displacement questions.

Given the seeming desirability of respondent awareness of the inherent tradeoffs associated with carrying capacity, it is especially important to note the general lack of statistically and substantively significant differences between the crowding-related norms of the two samples included in this study. The respondents who participated in the verbal protocol analysis were asked to "think aloud" as they answered the crowding-related normative questions, and study findings indicate that most respondents were actively considering at least some of the issues associated with the tradeoffs between resource/experiential quality and visitor access, and that many were actively considering both. The lack of differences in crowding-related norms between this sample and the sample that was not asked to participate in the verbal protocol analysis suggests that many, perhaps most respondents are thinking about such issues even when not prompted to report what they are thinking. This finding may be attributable at least partially to the deliberately normative nature of the management-action and displacement questions. From a methodological standpoint, the lack of differences between the two samples also suggests that "reactivity"—the potential influence of the verbal protocol on responses—was not an issue in this study.

This study may illustrate the potential value of employing both quantitative and qualitative research in park and outdoor recreation management (Borrie et al. 2001; Davenport et al. 2002). Conventional quantitative study of visitor norms leads to numerical estimates that can be useful in helping to formulate standards of quality for important indicator variables related to park and wilderness management. However, qualitative research can provide insights into how such normative standards of visitors are derived and the ways in which conventional quantitative studies might be refined to enhance their validity and usefulness. For example, findings from this study suggest that questions that introduce (at least implicitly) the need to consider inherent tradeoffs in carrying capacity may lead to more realistic estimates of the maximum acceptable level of recreation-related impacts.

CONCLUSIONS

Study findings suggest several conclusions concerning normative research applied to carrying capacity. First, it appears as though many respondents are conscious of and thoughtful about many of the issues associated with carrying capacity when formulating and reporting normative standards for acceptable resource and social conditions in parks and related areas. Most respondents in the verbal protocol analysis identified a number of dimensions of the fundamental tradeoffs involved in carrying capacity (protecting the quality of park resources and the visitor experience and maintaining reasonable public access), and many carried on an "internal debate" about these issues. The fact that few statistically or substantively significant differences were found between the sample of visitors who participated in the verbal protocol analysis and the sample of visitors who did not suggests that crowding-related norms as measured through conventional quantitative approaches may be reasonably well informed and thoughtful.

Second, research can (and perhaps should) be designed in ways that further enhance the knowledge and sensitivity of respondents regarding tradeoffs inherent in carrying capacity. In this respect, "preference"-based questions may offer the least valid or informed approach to formulating standards of quality in parks and outdoor recreation. Questions that at least implicitly ask respondents to consider the fundamental tradeoffs associated with carrying capacity may lead to more "valid" estimates of crowding and related norms, and provide data that might be incorporated more directly into management decisionmaking regarding appropriate standards of quality. This approach may help move normative research more toward the "prescriptive" type of data that ultimately are needed in managing carrying capacity (Manning 2003b; Manning and Lawson 2002; Shelby and Heberlein 1986; Stewart and Cole 2003).

Finally, quantitative and qualitative research probably should be used more often in ways that complement their respective strengths and weaknesses. In the case of this research, the qualitative method of verbal protocol analysis provided insights into the thinking of park visitors as they responded to a series of conventional quantitative questions. Study findings are somewhat reassuring that many visitors are consciously aware of many of the tradeoffs associated with managing carrying capacity, but also offer some guidance concerning how such questions might be refined and applied to ensure that both questions and answers are as informed and thoughtful as possible.

PART II Monitoring

15 Monitoring Recreation Visits to Acadia National Park

One of the most fundamental indicators for analyzing and managing outdoor recreation is the number of visits that are accommodated in a park or related area. Visits are at least an approximation of the level of public enjoyment or satisfaction that is generated, as well as the resource and experiential impacts associated with this use. Number of visits is also a guide to the level of facilities and services that should be provided. Systematic data on visitation also generates important information on trends in public use.

The NPS places considerable emphasis on measuring and reporting public use in the form of visits. In fact, the agency has collected information regularly about visits since 1904. In the early days when park visitation was low and sporadic, superintendents themselves counted park visitors and recorded where they came from and how they got to the parks. In today's world, where visits to the national parks number in the hundreds of millions annually, this system will no longer suffice! Public use measurement and reporting have become more sophisticated.

The primary objective of the NPS public use reporting system is to design and implement a statistically valid, reliable, and uniform method of collecting and reporting public use data for each park. Among the most important components of the public use reporting system are definition of terms, counting and reporting instructions, surveys and audits.

A "visit" is the central unit of analysis in the NPS public use reporting system. A visit is defined as the entry of any person, except NPS personnel,

This chapter is an edited version of the following paper: Ken Hornback and Robert Manning, "When Is a Visit Really a Visit? Public Use Reporting at Acadia National Park," *Park Science* 13 (1992):23.

onto lands or waters administered by the agency. However, there are three kinds of visits that must be counted and reported separately. "Recreation visits" are visits for recreation purposes. "Nonrecreation visits" are visits for nonrecreation purposes, including persons going to and from private land within parks, commuter traffic, other through-traffic, tradespeople with business in the park, any activity that is a part of or incidental to the pursuit of a gainful occupation, government personnel other than NPS employees with business in the park, and citizens in the park to discuss or hear about park business (e.g., public hearings). "Nonreportable visits" are visits by NPS employees, their families, concessioner employees, members of Cooperating Associations, activities associated with NPS cooperative agreements, tenants of NPS property if not crossing significant NPS territory for access, persons engaged in pursuit of specific legal rights of use (e.g., subsistence hunting and fishing), and NPS contractors.

Finally, duplicate counting (multiple entries on a single day) must be avoided. The major forms of duplicate counting are associated with commuter traffic back and forth through the park, visits to more than one area of a park with discontinuous boundaries, visitor traffic back and forth to visit outside vendors, and visitors residing outside the park making multiple daily visits.

Consequently, counting and reporting instructions (CRIS) are prepared to reflect the unique site characteristics of each park. CRIS contain the procedures for measuring, compiling, and recording public use. For very straightforward and small-scale areas, CRIS can be prepared informally. For larger and more complex areas, formal audits are needed. Audits of each NPS unit are conducted periodically. Audits constitute detailed studies of the public use complexities of each park.

Measurement of public use requires some knowledge of and about park visitors. This information is derived from periodic surveys. Visitor surveys produce multipliers or conversion factors used in public use reporting. Surveys are conducted to keep up with local economic, transportation, and demographic changes.

Acadia is especially complex from the standpoint of public use reporting. It occupies about half of Mount Desert Island, and consists of a patchwork of public lands interspersed with private lands. The park includes numerous uncontrolled entrances and exits and park roads are traveled by large numbers of visitors, local residents, and others.

STUDY METHODS

Acadia was audited by the NPS and, because of its complexity, a survey was deemed necessary in order to develop CRIS. The emphasis of the public use reporting system was to be based on a "double sampling" procedure. This technique is used commonly where visits are highly dispersed and difficult and expensive to count directly. A second, more easily measurable variable is created and statistically related to visitation. Visitation then can be estimated by means of this new variable. In automobile-oriented parks such as Acadia, this new or second variable is often an automated automobile traffic counter. A traffic counter at Sand Beach, a principal park attraction, was designated as the focus of the double sampling system at Acadia.

The survey was conducted in each of the four major use seasons. Thirty park sites were chosen for sampling, representing the diversity of visitor attractions. Sampling was done on 70 days, and 2,873 visitors were administered a short questionnaire. Variables of principal interest included reason for visit (recreation, nonrecreation, nonreportable), persons per vehicle, length of stay, and whether visitors tripped the Sand Beach traffic counter (i.e., drove by Sand Beach) on the days they were interviewed.

STUDY FINDINGS

Survey findings are presented in table 15.1. The first variable, the Sand Beach traffic-counter multiplication factor, was calculated on the basis of the per-

TABLE 15.1 Summary of study findings.

Variable	Season			
	Summer	Fall	Winter	Spring
Sand Beach traffic-counter multiplication factor	1.81	1.73	5.88	4.02
Persons per vehicle	2.99	3.01	2.42	3.75
Type of visit				
Recreation	96.6%	97.8%	97.1%	99.2%
Nonrecreation	2.8%	2.0%	1.2%	0.8%
Nonreportable	0.6%	0.2%	1.7%	0.0%
Length of stay				
Recreation, day use	5.05 hrs.	6.54 hrs.	6.57 hrs.	5.79 hrs.
Recreation, overnight use	101.47 hrs.	54.67 hrs.	42.71 hrs.	56.31 hrs.

centage of visitors who tripped the Sand Beach traffic counter. For example, during the summer season, 46.9 percent of visitors sampled did not trip the counter on the day they were interviewed (i.e., they did not drive by Sand Beach). This means the traffic counter is underestimating the number of visitor vehicles in the park and its reading must be adjusted upward accordingly. A majority of visitors (51.2 percent) tripped the traffic counter once, thus no adjustment is needed for these visitors. However, 1.8 percent of visitors tripped the counter twice, and an additional 0.1 percent tripped it three times, requiring an appropriate downward adjustment of the counter reading.

Aggregating all these adjustments, Sand Beach traffic-counter readings should be adjusted upward using a multiplication factor of 1.81 for the summer season. Other variables needed to estimate public use are persons per vehicle (2.99 for the summer season) and type of visit (recreation visits were 96.6 percent, nonrecreation visits 2.8 percent, and nonreportable visits 0.6 percent for the summer season). Finally, length of stay can be factored in to quantify public use further. Seasonal differences found among several of these variables suggest that it may be important to adjust multiplication factors by season.

CONCLUSION

Based on the above survey findings, a new CRIS was prepared and implemented at Acadia. The survey provided an information base that substantially enhances the validity and reliability of public use reporting and ensures that the public use reporting system is in conformity with NPS guidelines. Resulting data on visitation provides an important measure of recreation use that can be used to help guide management and track associated trends.

16 Design and Implementation of a Monitoring Plan for the Carriage Roads

Application of the Visitor Experience and Resource Protection (VERP) framework to the Acadia carriage roads resulted in a series of indicators and standards of quality for the visitor experience (Jacobi and Manning 1997). (Research supporting formulation of these indicators and standards is described in chapter 2.) Accordingly, these indicators must be monitored to determine if standards of quality are being maintained and to guide management of the carriage roads (National Park Service 1997). This chapter briefly reviews the indicators and standards that were formulated, describes several methods that are used to monitor indicator variables, outlines principal findings from this monitoring program, and offers some conclusions on the lessons learned from this monitoring program.

Indicators and Standards of Quality

Since the carriage roads are a highly engineered and "hardened" system of gravel roads, few resource-related impacts are associated with their use. Accordingly, indicators and standards for the carriage roads focused on experiential concerns, including crowding and conflicting uses (or "problem behaviors"). Indicators of crowding were expressed in three equivalent ways: (1) persons-per-viewscape (PPV) seen along typical 100-meter sections of the carriage roads, (2) the total number of visitors using the carriage roads per day, and (3) the percentage of visitors having a "high-quality" experience on the carriage roads (defined as the percentage of visitors reporting an acceptability value of at least two on the nine-point response scale used in the program of research (Manning, Negra, et al. 1996; Manning, Valliere, Wang,

---

This chapter is a compiled and edited version of periodic National Park Service monitoring reports (as cited in the chapter) prepared by Charles Jacobi.

et al. 1998; Manning, Valliere, Ballinger, et al., 1998). (The ways in which these standards were formulated and expressed in equivalent terms are described in chapters 2 and 17.) Standards for these indicators were set for two spatial and temporal zones that had been established for the carriage roads.

Indicators of conflict focused on four problem behaviors identified by hikers and bikers: (1) excessive bicycle speed, (2) bicycles passing from behind without warning and startling hikers, (3) hikers walking abreast and obstructing bikers, and (4) dogs off-leash (Manning, Negra, et al. 1996; Manning, Valliere, Wang, et al. 1998; Manning, Valliere, Ballinger, et al., 1998). Standards for these indicators were expressed in terms of the percentage of carriage road visitors experiencing more than two occurrences of these behaviors per two-hour period (the average length of stay on the carriage roads). Standards were set for the two spatial and temporal carriage road zones.

MONITORING CROWDING

A simulation model of carriage road use (described in chapter 17] estimates that as long as total daily use of the carriage roads remains under 3,000 visitors, then PPV standards in each zone will be met and 80 percent of carriage road visitors will have a high-quality experience, at least from the standpoint of crowding. Therefore, much of the monitoring program for crowding is directed at estimating the total daily use level of the carriage road system. This is done by using an electronic trail counter at one location along the carriage roads (a busy site on Eagle Lake, 0.3 miles from the nearest parking lot) and estimating total carriage road use based on the statistical relationship between trail-counter readings and a series of censuses of carriage road use. Twelve one-day censuses were conducted in which park staff and volunteers counted all visitors entering the carriage roads at all major access points between the hours of 9:00 a.m. and 6:00 p.m. (Jacobi 1997). The resulting statistical relationship between trail-counter readings on those days and total use levels allows estimation of total use levels based on trail-counter readings.

When the Island Explorer shuttle bus system began operation in 1999, there was concern that visitor use patterns on the carriage roads may change and that this might invalidate the assumptions of the simulation model of carriage road use. So additional censuses of carriage road use were conducted, and a new statistical relationship was developed between trail-counter readings and total carriage road use (Jacobi 2003).

Eleven years of monitoring have found no violations of the total daily carriage road use level and PPV standards that were set. In 2000, the estimated total carriage road use level for one day was 3,132, the only day the 3,000 figure has been exceeded (Jacobi 2001b). However, this figure does not exceed the 80 percent confidence interval for the standard of 3,000 visitors, so this was not considered a violation of the crowding-related standards. An 80 percent confidence interval is used because of the substantial variation in daily carriage road use. Typically, there are three or four days in July and ten to twelve days in August when total daily carriage road use is estimated at more than 2,000 visitors, and sometimes a day or two approaches 3,000 visitors (Jacobi 2007). Over the past eleven years, average total daily use in July ranged from 1,379 to 1,663 and in August it ranged from 1,552 to 1,984 (Jacobi 2007).

To validate the use of the trail-counter and simulation model, field-based counts of PPV levels are conducted every three years. For one-hour periods, park staff or volunteers are stationed at the end of a 100-meter section of carriage roads and "instantaneous" counts of the number of visitors seen are conducted at 15-second intervals. These counts are conducted for ten randomly selected days in July and August. Counts are conducted at five sites in both the high- and low-use zones of the carriage roads.

PPV counts for 2007 for the high-use zone are shown in table 16.1 (Jacobi 2008). Four violations of PPV standards are shown in bold. However, these violations are probably not of great concern since the counts are just barely above the standards. Moreover, violations of standards of PPV levels above ten are inherently difficult to manage. It seems likely that two relatively large groups of carriage road users occasionally will cross paths at one or more of the observation sites along the carriage roads, especially in the high-use zone. No group-size restriction has been set for the carriage roads, but this management practice might be considered if violations of higher PPV standards are found more commonly and can be tied to large groups (as opposed to simple increases in total carriage road use levels). Moreover, it may be wise to reconsider the standard of "0" for PPV levels above ten, as high PPV levels are likely to occur at least occasionally, simply by chance; this standard might be set most appropriately at a very low level (but not at zero), allowing it to be reached or exceeded a small percentage of the time.

TABLE 16.1 Number of minutes per hour in each PPV range for field counts in the high-use zone, 2007.

PPV range	Standard of quality	Date 7/11 (N = 5)	7/12 (N = 5)	7/17 (N = 5)	7/30 (N = 3)	8/3 (N = 4)	8/5 (N = 4)	8/10 (N = 5)
0	Not < 31	48.2	51.4	42.6	42.0	42.0	51.2	38.4
1–5	Not > 27	11.5	8.6	16.1	17.0	17.0	8.7	19.5
6–10	Not > 2	0.4	0.1	1.2	1.0	0.9	0	**2.1**
11–15	Not > 0	0	0	**0.1**	0	**0.13**	0	**0.1**
16–20	Not > 0	0	0	0	0	0	0	0
21–30	Not > 0	0	0	0	0	0	0	0

Note: Violations of PPV standards are shown in bold.

MONITORING CONFLICT

Conflict (or problem behaviors) is monitored every three years through a brief questionnaire administered to a representative sample of visitors exiting the carriage roads. The sample is stratified by entry location and time as determined by findings from the censuses of carriage road use. Sampling dates are selected randomly. The questionnaire collects information on the zone of carriage road use, number of the four problem behaviors/indicators experienced, length (time) of carriage road use, and type of activity (hiker or biker). A minimum of 250 completed questionnaires for each of the two spatial carriage road zones is sought (Jacobi 2007).

Summary findings for this monitoring effort are shown in table 16.2. Data are the percentages of time the standards are violated. Violations and near-violations are shown in bold. Only two violations have occurred: in 1997 for bicycles passing from behind without warning in the low-use zone, and in 2000 for dogs off-leash in the low-use zone. If violations become more frequent, then management practices will need to be applied.

CONCLUSIONS

Crowding and conflict are important in determining and maintaining the quality of visitor experience on the carriage roads. Consequently, indicators and standards have been formulated to guide carriage road management, and a related program of monitoring has been designed and implemented. This monitoring program relies on several methods, including an automatic

TABLE 16.2 Percentages of 1997, 2000, 2003, and 2006 carriage road visitors experiencing more than two occurrences in two hours of four problem behaviors in the high- and low-use zones compared with associated standards of quality.

	Low-use zone					High-use zone				
	1997	2000	2003	2006	Standard	1997	2000	2003	2006	Standard
Bicycles passing from behind without warning	5.20	4.93	1.15	2.65	Not > 5%	3.42	3.28	3.40	4.76	Not > 5%
Excessive bicycle speed	3.72	**4.04**	2.69	3.41	Not > 5%	6.41	6.15	3.40	7.54	Not > 10%
Dogs off-leash	**4.46**	**6.28**	3.08	**4.17**	Not > 5%	1.28	3.28	2.91	1.19	Not > 5%
Hikers obstructing	1.86	3.59	2.31	2.65	Not > 5%	4.70	7.38	7.28	9.92	Not > 10%

Note: Violations and near-violations of standards are shown in bold.

trail counter, occasional censuses of total carriage road use, a computer-based simulation model of visitor use, instantaneous counts of PPV levels, and a short visitor survey. Findings from the carriage road monitoring program suggest that standards of quality are being violated only rarely. The park instituted several management actions to guide carriage road use in the late 1980s and early 1990s when concern over the carriage roads emerged and application of the VERP framework and associated research were undertaken. Courtesy guidelines (also called "rules of the road") were established through a brochure that is distributed widely to carriage road users. Rules-of-the-road signs were installed at all major entry points to the carriage roads. Park staff roved the carriage roads on bicycle educating visitors for several years. Local bike rental shops were engaged as education partners. A local bike association was formed and a volunteer bike patrol instituted. The bike association also produced an educational video and public service announcements for local television. Friends of Acadia, a "friends of the park" group, supported some of these efforts financially. Finally, there was a great deal of publicity in the local newspapers about planning for the carriage roads and the associated program of research.

Over time, volunteer bike patrols, staff carriage road roving, and the video and public service announcements largely have been discontinued for lack of funding or declining need. The signs, the brochure, and the bike shop partnership all continue to educate carriage road visitors. Park staff continue to educate visitors one-on-one as they inquire about carriage roads at the park visitor centers. Occasional law-enforcement patrols also occur throughout the summer season, including horse patrols. Rangers on horse-back educate visitors about the courtesy guidelines.

The carriage road monitoring program will continue into the future, every year for crowding and every three years for conflict/problem behaviors. While the management practices for conflict described above appear to have been effective, managing crowding will be more challenging. Some carriage road visitors might be persuaded to use the Park Loop Road instead of the carriage roads for biking. Controls on parking to limit use will require cooperation from the state and local towns because most parking lots serving the carriage roads are not on park land. A permit system or fees to control use would be a last resort because these options likely would be unpopular and may not be feasible.

Experience with the monitoring program on the carriage roads suggests that it is needed to determine the degree to which the park is successful in meeting the standards of quality it has set. Data derived from monitoring also can help determine the reasonableness of standards that have been set and guide revisions of standards where needed. Moreover, multiple methods can be used to monitor indicators, each of which has strengths and weaknesses, and some of which are complementary. Monitoring can require a substantial commitment of time and staff, and a long-term commitment to monitoring is needed. The long-term nature of monitoring programs suggests that monitoring protocols need to be documented and institutionalized to deal with inevitable changes in park staff.

17 Computer Simulation Modeling as a Monitoring Tool for the Carriage Roads

Growing popularity of outdoor recreation is challenging researchers and managers as they attempt to protect park resources and the quality of the visitor experience. One important issue is the complexity of trail and other travel systems in parks and related areas. Little research has been aimed at describing the way that visitors travel and distribute themselves within a park or recreation system. This study seeks to fill this gap by meeting two objectives. One is to gather descriptive data on visitor travel on the carriage roads in Acadia to strengthen knowledge concerning travel patterns. The second objective is to explore the usefulness of computer simulation as a monitoring tool through this process.

Simulation Modeling Applied to Outdoor Recreation

Simulation modeling is a simplification of the structure and operation of a complex system. Simulation modeling enables the study of, and experimentation with, the internal interactions of a real-world system. The approach is especially suited to those tasks that are too complex for direct observation, manipulation, or even mathematical analysis (Banks and Carson 1984; Law and Kelton 1991; Pidd 1992).

Beginning in the mid-1970s, researchers explored computer simulation modeling as a tool to assist recreation managers and researchers (Manning and Potter 1984; McCool, Lime, and Anderson 1977; Potter and Manning 1984; Schechter and Lucas 1978; Smith and Headly 1975; Smith and Krutilla

This chapter is an edited version of the following paper: Ben Wang and Robert Manning, "Computer Simulation Modeling for Recreation Management: A Study on Carriage Road Use in Acadia National Park, Maine, USA," *Environmental Management* 23 (1999): 193–203.

1976). The main goal of the resulting "wilderness travel simulation model" was to estimate the number of encounters that occurred between recreation groups in a park or wilderness area. The model required input variables such as typical travel routes and times, arrival patterns, and total use levels. Outputs included the number of encounters between visitor groups of various types and the date, time, and location of encounters. Initial tests established the validity of the model, but the model soon fell into disuse because computers were relatively inaccessible at the time, and little was known about the maximum number of encounters between groups that was acceptable to visitors.

Recent changes in computing power and accessibility complemented advances in research on the carrying capacity of parks and related areas. These developments provided the context and impetus for the present study to revisit computer simulation for recreation research and management. Simulation-capable computers have become more accessible, and exponential growth in the power of personal computers has facilitated the use of graphic user interfaces and visual interactive modeling technologies to make the simulation process accessible to nonspecialists (Pidd 1992). These advances have led to the wide proliferation of simulation in a variety of fields including engineering, business management, and manufacturing.

Moreover, advances in research on carrying capacity, including development and application of management frameworks such as VERP have enabled formulation of indicators and standards of quality that can be used to help guide park management. Given the advances in carrying capacity research and computer simulation modeling, application of simulation modeling to carrying capacity was warranted.

In concert with an ongoing program of research at Acadia, it was decided to apply this work to the park's carriage roads. The carriage road system has eight major entrance/exit points and twenty-six intersections, with peak daily use levels approaching 3,000 visitors. Approximately 71 percent of visitors are cyclists, 26 percent are hikers or runners, and 5 percent are on horseback or in horse-drawn carriages (Manning et al. 1997).

Initial research on the carriage roads found that the number of visitors seen along the carriage roads (expressed as "persons per viewscape" or PPV) was an important indicator of the quality of the visitor experience, and that visitors reported that the maximum PPV that could be experienced without diminishing the quality of the recreation experience to an unacceptable degree was approximately 15. (This research is described in more detail in Chapter 2.) This indicator and standard were used to guide development and application of a computer simulation model of visitor use of the carriage roads. The objectives of the model were to facilitate monitoring PPV levels on the carriage roads and to estimate the maximum daily use level of the carriage roads without violating the PPV-related standard of quality.

STUDY METHODS

Data Collection

A variety of methods were employed to gather data necessary for building a model of carriage road use. These were visitor census counts, on-site visitor surveys, geographic information system (GIS) analysis, a field visit, examination of engineering maps, and computer timing of visitor arrival patterns. These are described below.

Data on where, when, and how many visitors entered the carriage roads system were gathered using five one-day visitor censuses. The dates were selected randomly from the summer use season. From 9:00 a.m. to 5:00 p.m. on each of those days, observers stationed at all eight main entrance/exit points recorded the number of visitors who entered per hour.

Information on visitor characteristics and travel patterns were gathered with an on-site visitor survey. A total of 514 questionnaires were administered at the eight main entrance/exit points during the summer use season. The number of surveys gathered at each site was proportional to that site's share of total exits from the entire system as determined by a census of visitor use. One visitor from each group was asked about their group size, their mode of travel (walking versus biking), the total amount of time they had spent on the carriage roads that day, and where and how long they paused during the visit. (Equestrian-related cases were not included in the study since these uses constitute such a small percentage of all carriage road use.) Finally, with the aid of a map, visitors were asked to list, in order, all of the intersections they passed during their trip. This produced a total of 381 unique travel routes.

The length of carriage road sections between intersections was calculated from a digital coverage using GIS analysis. The length of each unique route that respondents traveled was then calculated.

A field visit to the carriage roads and an examination of engineering maps determined that the length of a typical viewscape was approximately 100 meters. That is, this is the typical length of carriage road that can be seen at any one time.

The precise timing of visitor arrival patterns was measured using a program written for a laptop computer. Data were gathered over four half-hour periods with similar use levels near one entrance point on the carriage roads. Each time a visitor group arrived, a key was hit on the computer to record the time of arrival and travel mode (walking or biking) of visitor groups. Sixty-five data points were recorded. These data were gathered to verify the use of an exponential distribution to simulate arrival patterns. The use of an exponential distribution assumes that visitor groups arrive independently.

MODEL ALGORITHM AND PROGRAMMING

The simulation model was built using the object-oriented dynamic simulation package called Extend (1996). The structure of the model was built with hierarchical blocks that represented specific parts of the carriage road system. The three main types of hierarchical blocks that comprised the model were entrance/exit blocks, intersection blocks, and road section blocks.

The entrance/exit blocks were built to generate simulated visitor groups. Visitor groups were generated using an exponential distribution varying around mean values from the census counts. The groups were then randomly assigned travel modes (walking or biking) and group size, both according to probability distributions derived from the visitor survey. Simulated visitor groups were then randomly assigned travel speeds according to a lognormal distribution. The means and standard deviations were calculated from the travel times reported by survey respondents and the lengths of their travel routes. Lastly, visitor groups were randomly assigned a route identification number according to frequencies of actual routes reported by survey respondents.

The intersection blocks were built to direct simulated visitor groups in the right direction when they arrive at carriage road intersections. Lookup tables unique for each intersection direct each group toward the correct next intersection as indicated by their route identification numbers.

The road section blocks were built to serve two functions. The first was to simulate travel through the road section by delaying simulated visitor groups for the appropriate period of time, according to their assigned travel speeds. The second function was to gather PPV data. Within each road section block, a simulated 100-meter road segment was built. The number of visitors traveling on that 100-meter segment was counted and recorded once every minute of each simulation run.

Model Runs

Model runs were conducted to generate information on average PPV. Each run simulated carriage road use from 9:00 a.m. to 5:00 p.m. (the hours of peak use), but only recorded output from 10:00 a.m. to 5:00 p.m. Output from the first hour was considered unreliable because people who would have entered carriage roads before 9:00 a.m. were not simulated. The completed model was run for six levels of total daily use of the carriage roads: 375, 750, 1,500, 3,000, 6,000, and 12,000 visitors per day. The model runs were repeated five times at each use level to capture stochastic variation and generate confidence intervals. PPV conditions were recorded for four use zones: the entire carriage road system, road sections designated as high-use zones, road sections designated as low-use zones, and the road section between intersections 6 and 9 (a particularly heavily traveled section).

The model was also run for validation purposes. Data on how many simulated visitor groups exited at each exit point each hour were gathered for 20 model runs. Data on how many groups passed by the west side of Eagle Lake (the site of a permanent infrared trail counter) were gathered for 16 runs.

STUDY FINDINGS

Results are presented first on PPV conditions, and then on the results of model verification and validation. An alpha level of 0.05 was used for all statistical tests.

Persons per Viewscape

Figure 17.1 summarizes results estimating PPV conditions across all carriage road sections for different daily use levels. The results of the simulated days are expressed in the number of minutes out of an hour that a typical visitor will see selected PPV levels. For example, in figure 17.1, when 1,500 visitors

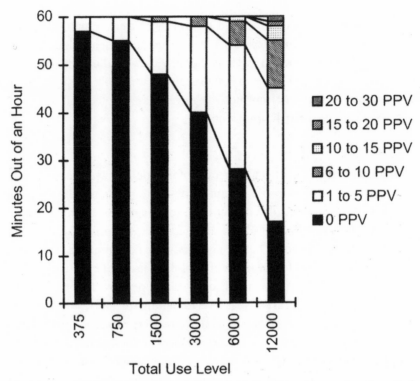

Figure 17.1 *PPV distribution for six daily use levels for all carriage road sections. Each value is a mean from five model runs.*

use the roads in a day, a typical visitor would see no one else (0 PPV) for 48 minutes out of an hour, one to five other visitors for 11 minutes out of an hour, and six or more other visitors for 1 minute out of an hour. Each data point shown represents the mean values, rounded to the nearest minute, from five model runs. Standard deviations calculated for these mean values range from 1.10 minutes (total use 6,000, 0 PPV) to 0.03 minutes (total use 12,000, 21–30 PPV).

Figure 17.2 provides a comparison of PPV results among the four use zones when 3,000 visitors use the carriage road system in a day. The use zones are: (1) low-use road sections, (2) all of the road sections in the system, (3) high-use road sections, and (4) the road section between intersections 6 and 9, the most heavily used road section in the system. Each data point shown represents the mean values, rounded to the nearest minute, from five model runs. Standard deviations calculated for these mean values

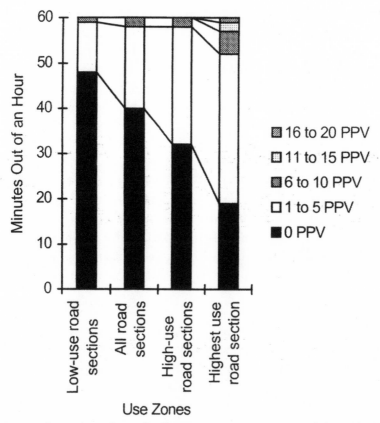

Figure 17.2 *Comparison of* PPV *distributions among use zones at a daily use level of 3,000. Each value is a mean from five model runs.*

range from 1.58 minutes (highest-use road section, 0 PPV) to 0.10 minutes (all road sections, 11–15 PPV).

Model Validity

Statistical tests were conducted comparing observed data with theoretical distributions used in the model. For example, the empirical distribution of interarrival times (amount of time between arrivals of visitor groups) gathered with the laptop computer at entrance points was compared to a theoretical exponential (M = 103.94) distribution. Chi-square statistical tests give no reason to conclude that the field data are poorly fitted by the exponential distribution. The distribution of average biker travel speeds calculated from visitor surveys also were compared to a theoretical lognormal

(M = 0.799 min/100 m, SD = 0.431) distribution. Again, chi-square tests give no reason to conclude that the data are poorly fitted by the lognormal distribution. The distribution of hiker travel speeds gathered with visitor surveys and calculated with a GIS program were compared to a theoretical lognormal (M = 1.615 sec/100 m, SD = 0.879) distribution. A chi-square test suggests that the data may be poorly fitted by the lognormal distribution. A Kolmogorov-Smirnov (K-S) test, on the other hand, gives no reason to conclude that the data are poorly fitted by the lognormal distribution.

Finally, three comparisons were made between observed data and model outputs: (1) the distribution of visitors across exit points, (2) the distribution of visitor exits across time, and (3) the distribution of visitors who passed by the Eagle Lake infrared trail-counter site through the hours of the day. Chi-square tests give no reason to conclude that the observed data are poorly fitted by the model output for all three comparisons.

DISCUSSION

Study findings support the use of computer simulation as a recreation research and management tool with respect to model utility and validity. PPV outputs for different total use level conditions and use zones provide an efficient and sophisticated view of the visitor experience that is related directly to crowding-related standards of quality. These results shed light on several aspects of visitor carrying capacity. First, PPV outputs show that, even at frontcountry areas such as the Acadia carriage roads, visitors generally see very few other visitors during most of the duration of their visits. Second, the outputs show that PPV conditions react consistently to increased total use level and that conditions vary by use zones. Third, the outputs show that free-access recreation use is distributed very unevenly, meaning that the number of persons in any visitor's viewscape will change throughout the duration of the visit.

The results also suggest that a temporal component is very important in setting standards of quality for carrying capacity management. It is common for managers to allow standards of quality to be violated for some percentage of time before management action is required. However, the percentage of time (or minutes out of an hour) that conditions can be permitted to exceed a certain PPV level is a very sensitive variable. From figure 17.1, use of the carriage roads would violate standards of quality at a total use level of 6,000 visits per day if managers decide that there can be more than 10 PPV for no more than 2 minutes out of an hour. However, standards of quality would not be violated until use reached 12,000 visits per day if managers decide there can be more than 10 PPV for no more than 5 minutes out of an hour.

The model-validation process used in this study followed the three-step process developed in the simulation modeling literature (Naylor and Finger 1967; Law and Kelton 1991). Results suggest that model outputs are accurate representations of actual conditions. All tests comparing observed data to model outputs gave no reason to conclude that the observed data are poorly fitted by the model output.

All tests comparing input distributions to observed data failed to cast doubt on the theoretical distributions, except for one. The significant difference indicated by a chi-square test comparing the distribution of hikers' average travel speeds against a lognormal distribution should be interpreted cautiously. It may be that a lognormal distribution is not the best theoretical distribution for simulating hiking speeds. On the other hand, reasonable confidence can be placed in the K-S test results that show no significant difference. It has been recognized in the literature that K-S tests are often superior to chi-square tests when sample sizes are relatively small (Banks and Carson 1984; Law and Kelton 1991). This may be the reason why the tests for bikers (sample size 316) showed no significant difference, while the tests for hikers (sample size 65) did.

The goodness-of-fit tests comparing model outputs to census and Eagle Lake counter data suggest that the model accurately simulates travel patterns on the carriage roads. The time and place of exit comparisons plus the Eagle Lake counter site comparisons suggest that simulated visitor groups follow realistic spatial and temporal travel patterns.

The correlated comparison between field PPV counts and model outputs suggests that the model's PPV estimates may be close to real PPV conditions. More cannot be concluded from the field counts due to the small number of observations.

The ability of the model to estimate PPV conditions under hypothetical use levels has not been tested directly. Such tests would require studies over much longer periods of time. An area that deserves attention is the model's assumption that the distributions of travel routes remain relatively similar under conditions of increasing use. While no studies have yet dealt with this issue directly, there is evidence that visitors who feel crowded may adopt coping behaviors, which may include adjusting their travel routes. (The issue of coping is described more fully in chapter 11.)

CONCLUSIONS

This study suggests that computer simulation has promise as a tool for recreation research and management. The carriage roads simulation model demonstrated that valid models can be built to simulate recreation travel patterns and provide substantial detail about park use patterns. By relating management parameters such as total use to indicators of quality such as PPV, simulation models can provide information on current carrying capacity conditions and also predict future conditions.

There are two important management implications of the research. First, simulation modeling can be a powerful tool to assist in monitoring indicators of quality. Without computer simulation, managers often have to measure impact conditions directly with field observations, and this can be especially challenging where recreation use is distributed widely in both space and time and use conditions are subject to rapid change. By establishing reliable relationships between management parameters (e.g., total use) and indicators of quality (e.g., PPV), simulation models can save managers valuable personnel time and other resources. In Acadia, managers can use the carriage road model to estimate PPV conditions by using information on total daily use level. (Use of simulation modeling in the park's monitoring program is described in chapter 16.) The second way in which computer simulation can be a powerful management tool is through its ability to predict impact conditions under hypothetical scenarios. In addition to possible future conditions such as increasing use levels, managers can simulate results of management actions that redistribute spatial or temporal patterns of use. Simulation modeling increases managers' ability to make informed carrying capacity policy decisions.

18 Monitoring and Assessing Trail Conditions at Acadia National Park

Trails are vital in parks and related areas, because hiking is a popular recreation activity and trails provide access to destinations of interest to both visitors and managers. Therefore, maintaining trails in good condition is important. While various forms of trail hardening and surfacing can enhance the durability of trails, these options can be costly or inappropriate due to management objectives or visitor preferences (Cahill, Marion, and Lawson 2008). Trail management requires objective and timely information about resource conditions of trails and how they change over time (Marion and Leung 2001). Trail condition assessment and monitoring methods have been developed to provide such information (Leung and Marion 2000). Resulting data can be used to document and evaluate long-term trends in trail conditions, and relational analyses can improve understanding of the relative importance of the use-related, environmental, or managerial factors that influence trail conditions (Farrell and Marion 2002). Finally, monitoring is a critical component in contemporary park and outdoor recreation management frameworks that require periodic assessments of trail conditions for comparison to standards of quality, with subsequent monitoring to evaluate the efficacy of corrective management actions (Leung and Marion 2000; Newsome, Moore, and Dowling 2002).

This chapter describes research and resulting data from an assessment of the 114 miles of trails on the MDI portion of Acadia. The principal objective of this research was to develop and apply efficient trail-condition assess-

---

This chapter is an edited version of the following report: Jeffrey Marion, Jeremy Wimpey, and Logan Park, "Monitoring Protocols for Characterizing Trail Conditions, Understanding Degradation, and Selecting Indicators and Standards of Quality, Acadia National Park, Mount Desert Island." Blacksburg, Va.: USDI, U.S. Geological Survey, Virginia Tech Field Station (forthcoming).

ment procedures able to characterize trail resource conditions accurately as part of a long-term monitoring program under the auspices of the NPS's VERP framework.

TRAIL MONITORING SYSTEMS

A variety of methods for monitoring trail conditions have been developed (Cole 1983; Leung and Marion 2000). At the most basic level, a trail inventory may be employed to locate and map trails and to document trail features such as type of use, segment lengths, hiking difficulty, and natural and cultural features. Trail location information can be documented accurately using a Global Positioning System (GPS) device, which can be input to a Geographic Information System (GIS) for display and analysis of trail attributes (Leung et al. 2002; Wolper et al. 1994; Wing and Shelby 1999).

Trail condition assessments seek to describe resource conditions and impacts for the purpose of documenting trends in trail conditions, investigating relationships with potential causal factors, and assessing the efficacy of management actions. Trail monitoring methods generally are classified as either sampling- or census-based (Leung and Marion 2000). Sampling-based approaches employ either systematic point sampling, where assessments are conducted at a fixed interval along a trail (Cole 1983, 1991), or stratified point sampling, where sampling varies in accordance with strata such as level of use or vegetation type (Hall and Kuss 1989). Census-based approaches employ either sectional evaluations, where trail assessments are made for entire trail sections (Bratton et al. 1979), or problem evaluations, where continuous assessments record all occurrences of predefined impacts (Leung and Marion 1999a; Marion 1994; Wenjun et al. 2005). These assessment approaches also can be integrated and applied simultaneously (Aust et al. 2005; Bayfield and Lloyd 1973). Methods for characterizing vegetation changes (Hall and Kuss 1989) and soil loss (Farrell and Marion 2002; Leonard and Whitney 1977; Marion, Leung, and Nepal 2006) also have been developed.

Guidance has been developed for selecting between a sampling-based or census-based approach (Marion, Leung, and Nepal 2006). Selection of a sampling method may not necessarily confer a substantial savings in assessment time as the systematic point sampling and problem census methods both require hiking nearly all of the trails under study. The problem census method requires less assessment time, particularly when trails are in good condition. However, an evaluation of these methods in Great Smoky Mountains National Park found the point sampling method to provide more accurate and precise measures of trail characteristics that are continuous (e.g., width or depth) or frequent (e.g., exposed soil) (Marion and Leung 2001). The problem census method is a preferred approach for monitoring trail conditions that can be defined easily (e.g., excessive erosion) or are infrequent, particularly when managers need information on the location and lineal extent of specific trail impact problems. One deficiency of this method is the need for subjective judgments of where specific impacts begin and end.

STUDY METHODS

Study Area

The study area for this assessment of trail conditions was the MDI portion of Acadia. The terrain on MDI is highly varied; beaches and cliffs along the rocky coast give way to steep bedrock-strewn ridges interlaced with woodlands, numerous clear lakes, and a glacial fjord. Glacial activity shaped much of the island, resulting in the current landscape dominated by long, gently sloped, north-south ridges with steep east-west faces. Trails were crafted during the late nineteenth and early twentieth centuries. Many of the MDI trails are unusual due to the exceptional amount of stone crafting used in their construction. For historic preservation reasons, the steep, direct-ascent alignments of the oldest trails are preserved by the NPS as historic park features. A few of the steepest trails resemble *via ferrata*–style hikes, featuring staircases, metal handholds, ladders, and rails.

Monitoring Procedures

This study's primary objectives were to develop efficient trail-condition monitoring protocols and provide baseline data for use in selecting VERP-related indicators and standards. Point sampling methods provide more useful and appropriate data for these purposes than problem assessment methods (Marion and Leung 2001). Based on the findings of Leung and Marion (1999c), the substantial trail mileage in the MDI network, and the need for an efficient method that NPS staff can sustain, a 500-foot (152.4 meter) point-sampling interval was selected. This interval provided more than a thousand sample points for statistical procedures and placed enough points along trails to characterize conditions adequately across the entire trail network. An analysis using the GIS layer of the MDI trail network revealed that this sample interval would place at least three sample points on most trail segments.

Traditionally, point-sampling trail surveys involved pushing a measuring wheel along the trail tread and stopping at a fixed interval following a random start. The use of a measuring wheel introduces an unknown amount of measurement error that varies with each survey. The rugged MDI terrain, crafted stone stairs, and vertical ascents involving metal railings and rungs also increase the difficulty of using a measuring wheel. Instead, a GIS layer of the MDI trail system was used to select trail-survey sample points and a sub-meter accuracy GPS unit was used to navigate to each sample point.

Sample points were located along the trail network at the specified 500-foot interval. At each sample point, a transect was established perpendicular to the trail tread with endpoints defined by the most visually obvious outer boundary of trampling-related disturbance (omitting maintenance disturbance). These boundaries are defined by pronounced changes in ground vegetation height, cover, composition, or, when vegetation cover is reduced or absent, by disturbance to organic litter. The objective was to define the trail tread receiving the majority (greater than 95 percent) of traffic, selecting the most visually obvious outer boundaries that can be identified most consistently. The distance between these disturbance boundaries was measured as tread width (table 18.1). If tread boundaries were not able to be determined (e.g., trail on bedrock), tread width was coded as "missing."

At each transect, survey staff assessed the grade of the trail and the trail slope alignment angle—the difference in compass bearing between the prevailing landform slope (aspect) and the trail's alignment at the sample point (Leung and Marion 1996). A trail aligned along the contour would have a slope alignment angle of 90 degrees, a "fall-line" trail aligned congruent to the landform slope would be 0 degrees. Trail position relative to the local topography was determined as side-hill or fall-line. Tread surface composition was assessed in the following categories: bare soil, vegetation, organic litter, roots, natural rock, stone work, and man-made materials (wood or gravel). For each category, the percent of tread width was recorded to the nearest 10 percent (5 percent when needed).

Three measures of soil loss were included in the survey (table 18.1). A traditional, rapid assessment method has been to measure the maximum

TABLE 18.1 Description of trail impact indicators and calculation methods.

Impact indicator	Calculation method
Trail width	Width of trail tread based on the most visually obvious outer boundary of trampling-related disturbance estimated to capture > 95 percent of traffic.
CSA soil loss	The cross sectional area from the estimated pre-trail use land/tread surface to the current tread surface. Calculated square inches at each transect. This measure can be extrapolated to provide a volume (cubic yards) estimate of trail soil loss by multiplying mean CSA for a trail by trail length. Mean CSA computations include o values for sample points where CSA was unable to be assessed.
Maximum incision	Maximum vertical measure from the estimated pre-trail use land/tread surface to the current tread surface.
Mean trail depth	Calculated by dividing mean CSA by mean tread width, including o values for sample points where CSA was unable to be assessed.
Area of disturbance	Calculated by summing the product of mean tread width and trail length.

incision or depth of the trail tread along a perpendicular transect defined by a taut line connected to stakes at the trail borders. A cross-sectional area (CSA) measure of total soil loss also was assessed using a fixed-interval method (Cole 1983). Temporary stakes were placed at positions that enabled a tape measure to be stretched along what survey staff judged to represent the original land surface for fall-line trails, or the post-construction tread surface for constructed side-hill trails. In rare situations where "historic" tread erosion was evident, staff assessed only the soil loss associated with the current tread. The rationale for this procedure is that recreation-related soil loss that is relatively recent is of greater importance to land managers and monitoring objectives. Severe erosion from historic activities that often preceded recreational trail uses is both less important and more difficult to measure reliably. Historic erosion is defined as erosion that occurred more than ten to fifteen years ago and is judged most readily by the presence of trees or shrubs growing directly from the eroded side-slopes.

CSA was assessed by taking vertical measurements along the tape measure at a fixed interval of 0.3 feet (1-foot intervals for wider trails). Excel spreadsheet formulas were developed to calculate CSA and mean trail depth (table 18.1) based on these data. CSA measurements were not able to be assessed when sample points fell on man-made materials (boardwalks, elevated treads, stonework) or on bare bedrock. As a consequence, CSA measures were completed for 492 of the 1,117 transects in the sample population. This proportion indicates the rocky and crafted environment of the Acadia trail system.

A high-resolution digital photograph of each sample location was taken and photo numbers were recorded in the GPS. Monitoring protocols call for field staff to return to the same sample points during future assessments. While a GPS can return staff to the general vicinity, the photographs can be referenced to position transects that closely approximate those used in the first monitoring cycle. Photographs also can be used in interpreting data and for direct visual comparisons of changes in trail conditions.

STUDY FINDINGS

This section reports results from the assessment of trails on MDI to illustrate the types of data that can be derived and their application to the VERP framework. Data from two trail indicators are presented to evaluate trail design attributes and characterize current trail system conditions. Finally, a relational analysis and statistical testing illustrate how monitoring data can be evaluated to improve understanding of current trail conditions and impact processes, and to enhance trail design and management.

The trail survey assessed conditions at 1,117 sample points selected to be representative of the 114-mile MDI trail system. While trail-condition assessment surveys are focused on achieving long-term monitoring objectives, they also provide an opportunity to collect useful data that characterizes physical attributes of the trail system. These attributes can be used to evaluate the sustainability of trails and in relational analyses with impact indicator data. Two such indicators assessed in this survey are trail grade and trail slope alignment angle. Soil loss on trails is strongly influenced by trail grade. The speed of surface-water runoff intercepted and carried downhill along trail treads increases exponentially with increasing trail grade (Dissmeyer and Foster 1984). In contrast, trails located in flatter terrain exacerbate two other core trail impact problems, tread muddiness and excessive widening.

The distribution of trail grade values for MDI trails illustrates their susceptibility for all three core trail-impact problems. Approximately 18 percent of the trail system is located in flatter terrain (0 to 2 percent grade) where treads can be susceptible to tread widening and muddiness problems. Fortunately, substantial amounts of granitic rock and granules in most soils prevent muddiness from being particularly troublesome, and managers have used boardwalks and occasionally gravel effectively in many locations lacking such substrates. Such actions also effectively address tread widening, along with dense woody vegetation common to lowland settings. Of greater concern is that 30.7 percent of the trail system has grades exceeding 15 percent. Trail manuals generally recommend keeping trail grades below 10 percent (Hooper 1988) or 12 percent (Hesselbarth and Vachowski 2000) to limit soil erosion, with rockwork often needed to harden and reduce erosion on treads greater than 15 percent. However, the mean grade of MDI trails is 13.2 percent and 10 percent of the MDI system has trail grades exceeding 30 percent. Many, but by no means all, of these excessively steep alignments have constructed rock steps or ascend exposed rock faces with anchored metal rungs. Analyses presented later in this section investigate the relationship between trail grade and soil loss.

As described in the methods section, a trail's slope alignment angle is the angle between the prevailing landform slope (aspect) and the trail's alignment extending downhill from the sample point. In contrast to trail grade, the influence and importance of this indicator is not widely known or investigated, though recent studies suggest it may be as influential as trail grade (Aust et al. 2005; Marion and Olive 2006). Remarkably, half (49.8 percent) of MDI trails are aligned within 22 degrees of the landform aspect or fall line, the path naturally taken by water running down a mountain slope.

Once a fall-aligned trail becomes incised, water trapped within the tread is exceptionally difficult to direct off. In flatter terrain, such treads are susceptible to muddiness and tread widening. When fall-line trail grades are steep, treads are particularly prone to soil erosion unless their substrates are exceptionally rocky or stonework is used. Rerouting fall-aligned sections generally is preferred, although alternative routes may not be possible due to cliff-lines or land ownership. On MDI, park staff feel compelled to retain most of these alignments on the basis of their historic values, including the protection of historic stonework along many segments. Fall-line trails with grades exceeding 15 to 20 percent frequently require significant investments in rockwork and ongoing maintenance to keep them sustainable. However, water still will drain under or over such work, which can increase danger to trail users or harm and loosen the rockwork during winter freezing.

Trail Condition Indicators

Trail width ranged from 0 to 197 inches with a mean of 37.8. One-quarter of the trails exceed 4 feet in width. The total area of intensive trampling disturbance associated with the MDI trail system is estimated to be 43.6 acres, based on calculations extrapolating mean trail width to the 114-mile MDI trail system. This amounts to 0.0013 percent of the park acreage on MDI.

Assessed soil loss is attributable to several causal factors, including erosion from water or wind, compaction from hikers, and soil displacement to the trail sides or downslope. At the locations where it was possible to apply this procedure (N=490), maximum incision ranged from 0 to 17 inches with a mean of 3.1. However, 627 sample points were located on bedrock, crafted stonework, or wooden boardwalk where such measures were inappropriate. Assuming no soil loss at these locations (i.e., incision = 0) yields a more valid trail-system mean maximum incision measure of 1.4 inches.

Cross-sectional area soil loss measurements, while more time-consuming, provide a more accurate estimate of soil loss. CSA ranged from 0 to 744 square inches, with a mean of 83.7 square inches. As with incision, staff were unable to assess CSA at many locations (N=628) and assuming no soil loss at these locations yields 36.7 square inches as a more valid estimate of mean soil loss for the MDI system. A calculation extrapolating this measure by the trail system length yields an estimated aggregate soil loss of 153,405 cubic feet (5,681 cubic yards or 568 ten-cubic-yard dump trucks). On a per-mile basis, soil loss is approximately 1,346 cubic feet per mile (49.8 cubic yards per mile).

A more representative measure of trail incision is provided by calculating mean tread depth from the vertical measures recorded to compute CSA. This measure ranged from 0 to 12.6 inches with a mean of 2.1 inches. Substituting 0's for locations where incision and CSA could not be assessed provides a more valid mean measure of 0.9 inches.

Finally, field staff assessments of the tread substrate as a proportion of transect width are used to characterize the typical trail-system substrates. The predominant tread substrate is rock (34.4 percent), followed by organic surface litter (26.6 percent) and soil (14.7 percent). The man-made category (12.9 percent) includes wood surfacing associated with boardwalks and human-placed gravel. Highly crafted stonework tread surfacing contributes 5.9 percent, followed by roots (3.7 percent) and vegetation (1.9 percent). Field staff did not assess mud or standing water, as these were rarely encountered.

Understanding Soil Loss

As previously noted, trail degradation can be minimized through proper trail design, including trail grade and its alignment to the prevailing slope. This section applies a relational analysis and statistical testing to evaluate

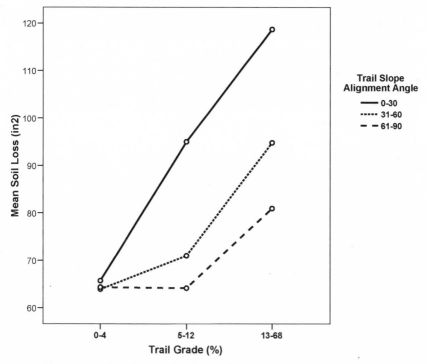

Figure 18.1 *The influence of trail slope alignment angle and trail grade on soil loss as measured by cross-sectional area.*

the relative influence of these two factors on trail soil loss, as assessed with CSA measures. Our hypothesis is that trail alignments with steep grades and/or fall-line orientations are more susceptible to soil erosion and will have larger CSA values. The influence of both these factors was tested statistically with ANOVA (General Linear Model) and found to be highly significant (F/p-value: model = 4.1/0.000; grade = 4.2/0.015; slope alignment = 3.1/0.047). Mean CSA values for three levels of trail grade and trail slope alignment angle are graphed in figure 18.1. These findings are dramatic, illustrating the strong influence of both these trail design factors. The least-eroded trail segments are those aligned closest to the contour (slope alignment = 61–90) with grades of up to 12 percent. The influence of trail grade increases as trail slope alignment angles decrease from 90 (contour) to 0 (fall-line). In particular, substantial increases in CSA values are shown to occur for trails in the 0 to 30-degree trail slope alignment category and for trails with grades in excess of 12 percent.

We expect that soil loss could have been substantially higher if not for the amount of exposed bedrock and rock present in the soils. As previously noted, soil loss could not be assessed at 56 percent of the sample, often due to the presence of bedrock, and in locations where measurements were possible, rock comprised the largest percentage (34.4 percent) of the tread surface. A principal management implication of these findings is that park staff could effectively reduce soil loss in locations where soils are a predominant substrate component by relocating segments with steep grades and low slope alignment angles (e.g., grades greater than 12 percent and alignment angles less than 30 degrees). Relocations to reduced grades would also likely create safer and more enjoyable hiking experiences. Improving tread drainage and installing rockwork in these locations also would be effective management responses.

CONCLUSIONS

Park managers are increasingly implementing VERP and related frameworks for managing park use and its potential impacts to park resources. The ability to monitor changes in resource conditions caused by visitor use is an essential component of such frameworks. Monitoring provides a variety of information about changing resource conditions that managers can use to describe the nature and severity of visitor impacts, evaluate their acceptability in comparison to standards of quality, conduct relational analyses, and evaluate the efficacy of management actions.

A variety of efficient methods for monitoring visitor impacts on trails have been developed. This chapter describes application of a point-sampling trail-monitoring method applied to assess the condition of trails at Acadia. This assessment yielded data used to characterize baseline conditions for the Acadia trail system and develops protocols that can be used to monitor changes in trail conditions periodically over time. Data from two trail indicators, trail grade and trail slope alignment angle, revealed some significant vulnerabilities, with about 31 percent of the trail system exceeding grades of 15 percent, and 50 percent of the trail system aligned within 22 degrees of the landform aspect or fall line.

Study findings describe current trail conditions by characterizing tread substrates and tread width and soil loss. Trail conditions are generally good, although soil loss was estimated at 5,681 cubic yards for the entire trail system. Large amounts of exposed bedrock and rockiness in the soils have prevented soil loss from being even more substantial. A relational analysis illustrated how monitoring data can be used to improve understanding of factors the influence soil loss. Both trail grade and trail slope alignment angle were found to be related significantly to trail soil loss, as assessed by CSA measures. These findings suggest that if soil loss is found to occur at unacceptable levels, relocating trails with steep grades or alignments close to the fall line would be an effective means for reducing soil loss.

19 Monitoring Visitor Impacts on Cadillac Mountain Using Remote Sensing

Contemporary park and outdoor recreation management frameworks such as VERP rely on a long-term program of monitoring. Monitoring is focused on indicators of quality that serve as the proxies for management objectives and desired resource and experiential conditions in parks and related areas. Data derived from monitoring suggest the degree to which standards of quality for indicator variables are being maintained and the need for and effectiveness of management actions.

Methods for inventorying and assessing resource-related impacts of visitor use have been developed, but these methods often require substantial field work and may not be well-suited to monitoring changes in resource conditions over time (Leung and Monz 2006). (Examples of these methods are described in chapters 4 and 18.) Remote sensing technology may offer a useful approach to monitoring long-term changes to park resources caused by visitor use. Potential advantages of remote sensing include collection of large amounts of data very quickly and the availability of archived data that can be used to identify trends in resource conditions. A growing body of research has begun to explore the potential usefulness of remote sensing technologies for (1) inventorying park resources (MacConnell and Stoll 1968), (2) identifying trends in park resource conditions (Price 1983; Nassauer 1990), and (3) assessing the usefulness of remote sensing in park and outdoor recreation management (Hammitt and Cole 1998; Rochefort and Swinney 2000; Ingle et al. 2004; Gross et al. 2006). Recent advances in remote sensing technologies and image resolution suggest a growing poten-

This chapter is an edited excerpt of the following: Min Kim, "Monitoring Vegetation Impact Using Remote Sensing Technology: Cadillac Mountain Summit, Acadia National Park." Ph.D. dissertation, University of Maine, 2009.

tial as a resource monitoring approach (Loveland et al. 2002; Weis et al. 2005; Gross et al. 2006; Alexandre and Eleonore 2007).

THE STUDY

This study was designed to assess the application of remote sensing to monitor visitor-caused impacts to soil and vegetation on the summit of Cadillac Mountain at Acadia. Cadillac Mountain is an important destination for many visitors to Acadia and is readily accessible by road and trails. Moreover, the summit of the mountain is characterized by thin soil and low-lying subalpine vegetation, making the area especially vulnerable to visitor-caused impact.

Efforts to concentrate visitors and limit impact to soils and vegetation on the summit were initiated many years ago by installing a short, paved loop trail. Interpretive stations were placed along the summit trail. However, given the generally open nature of the area, and the tendency for many visitors to walk off the trail, the summit still has experienced impacts to vegetation and loss of soils to support regeneration of vegetation. In 2000, park staff instituted a more intensive management program using physical barriers along the margins of the trail and low-impact education messages. To better understand the effectiveness of these management actions, remote sensing technologies were used to examine pre- and post-conditions of vegetation surrounding the summit loop trail. A sequence of study objectives was developed to accomplish the broader goal of assessing the usefulness of remote sensing technologies as part of a visitor-impact monitoring program: (1) map vegetation biomass using remote sensing, (2) examine vegetation biomass before and after the changes in management in 2000, (3) evaluate the efficacy of visitor management strategies to keep visitors on the trail and durable surfaces by examining different spatial scales of vegetation change detection in proximity to management actions, and (4) propose possible locations of future enclosures or other management actions.

STUDY METHODS

Two multi-spectral remote sensing datasets with high spatial resolutions, an IKONOS satellite image taken in August 2001 and another image captured by aircraft in June 2007, were utilized to detect vegetation biomass changes on the summit of Cadillac Mountain. Using remote sensing software, the IKONOS 2001 image was modified to match the higher ground-resolution format of the aircraft-generated image. A Normalized Difference Vegetation Index (NDVI) was used to detect vegetation biomass changes (Crist 1985; Xavier and Vettorazzi 2004; Jensen 2005; Lunetta et al. 2006; Myeong et al. 2006). NDVI is the most commonly used formula using two different reflective bands of multi-spectral remote sensing dataset for estimating vegetation cover and green biomass (Sader 1987; Michener and Houhoulis 1997; Song et al. 2001).

Based on methodologies from landscape ecology, a multi-scaling approach was applied to detect vegetation increase and decrease at different spatial scales (Levin, 1992; Turner, Gardner, and O'Neill 2001). For this analysis, three spatial scales were used to identify vegetation biomass changes in the vicinity of the summit loop trail: small (within 30 meters of the trail), medium (within 60 meters of the trail), and large (within 90 meters of the trail). This design enabled testing of the following hypotheses: (1) the rate of increased vegetation biomass would be higher than the rate of decreased vegetation biomass at all three spatial scales due to the management actions initiated in 2000, and (2) the rate of increased vegetation biomass would decrease from the small to large scale due to the management actions focused close to the trail and associated compliance of visitors as compared to vegetation increase that typically would occur in a more undisturbed environment at the larger scale. Also, analysis included investigation of vegetation biomass changes in the physical barriers as well as areas in the vicinity of the summit loop trail on the summit of the mountain.

STUDY FINDINGS

The biomass change detection analysis in 1-meter ground resolution was mapped using GIS. The results of the spatial scale analysis generally supported the hypothesized relationships regarding efficacy of management actions. The rate of increased biomass was higher than the rate of decreased vegetation biomass at all three different spatial scales as well as inside the three physical barriers located around the summit loop trail. Also, the rate of increased biomass was diminished going from the small scale to larger landscape scale in the vicinity of the summit loop trail: 12.80 percent within 30 meters to 10.16 percent within 60 meters to 8.77 percent within 90 meters.

Similar biomass change detection analysis in the 4-meter ground resolution revealed mixed results regarding the study hypotheses. Again, the rate of increased biomass was higher than the rate of decreased biomass at all three spatial scales. However, it was impossible to detect increased and decreased biomass within the three enclosures and the rate of increased biomass was nearly identical at all three spatial scales in the vicinity of the summit loop trail: 4.09 percent within 30 meters to 3.64 percent within 60 meters to 4.02 percent within 90 meters.

In both ground-resolution analyses, the rate of increased vegetation biomass was always higher than the rate of decreased vegetation biomass at the three spatial scales. These results support the efficacy of management actions designed to keep visitors on maintained trails and other durable surfaces. Previous observational studies of visitor behavior on Cadillac Mountain found that many visitors wander off the maintained trail, primarily within the 30-meter spatial scale, but sometimes occurring as far away as 90 meters from the trail (Turner and LaPage 2001). (This issue is discussed more fully in chapter 21.) In addition, the different rate of increased biomass observed closer to the trail, at least with the 1-meter ground resolution, further supports the positive effect of management and that the change is not due to random natural variation of increases and decreases in vegetation. Also, it should be noted that less biomass was detected within the total area within the 30-meter spatial scale, suggesting that nonvegetative surfaces such as soil and bare rocks are more predominant than vegetation. Although these results seem to support a clear positive direction, any future increases in biomass may at some point be limited if no substrate exists to support vegetation growth. While detection of vegetation increases over time can be used as a measure of the efficacy of management actions, the detection of no vegetation loss might be equally important at this spatial scale.

Finally, analysis included investigation of biomass changes directly in the vicinity of the summit loop trail. Relatively little biomass change was found around the summit loop trail itself, but more increases than decreases in biomass were found. However, away from the summit loop trail, more decreases than increases in biomass were found at two specific locations: (1) near the gift shop and a nearby trail not associated with the summit loop trail; and (2) a high ridge located on the west side of the parking lot. In these locations, fewer visible forms of intensive visitor management actions such as physical barriers and educational signs have been installed. It is possible that many visitors may be going to these locations before they walk the summit loop trail and are unaware that they should remain on maintained trails and other durable surfaces. The gift shop was renovated recently with new interpretative exhibits and the toilet facility was rebuilt with eco-friendly technology. A high ridge located on the west side of the parking lot has been used for a tour bus stop associated with cruise ship visits. It is plausible that the vegetation impacts at these locations could be attributed to increased visitor uses associated with the updated facilities and tour bus stop. Additionally, a lower parking lot near the summit of Cadillac Mountain was re-signed from "Sunset Point" to the less enticing "Blueberry Hill" because of the popularity of this area, parking congestion, and vegetation degradation occurring in this vicinity. Some of the visitors once at this site in the early evening hours might be re-directed to western locations closer to the top of the summit of Cadillac Mountain. Therefore, more intensive management actions might be warranted for these two specific locations or re-evaluation of the management of the Blueberry Hill parking area near the summit may become necessary.

CONCLUSION

The findings from this study indicate that by using NDVIs from two different remote sensing datasets, it was possible to measure vegetation changes at the summit of Cadillac Mountain between 2001 and 2007. These measures of change in vegetation in the vicinity of the summit loop trail provide baseline data for determining trends in vegetation change over longer periods of time. In this regard, remote sensing technology offers a feasible approach for assessing visitor-caused vegetation impact and the efficacy of associated management actions. Study findings suggest that management actions instituted in 2001 designed to encourage visitors to stay on the maintained summit loop trail and other durable surfaces are meeting with some success in limiting visitor-caused impacts to soil and vegetation.

While the methods employed in this study can be used to measure trends in biomass, more detailed analyses about changes at the levels of vegetation species or genus will be required to assess fragile vegetation types in the study area. Research has shown that re-vegetated sites often consist of more resilient and resistant species and overall less natural diversity than sites that have not been impacted by visitor use (Hammitt and Cole 1998). Future research on remote sensing is planned to incorporate a pixel-based post-classification change-detection component to analyze changes in diversity of vegetation. Control sites of relatively undisturbed vegetation will be integrated into the analysis of change detection using remotely sensed imagery. While this approach is not intended to be a substitute for the more conventional on-the-ground inventory and assessment procedures developed in the field of recreation ecology, remote sensing technology may complement these approaches while adding an important degree of efficiency (Manning, Jacobi, and Marion 2006).

20 Monitoring Parking Lot Conditions to Assess the Effectiveness of Alternative Transportation and Travel Information Technologies at Acadia National Park

Many of the most popular attractions in Acadia such as Cadillac Mountain, Sand Beach, and Jordan Pond House experience parking problems. In addition to anecdotal information on parking conditions from park staff and visitors, parking was identified as a long-standing problem in the park's General Management Plan. This plan identified public transportation as the preferred approach for both protecting park lands and providing a quality visitor experience.

In 1999, Acadia introduced the Island Explorer bus with the help of state and federal government transportation agencies, the nonprofit organization Friends of Acadia, and communities on MDI. Unlike other new alternative transportation systems being introduced in national parks that charge riders, this is a free service operated by a nonprofit organization and relies on voluntary use (Turnbull 2003). From late June through early September of the first season, the buses carried a total of 142,260 passengers over six routes through the park and MDI towns (Daigle and Lee 2000). The success of the Island Explorer bus has led to a number of other developments, including a corporate sponsor and subsequent expansion of service and increased bus capacity. During the 2002 operation season, the buses carried 281,142 passengers over seven routes, an increase of almost 100 percent (Zimmerman, Coleman, and Daigle 2003). The design of the Island Explorer bus system relies on the cooperation of local communities and private businesses on MDI so that visitors can gain access to the bus from where they stay, thus leaving their privately owned vehicles at lodging fa-

This chapter is an edited version of the following paper: John Daigle and Carole Zimmerman, "Alternative Transportation and Travel Information Technologies: Monitoring Parking Lot Conditions over Three Summer Seasons at Acadia National Park," *Journal of Park and Recreation Administration* 22 (2004): 82–103.

cilities. The central artery of the Island Explorer bus system is located in the town of Bar Harbor, which is in close proximity to where most visitors stay and serves other important visitor needs such as shops and restaurants. Visitors gain access to the park via buses departing Bar Harbor with stops at popular destinations such as Sand Beach, Eagle Lake, and Jordan Pond House.

In 1999, as part of a continued collaborative planning effort, Acadia was chosen for a study of the effectiveness of intelligent transportation system (ITS) technology in helping to solve national park transportation problems. During the summer of 2002, ITS technologies were installed, with many components intended to enhance the operation of the Island Explorer bus system (Zimmerman, Coleman, and Daigle 2003). These included two-way voice communications, automatic vehicle location, electronic bus departure signs, automated annunciators on-board the buses, and automatic passenger counters. Real-time travel information was collected and integrated with Island Explorer buses and disseminated to visitors via an automated annunciator that transmitted an audio message and displayed the next bus stop on an electronic sign within the bus for all seven bus routes. Also, electronic signs displayed real-time departure times of the next Island Explorer bus at the Visitor Center and Jordan Pond House bus stops in Acadia and the Village Green in Bar Harbor. ITS traffic-management components within the park included parking lot monitoring and traffic volume recorders at park entrances. Traveler information was provided to visitors, including real-time parking conditions at two popular destinations in the park, Sand Beach and Jordan Pond House. This information was available on the Acadia web page and displayed on signs at the Visitor Center, Blackwoods Campground, and Seawall Campground. The overall goal was to enhance the visitor experience and to divert visitors from using their private vehicles to using the Island Explorer bus for traveling around MDI and in the park.

This chapter reports the results of field observations conducted over three summer seasons at eight parking areas in Acadia that were served by Island Explorer buses. Years 2000 and 2001 represented baseline conditions, and 2002 represented the post-deployment phase of ITS. An important goal related to the ITS technologies was to divert use from privately owned vehicles to the Island Explorer bus. One objective of the investigation was to examine whether the availability of this information led to a reduction in the number of privately owned vehicles parked outside of designated parking spaces at the popular attractions of Sand Beach and Jordan

Pond House. By making real-time parking information available at these two areas, it was hoped that visitors might alter their travel plans and decide to use the Island Explorer bus instead of their privately owned vehicle or change the time of day to visit the attraction. Therefore, a second objective was to assess whether ITS helped to distribute the demand for parking more evenly among parking lots. Data sources such as park use statistics, Island Explorer ridership statistics, and a 2002 visitor survey examining use of the travel information technologies are presented in relation to the parking lot conditions data. These data can help improve understanding of the effectiveness of ITS in solving parking and related transportation problems.

STUDY METHODS

Park staff were interviewed about parking, and eight areas were selected as potential study sites. These areas included parking lots at Sieur de Monts, Sand Beach, Bubble Pond, Jordan Pond, Ikes Point, Eagle Lake, Acadia Mountain, and Echo Lake. These sites were verified through a meeting of stakeholders. Criteria for selecting sites included the travel information technologies to be deployed and, in particular, the technologies associated with the Island Explorer bus that serviced the parking lots specified above.

The study design incorporated information beyond "illegally" parked vehicles, to include other vehicles causing safety and aesthetic problems, such as the number of legally parked vehicles along the Park Loop Road leading to the entrance of the Sand Beach parking lot. In addition to the data collected in the parking lot study, a visitor survey assessing travel experiences also included data regarding parking. For example, questions asked visitors about their travel experiences and if they had encountered any parking problems using their privately owned vehicles, how they responded, and time of day they first encountered the parking problems.

Maps of the parking areas and written instructions were created to develop an efficient protocol and to identify specific locations for field data-collection staff to count the number of vehicles not in paved parking spaces. Data sheets were used to record the date, weather conditions, time of day for parking area observation, number of vehicles not in paved parking spaces for each specified section of the parking lot, total vehicle count not in paved parking spaces for the parking lot, and grand total of vehicles not in paved parking spaces counted for the day. For example, vehicles were counted if parked outside of a designated parking space in the parking area or along the shoulder of the entrance road leading to a parking lot.

Using a multi-stage cluster sampling design, a total of 86 parking observations were recorded over three summer seasons. Planning for the study did not start until May 2000. Consequently, it was not possible to begin baseline data collection until August 2000, after stakeholders agreed upon the methods and locations for the parking counts. In 2001, parking counts began in late June and ran through Labor Day weekend to capture the entire tourist season coinciding with the operation of the Island Explorer bus system. The majority of the parking observations (53 percent) occurred in the month of August. For the months of June and September, fewer sample days reflects the operation of the Island Explorer bus system, which started in late June and ended after the Labor Day weekend during the study period.

STUDY FINDINGS

Parking Lot Counts

Generally, a consistent use pattern was observed over the three summer seasons in terms of the proportion of vehicles exceeding the capacity of individual parking lots. Figure 20.1 contains a graph showing the mean number of vehicles exceeding the capacity of the eight parking locations by year. The margin of error was calculated for a 95 percent confidence interval. A range of conditions was observed. For example, a mean of 81 to 124 vehicles exceeded the capacity for the Sand Beach parking lot over the three summer observation periods as compared to a mean of five or fewer for Sieur de Monts, Bubble Pond, Ikes Point, and Echo Lake parking lots. The data do not demonstrate an overall redistribution of vehicles among the parking lots as a result of ITS, as there was no significant increase or decrease in the mean number of vehicles exceeding the capacity of the parking areas. However, it is possible that a redistribution occurred but was not measured by the data collected, which focused solely on excess parking. For example, it is possible that the total number of vehicles increased at Echo Lake during 2002, but vehicles would not have been counted if parked legally within the capacity of the parking lot. The Echo Lake parking lot has a very large parking capacity and the number of vehicles rarely exceeded the capacity of the parking lot. Future studies should consider a design to count all vehicles

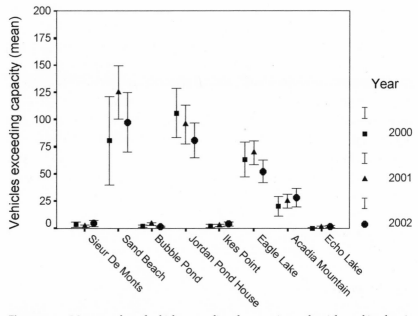

Figure 20.1 *Mean number of vehicles exceeding the capacity at the eight parking lots in Acadia National Park, summers 2000 to 2002. Error bars indicate the 95 percent confidence levels.*

whether or not they are parked illegally or parked outside of designated lots to better assess redistribution within the park.

Sand Beach and Jordan Pond House Parking Lot Conditions by Day, Month, and Year

A similar use pattern was evident at the Sand Beach and Jordan Pond House parking lots, with peak use occurring during the month of August and more frequent use during the middle of the week as compared to weekends. However, a decrease was observed in the number of vehicles that exceeded the parking lot capacity in 2002 as compared to 2001, even though total visitors to the park increased.

The number of vehicles exceeding the capacity of the Sand Beach and Jordan Pond House parking lots varied among the days of the week during the summer observation periods. No significant differences were detected between the mean number of vehicles counted as exceeding the capacity of the two parking lots by day of the week. However, the middle of the week generally had higher mean number of vehicles exceeding the capacity as compared to the first part of the week and weekends. A possible explanation of the daily parking use patterns observed may be related to the typical week of vacation with travel to and from the area occurring mostly on weekends (Littlejohn 1999; Daigle and Lee 2000).

As with parking use patterns for days of the week, variation was observed for months of the summer season and number of vehicles exceeding the capacity of the Sand Beach and Jordan Pond House parking lots. There were several days during the month of August (35 percent of days sampled) when the capacity of the two parking lots was exceeded by more than 300 vehicles. In fact, over half of the days sampled during the month of August (59 percent) had vehicle counts that exceeded capacity by more than 200 cars across the two study lots. Approximately half of the days sampled in July had between 151 and 250 vehicles exceeding the capacity. In August, the mean number of vehicles was 242 across the two lots as compared to 193, 179, and 130 for September, July, and June, respectively. A significant difference in the mean number of vehicles exceeding the capacity of the two study lots was detected between August and June. For these parking areas, there appears to be a relationship between the monthly park use statistics and the intensity of overflow parking conditions.

In 2001, on more than half of the days that the two parking areas were observed (57 percent), more than 200 vehicles were counted outside designated parking spots for the two parking lots. In contrast, in 2002, the number of excess vehicles was over 200 for the two parking lots on 30 percent of the days observed. These percentages show a similar trend in the numbers of vehicles exceeding the capacity of the two parking areas during the 2001 and 2002 summer seasons. No significant differences were detected between the mean number of vehicles counted as exceeding the capacity of the two parking lots and year but the decline from a mean of 215 vehicles in 2001 to 180 vehicles in 2002 suggests a trend in the desired direction. It should be noted that the total number of visitors to the park increased each of the three years, making the reduction in the parking excess statistics for 2002 especially notable.

Parking Availability Information and Travel Information Technologies

In order to test the impact of parking information on visitor behavior, Sand Beach and Jordan Pond House lots were selected as sites for which information on parking conditions would be made available to visitors. Sand Beach and Jordan Pond House are especially popular destinations in the park, and it is possible for visitors to park close to but outside the designated parking areas for these attractions. No significant difference was detected in mean number of vehicles exceeding the capacity of the two parking areas for the 2001 and 2002 summer seasons. Nevertheless, in 2002, the year that ITS was operational, a reduction in the mean number of vehicles exceeding the capacity of the Sand Beach and Jordan Pond parking areas occurred compared to 2001.

The magnitude of change for the Sand Beach and Jordan Pond House parking areas as compared to the other six parking areas might be partly related to the real-time parking information available for these two areas and not the other six areas. Participants in a 2002 visitor survey that examined visitors' use of travel information technologies provided some insight regarding changes in parking conditions at these two parking areas. (This survey is described in more detail in chapter 25.) First, a subset of survey participants were selected who specifically identified Sand Beach and Jordan Pond House as planned destinations. Second, participants were then compared on variables such as extent to which they used the travel information technologies, including real-time parking information, and use of the Island Explorer bus. Also, as noted above, Island Explorer ridership has increased each year; for example, 193,057 riders in 2001 as compared to 281,142 in 2002 for a 21 percent increase in total riders. Ridership statistics for specific bus routes servicing the Sand Beach and Jordan Pond House provide a context for interpreting the observed changes in parking conditions at these two parking areas.

Over one-third (35.7 percent) of the participants who identified Jordan Pond House as a destination indicated that they used the real-time parking conditions information. Nearly half (48.3 percent) of participants agreed or strongly agreed that the real-time parking information helped them decide to use the Island Explorer bus. Nearly half (47.3 percent) of the participants who identified Jordan Pond House as a destination reported use of the Island Explorer bus during their recent visit. Over three quarters (80.0 percent) of participants agreed or strongly agreed that the travel information technologies such as the real-time bus departure signs helped them decide to use the Island Explorer bus. The bus ridership statistics for the Jordan Pond House bus route suggest an influence of the travel information. While ridership increased on all designated bus routes by 21 percent, a much higher increase occurred in ridership on the Jordan Pond House bus route (nearly 34 percent), representing an addition of 11,547 riders in 2002.

Similar to the Jordan Pond House area, over one-third (40.3 percent) of the participants who identified Sand Beach as a destination area indicated that they used the real-time parking conditions information. Over half (54.8 percent) of participants agreed or strongly agreed that the real-time parking information helped them to decide to use the Island Explorer bus. More than half (61.3 percent) of the participants who identified Sand Beach as a destination reported use of the Island Explorer bus during their recent visit. Over three-quarters (85.1 percent) of participants agreed or strongly agreed that the travel information technologies such as the real-time departure signs helped them decide to use the Island Explorer bus. Similar to Jordan Pond House, bus ridership statistics for the Sand Beach route appear to be related to the provision of travel information. The Island Explorer bus route servicing Sand Beach experienced a 37 percent increase in riders—25,752 riders in 2001 to 40,891 riders in 2002—and had the highest percentage increase in riders as compared to the other bus routes.

In summary, no significant differences were detected between the mean number of vehicles counted as exceeding the capacity of the Sand Beach and Jordan Pond House parking lots and year. However, the magnitude of change for Sand Beach and Jordan Pond House from a mean of 215 vehicles in 2001 to 180 vehicles in 2002 as compared to the other six parking areas studied may in part be related to the real-time parking information available for these two areas and not the other six areas. Based on other data, including a visitor survey and ridership statistics, there appears to be a relationship between the travel information technologies, use of the Island Explorer bus, and the changes observed in parking conditions at these two areas. However, results suggest that ITS cannot be relied upon solely to reduce parking problems significantly and that additional measures are needed to reduce parking problems further.

Several reasons may help explain why no statistically significant differences were observed in parking conditions. While awareness of parking availability information and traveler information is an essential first step in attempting to change visitor behavior, the 2002 survey of visitors revealed that it did not always translate into use of the information. Some visitors chose not to use the traveler information or Island Explorer buses and expressed high satisfaction with their travel experiences and little concern about locating places to park near their intended destinations (Zimmerman, Coleman, and Daigle 2003). The vast majority of visitors contacted on the Island Explorer buses who reported being aware of one or more of the ITS travel technologies actually used the traveler information. However, only a slight majority of visitors contacted at other locations who reported being aware of one or more of the ITS travel technologies actually used the traveler information. For example, over half of visitors (55 percent) reported being aware of the information on parking availability, but only 30 percent reported planning to use the information for their travel (Daigle and Zimmerman 2004b). Also, the status of parking lots being full did not necessarily restrict visitors from gaining access to these attractions. Some visitors may have realized that these areas were still accessible by privately owned vehicles (e.g., by parking along the road) and despite knowing the condition of the parking lots did not plan to use the information. In other words, the traveler information or buses may have had little influence in deterring these visitors from using their privately owned vehicles to access the Sand Beach and Jordan Pond House parking lots.

Another reason for not seeing significantly fewer vehicles causing parking problems may be related to the parking policy in effect during the study period that allowed vehicles to park outside established parking spaces unless a blatant violation occurred, such as a vehicle parked over a parking barrier. This encouraged a "snowball effect": Once one car parked illegally without a warning or ticket, more visitors were likely to park illegally. If a more strict policy were to be implemented to regulate parking, especially at Jordan Pond House, more visitors may have sought out parking availability information and used the Island Explorer bus, thereby further reducing the number of vehicles exceeding the capacity of the lots at these two popular sites. Finally, there was a slight increase in total visitation to the park in 2002 compared to 2001. Some visitors who utilized the travel information technologies and who ultimately decided to ride the bus instead of driving their own personal vehicles to the Sand Beach and Jordan Pond House destinations simply may have been replaced by additional visitors who were unaware of the travel technologies or who knew about the information but still used their personal vehicles to access these destinations.

CONCLUSIONS

Parking lot monitoring revealed a reduction in the number of vehicles beyond capacity at Sand Beach and Jordan Pond House from 2001 to 2002. This reduction was in spite of an increase in total annual visits to the park and is presumably due to implementation of ITS technology and related alterative transportation. While this reduction was not statistically significant, it is a step in the right direction. Monitoring should be continued to assess parking conditions in the park and evaluate the effectiveness of management actions designated to address this issue.

Information may be needed to educate visitors about the potential impacts on vegetation and soil erosion caused by vehicles parked outside of designated spaces. More enforcement and signage, especially at the Jordan Pond House parking lots, may further reduce the number of illegally parked vehicles. For a less direct approach, management may want to make modifications to parking lots by strategically placing boulders or other natural barriers at problem spots. This approach may be a more effective and efficient method of reducing the number of illegally parked vehicles. Finally, most of the vehicles counted that exceeded the capacity of Sand Beach parking lot were parked legally along the right side of the one-way Park Loop Road leading to the entrance of the parking lot. In this instance, persuasive appeals to use public transit might focus on the aesthetic consideration of seeing more of the scenic beauty of the park rather than parked cars while traveling along the Park Loop Road.

PART III Management

21 | Managing Visitor Impacts on Cadillac Mountain

An accumulating body of research dating back several decades has documented the variety and severity of environmental impacts that visitors can have on parks, including trampling of fragile vegetation, soil compaction and erosion, water pollution, and disturbance of wildlife (Hammitt and Cole 1998; Marion and Leung 2001). A common finding of this research is that such impacts can occur even under relatively low levels of use. For example, an early study in the Boundary Waters Canoe Area Wilderness in Minnesota found that an average of 80 percent of groundcover was lost at campsites in a single season, even under use conditions that were described as "light" (Frissell and Duncan 1965). The urgency of this issue has been magnified over time as annual use levels of popular parks and related areas are now measured in the hundreds of thousands and even millions.

How can parks be managed to limit the environmental impacts of visitor use? How effective are these management practices? Why are some management practices more effective than others? How acceptable are alternative management practices to visitors? To help answer these and related questions, a multi-method study was conducted at the summit of Cadillac Mountain in Acadia. The study applied a range of management practices designed to control the impacts of visitor use ("treatments") along with associated "controls" and employed observational and survey methods to measure the effectiveness of the experimental management practices. The first component of the study used unobtrusive observation to determine

---

This chapter is an edited version of the following paper: Logan Park, Robert Manning, Jeffrey Marion, Steven Lawson, and Charles Jacobi, "Managing Visitor Impacts in Parks: A Multi-Method Study of the Effectiveness of Alternative Management Practices," *Journal of Park and Recreation Administration* 26, no. 1 (2008): 97–121.

the percentage of visitors who walked off an official trail (and therefore damaged surrounding soils and vegetation) under control and treatment conditions. The second component of the study used a series of surveys of visitors exposed to control and treatment conditions to understand how these management practices affected visitor behavior and how acceptable these management practices were to visitors. The combination of research design (experimentation and associated controls) and methods (observation and visitor surveys) used in this study provides multiple and complementary perspectives on the important issue of protecting park resources from the impacts of visitor use.

The summit of Cadillac Mountain is one of the most popular sites in the park, offering sweeping views of the park and surrounding areas, and is readily accessible by road and trails. Consequently, up to 5,500 visitors are drawn to the summit area on peak summer days (Turner and LaPage 2001; Baldwin and LaPage 2003). A 0.3-mile paved summit loop trail (along with a large parking lot and gift shop) is designed to accommodate this use. However, many visitors choose to walk off this formal trail, and off-trail walking has resulted in extensive and severe trampling impacts to surrounding soil and vegetation (Turner and LaPage 2001; Evans 2002). These impacts are exacerbated by the fragile character of the summit, which is comprised of low-lying sub-alpine vegetation and thin soils, and by the short, high-latitude growing season. The presence of rare plant species and concerns about visitor-caused impacts have prompted the state of Maine to designate the summit as a Critical Environmental Area (Turner and LaPage 2001).

MANAGING VISITOR USE

The literature on parks and outdoor recreation suggests that a variety of management alternatives might be applied to guide visitor use and minimize resulting impacts (Cole, Petersen, and Lucas 1987; Anderson et al. 1998; Manning 1999). For example, visitor use and impacts might be subject to four basic management strategies: limiting the amount of use, increasing the supply of recreation areas/opportunities, altering visitor behavior to reduce impacts, and hardening the resource to visitor use (Manning 1979b). A number of sub-strategies are available within each of these alternatives.

Another way to conceptualize management alternatives focuses on tactics or actual management practices. Management practices are actions or tools applied by managers to accomplish the strategic objectives outlined above. For example, restrictions on length of stay, differential fees, and mandatory use permits are all management practices designed to implement the strategy of limiting recreation use. Management practices may be classified along a spectrum according to the directness with which they act on visitor behavior (Lime, 1977b; Peterson and Lime 1979; Chavez 1996). As the term suggests, direct management practices act directly on visitor behavior, leaving little or no freedom of choice. Indirect management practices attempt to influence the decision factors upon which visitors base their behavior. As an example, a direct management practice for reducing campfire-related impacts would be a regulation to prohibit campfires and enforcement of this regulation. An indirect management practice would be an education program informing visitors of the undesirable ecological and aesthetic impacts of campfires and encouraging them to carry and use portable stoves instead.

The relative advantages and disadvantages of direct and indirect recreation management practices have received substantial attention in the professional literature. Generally, indirect management practices are favored when and where they are believed to be effective (Peterson and Lime 1979; McCool and Christensen 1996).

Emphasis on indirect management practices, however, has not been endorced uniformly (McAvoy and Dustin 1983; Shindler and Shelby 1993). It has been argued that indirect management practices may be insufficiently effective. Some visitors, for example, may ignore management efforts to influence the decision factors that guide behavior. The actions of a few, therefore, hamper attainment of management objectives. This problem may be especially germane to the issues of resource impacts because, as noted earlier, these impacts can be caused by low levels of use.

Since information and education programs are an indirect management practice, they commonly are applied to help manage visitor use (Marion, Roggenbuck, and Manning 1993; Abbe and Manning 2007). However, information or education can be seen as having varying degrees of application to a variety of recreation management problems (Roggenbuck 1992; Vander Stoep and Roggenbuck 1996; Hendee and Dawson 2003). Problem behaviors of visitors can be classed into five basic types along a spectrum. At the two ends of the spectrum, problem behaviors can be seen as either deliberately illegal (e.g., theft of cultural artifacts) or unavoidable (e.g., disposal of human waste). In these instances, information may have limited effectiveness. However, the other three types of problem behaviors—careless actions (e.g., littering), unskilled actions (e.g., selecting an inappropriate campsite), and uninformed actions (e.g., using dead snags for firewood)—may be considerably more amenable to information and education programs.

Information and education also can be considered in relation to theories of moral development (Christensen and Dustin 1989). This approach builds on two prominent theories of moral development (Kohlberg 1976; Gilligan 1982). Both theories suggest that people tend to evolve through a series of stages of moral development ranging from those that are very self-centered and are based on issues of immediate rewards and punishments to those that are highly altruistic and are based on principles of justice, fairness, and self-respect. Individual visitors to parks and recreation areas may be found at any of the stages of moral development. Management implications of this conceptual approach suggest that information and education programs (and perhaps management programs in general) should be designed to reach visitors at each of these stages of moral development. For example, to reach visitors at lower levels of moral development, managers might emphasize extrinsic rewards and punishments for selected types of behavior. However, communicating with visitors at higher levels of moral development might be more effective by means of emphasizing the rationale for selected behaviors and appealing to one's sense of altruism, justice, and fairness.

STUDY METHODS

While a variety of practices might be used to manage visitor use and its associated impacts, there is uncertainty about the effectiveness of these alternatives (Manning 1999). A number of studies have explored this issue (see, for example, Roggenbuck and Berrier 1982; Harmon 1992; Alpert and Herrington 1998), but resulting knowledge is spotty. Most research has focused on only a few management practices such as information or education and use limits. Moreover, much of this research has been hypothetical and attitudinal, not experimental and behavioral. The study described in this chapter was designed to test the effectiveness of alternative management practices that

TABLE 21.1 Summary of management actions for study controls and treatments.

| | Management actions[a] | | | | | |
| | Indirect | | | | | Direct |
Controls/Treatments	Educational signs	Appeal to remain on trail or bedrock	Appeal to remain on trail	Personal educational message	Prompter signs	Trailside fencing
Control 1 (control for treatments 1–4)	No	No	No	No	No	No
Treatment 1 (educational signage I)	Yes	No	No	No	No	No
Treatment 2 (educational signage II)	Yes	Yes	No	No	No	No
Treatment 3 (educational signage III)	Yes	Yes	No	Yes	Yes	No
Treatment 4 (fencing)	Yes	Yes	No	No	No	Yes
Control 2 (control for treatment 5)	Yes	Yes	No	No	No	No
Treatment 5 (personal message to tour bus passengers)	Yes	Yes	Yes	No	No	No

[a]Pre-existing management actions were held constant for all controls and treatments: paved trail with some coping stones, site map signs, and exclosures around several patches of vegetation.

ranged from indirect to direct, and to conduct this test in an experimental context. Moreover, multiple research methods—observation and visitor surveys—were used to capitalize on the strengths of each and to validate findings from each methodological approach. Management practices included in the study were designed to encourage visitors to the summit of Cadillac Mountain to stay on the paved summit loop trail in order to limit their impacts on surrounding soil and vegetation. The following range of controls and treatments were tested in this study. A summary of management actions by controls and treatments is shown in table 21.1.

Control 1 (control for treatments 1 through 4). Simple site maps of the summit loop trail were posted at both entrances/exits to the summit loop trail. Existing split-rail fence exclosures around some large patches of remaining vegetation on the summit and large coping stones defining the trail margin in selected locations were kept in place for this control and all treatments. Moreover, the existence of the paved trail itself could be considered a "treatment" designed to encourage visitors to confine their use to the developed, formal trail.

Treatment 1 (educational signage I: paved trail and rocks). Signs were posted at the site maps at the entrances/exits to the summit loop trail and at two intervals along the trail. These signs briefly described the damage caused by walking off the trail and asked visitors to walk only on the paved trail or on rock surfaces. This treatment was designed to test the effectiveness of the indirect management practice of information/education delivered through signs. As described above, it encouraged visitors to stay on the paved trail but also allowed them to walk off the trail if they stayed on rock surfaces.

Treatment 2 (educational signage II: paved trail only). This treatment was the same as treatment 1, but the second set of signs asked visitors to remain on the paved trail only.

Treatment 3 (educational signage III: paved trail only plus prompter signs). This treatment was the same as treatment 2. However, ground-level "prompter" signs constructed of 4×4-inch wooden blocks with a "no walking" graphic were installed at the twenty-four most prominent informal (visitor-created) trails branching off the paved summit loop trail.

Treatment 4 (site management). This treatment was the same as treatment 2 but added a low, symbolic rope fence lining the first 150 feet of the paved trail. The fence was designed to keep visitors on the paved trail. This treatment was designed to test the effectiveness of a direct management practice.

Control 2 (control for treatment 5). This control was the same as treatment 2. However, in this control, only visitors arriving at the summit by bus were selected for observation. This control and its companion treatment 5 were administered only on days when cruise ship passengers were driven to the summit on charter busses.

Treatment 5 (personal message to tour bus passengers). This treatment was the same as control 2. However, concessioner tour bus drivers delivered a brief oral educational message and request to visitors to stay on the paved trail. This message was delivered verbally as passengers were en route to the summit. This treatment tested information delivered in person.

Each of the above controls and treatments was applied for up to three randomly selected days over a two-week period during the peak summer use season. On each of these days, trained research staff unobtrusively observed a systematic random sample of visitors (every nth visitor), recording whether visitors walked off the paved trail and noting related information. Field staff consisted of sixteen trained observers. On a given day, up to ten observers worked singly or in pairs to collect data on individual visitors throughout a full observation. Interobserver reliability was checked during training exercises on-site at the study outset, and exceptional situations were clarified daily at start and break times. Observers dressed and behaved in a manner generally consistent with park visitors to conceal their identity (Burrus-Bammel and Bammel 1984; Turner and LaPage 2001). Observations were conducted only during peak use hours and fair weather when use levels were sufficient to ensure that observers would not be obvious. Visitors were followed at a discrete distance of approximately 50 feet. Sample sizes for treatments and controls ranged from 137 to 210, and totaled 1,135. Observers recorded relevant behavioral information, including time spent reading information signs, occurrence of walking off-trail, apparent reasons for walking off-trail, surfaces visitors walked on when off-trail, and whether or not visitors crossed trailside coping stones or the symbolic rope fencing that marked the margin of the trail in some sections when and where applicable. In addition, observers conducted rapid spot counts of other visitors visible and off-trail nearby (within 50 meters). A short list of common "apparent reasons for walking off-trail" was supplied to observers based on pre-test observations, with additional space to record other reasons as observers saw fit. General demographic data of visitors also were recorded as observed, including gender, apparent age, and apparent group type. Observations continued for the length of the subject's visit to the summit as long as the subject remained on the paved trail. If the subject walked off the paved trail, observation continued for a maximum of one minute or until the visitor's feet were no longer visible (at which point the observers could no longer see the surfaces on which visitors were walking).

A survey of representative samples of visitors was administered in conjunction with the observational study. The survey was administered on the same days that control 1 and associated treatments 1 through 4 were applied. (Control 2 and treatment 5, applied to tour bus passengers, could not be included in the survey component of the study because the short period of time spent on the summit by these visitors did not allow them to participate.) Visitors who were finishing their walk in the area of the paved sum-

TABLE 21.2   Type of problem behavior associated with walking off-trail.

	Control 1	Treatment 1	Treatment 2	Treatment 3	Treatment 4
I needed to walk off the paved summit loop trail (e.g., I had to get around other visitors)	23.3	23.3	30.4	23.5	20.7
I didn't know that walking off the paved summit loop trail might damage soils and vegetation	42.9	33.3	18.8	22.2	32.1
I didn't know that I was supposed to stay on the paved summit loop trail	70.7	43.6	19.1	31.6	55.2
I didn't mean to walk off the paved summit loop trail (i. e., I walked off the paved summit loop trail accidentally)	10.2	25.6	22.2	27.8	11.1
I feel visitors should be allowed to walk off the summit loop trail	66.7	54.1	35.6	27.8	55.6

Note: Data are percentage of respondents who agreed with each statement.

mit loop trail were selected randomly (every nth visitor) and asked to complete a self-administered questionnaire. It should be noted that visitors who participated in the survey were not necessarily the same visitors who were observed in the observational component of the study. The response rate to the survey was 71.7 percent. Sample sizes for the control and treatments 1 to 4 ranged from 100 to 161, for a total of 596 completed questionnaires. The questionnaire addressed several issues, including (1) whether visitors reported walking off the paved trail, (2) why they did or didn't walk off-trail, (3) whether or not they noticed (a) the study treatments (i.e., the management practices that were applied) and (b) the environmental impacts caused by visitors walking off-trail, (4) how the management practices included in the treatments affected their decision to walk off-trail or not, and (5) the degree to which they supported or opposed a range of management practices designed to keep visitors on the paved trail. Questions addressing why visitors did or didn't walk off-trail were guided by the conceptual frameworks outlined earlier. Statements were developed representing the five basic types of problem behaviors (illegal, unavoidable, careless, unskilled, uninformed) and respondents who reported walking off-trail were asked to indicate which of these statements applied to them (see table 21.2). Similarly, statements representing a range of moral devel-

TABLE 21.3   Reasons for not walking off-trail.

Statement	Percentage who replied "applies to me"
I was afraid I'd be reprimanded or fined	14.8
I was afraid that other members of my group would think poorly of me	11.4
I was afraid that other visitors in general would think poorly of me	20.1
It is not fair for me to walk off the paved summit loop trail when many other visitors don't	49.1
I feel better about myself by not walking off the paved summit loop trail	76.8

opment were presented and respondents who reported that they had not walked off-trail were asked to indicate which of these statements applied to them (see table 21.3).

STUDY FINDINGS: VISITOR OBSERVATION

Effectiveness of Treatments

The percentage of visitors walking off trail for all treatments and controls is shown in table 21.4. A substantial majority of visitors (73.7 percent) walked off-trail under control 1 (control for treatments 1 through 4) conditions. Treatment 2 (educational signage II) reduced walking off-trail to 63.0 percent of visitors, but this reduction from the control was not statistically significant. Treatment 1 (educational signage I) reduced walking off-trail to 59.1 percent of visitors, and this reduction from control 1 was statistically significant. The more aggressive treatment 3 (educational signage III) reduced walking off-trail to 24.3 percent of visitors, and this reduction from the control was also statistically significant. Treatment 4 (site management) reduced walking off-trail to 1.2 percent of visitors within the fenced portion of the trail, and to 24.2 percent of visitors beyond the fencing, and both of these reductions from control 1 were highly statistically significant.

Control 2 (control for treatment 5) found that 36.9 percent of bus passengers walked off-trail, and this reduction from control 1 was statistically significant, underscoring the importance of properly controlling for different types of users (i.e., tour bus passengers versus other visitors). (As noted earlier and in table 21.1, control 2 included the educational signage of treatment 1.) This effect may be due in part to the tightly controlled schedule of tour bus operations that allow passengers only a short time at the summit. Treatment 5 (personal message to tour bus passengers) resulted in 40.7 per-

TABLE 21.4 Percentage of visitors walking off-trail by controls and treatments.

Control treatments	Percentage	Self-reports
Control 1 (control for treatments 1–4)	73.7	67.7
Treatment 1 (educational signage I)	59.1[a]	39.4
Treatment 2 (educational signage II)	63.0	36.9
Treatment 3 (educational signage III)	24.3[b]	17.2
Treatment 4 (fencing)	1.2	25.2
	(within and beyond fence: 24.2[c])	
Control 2 (control for treatment 5)	36.9	
Treatment 5 (personal message to tour bus passengers)	40.7[d]	

[a]significantly different than control 1 at χ^2 (1, $N = 328$) $= 7.7, p < 0.001$.
[b]significantly different than control 1 at χ^2 (1, $N = 362$) $= 7.724, p = 0.005$.
[c]significantly different than control 1 at χ^2 (1, $N = 317$) $= 77.490, p < 0.001$.
[d]significantly different than control 1 at χ^2 (1, $N = 301$) $= 35.631, p < 0.001$.

cent of tour bus passengers walking off-trail, and did not differ to a statistically significant degree from control 2.

Attention to Signage

One reason for the limited effectiveness of the text-based educational management practices (treatments 1 through 3) may be due to the lack of attention to signs by most visitors. In no treatment did mean time spent reading signs exceed eight seconds. For the first sign encountered, a majority of visitors either ignored or only glanced at the sign regardless of the treatment. The second sign encountered contained less information (it did not include the site map or the educational message, but only asked visitors to remain on the trail or rock surfaces). This distinction may be why visitors spent even less time reading this sign (only about a third of the time spent on the first sign). The lack of attention to signs may be at least partly a function of crowding at the summit. When some visitors stopped to read the signs, they inadvertently may have blocked the view of other visitors. Visitors obstructing the signs obviously would reduce the potential effectiveness of this management practice.

Off-Trail Behavior

Why did visitors walk off-trail, and what did they do off-trail? Research staff recorded notes on their observations about these issues (using a short list of potential reasons as described earlier), although these questions cannot be answered fully by observation alone. (These issues are addressed more fully in findings from the visitor survey component of the study, described below.) The vast majority of visitors who walked off-trail (78.6 percent) simply seemed to be "exploring" the area. The next most common reason (13.0 percent) was to take photographs. Photographers seemed to be searching for a better vantage point and trying to take pictures that did not include large numbers of other visitors.

Once visitors walked off the trail, the vast majority (72.5 percent) did not evidence any visible effort to avoid stepping on vegetation or bare soil (i.e., by remaining on rock surfaces). The treatment in place had no statistically significant effect on this behavior.

Predictors of Walking Off-Trail

Several characteristics of respondents and other variables were tested to see if they were associated with walking off-trail (i.e., could these variables be used to help predict what type of visitors are most likely to walk off-trail?). Demographic and socioeconomic characteristics of respondents, including age and gender, generally were not associated strongly with walking off-trail or other off-trail behavior for any of the controls or treatments. However, group type was highly significant as a predictor of visitors going off-trail: family and friendship groups were significantly more likely to walk off-trail than couples were. The other variable that was associated strongly with walking off-trail was the presence of other visitors off-trail. Cross-tabulation showed that up to twenty other visitors were observed to be off-trail in nearby areas in over 80 percent of cases when subject visitors walked off-trail.

STUDY FINDINGS: VISITOR SURVEY

Walking Off-trail

Visitors were asked to report whether they had walked off the paved trail. Data for the applicable control and treatments are shown in table 21.4 (along with comparable findings from the observational component of the study as discussed above). During control 1, about two-thirds of respondents (67.7 percent) reported walking off-trail compared to 73.7 percent who were observed to walk off-trail. These proportions were significantly different. It should be remembered, as noted above, that even though the observational and survey components of the study were conducted simultaneously, survey participants were not necessarily—and most probably were not—visitors who actually were observed. To the extent that visitors observed and surveyed were representative of all visitors (both samples were randomly selected), survey respondents underestimated the extent to which they walked off-trail for the control and four of the five treatments. There is little reason to think that the observational data are not the most accurate measure of walking off-trail. Respondents may have underreported walking off-trail for several reasons. First, there may be some degree of "social desirability bias," so that respondents may have been hesitant to report that they engaged in a behavior that is officially discouraged (Godbey 1984). Second, there may have been some confusion about what constitutes "walking off-trail." The questionnaire was quite specific about defining this behavior, but many visitor-created trails diverge from the paved trail, and it is possible that some respondents considered at least some of these trails as part of the officially designated and maintained summit loop trail. Finally, some respondents may have had difficulty recalling the specific nature of their activities, including exactly where they walked over the duration of their visit to the mountain summit.

Why Visitors Walked Off-trail

As noted above, many visitors reported walking off-trail. These respondents were asked two follow-up questions to explore why they walked off-trail. The first question addressed the purpose of walking off-trail, much like research staff tried to note in the observational component of this study. Respondents were asked to indicate which of seven purposes of walking off-trail applied to them, and respondents were allowed to indicate as many of these purposes as applied. Large percentages of respondents reported the relatively generic purposes "to get a better view" (62.3 percent) and "to explore" (43.2 percent). Seeking out a better point to take a picture also was reported by a relatively large percentage of respondents (61.8 percent). These findings are generally in keeping with data derived from the observational component of the study. A total of 18 percent of respondents reported that they walked off-trail "to move past others on the trail" and "to get away from crowds on the trail." This raises potential connections between the ecological and social dimensions of carrying capacity and recreation management more broadly; crowding/congestion along the trail can lead to some visitors walking off the trail, and this leads to increasing environmental impacts. Relatively few respondents walked off-trail to participate in other recreation activities, including picnicking (7 percent) and picking blueberries (5 percent).

The second question was based on the conceptual framework of "types" of recreation management problems as described earlier. Respondents were asked to report whether each of five basic reasons for walking off-trail applied to them. Results are suggestive of the extent to which information/education programs (and perhaps indirect management practices in general) might be effective in addressing the issue of walking off-trail (table 21.2). Relatively large percentages of respondents (from 27.8 percent to 66.7 percent, depending on the control/treatment in place) reported that they walked off-trail because they felt visitors should be allowed to do so. This response generally corresponds to the "illegal" type of recreation management problem (especially when considered in the context of the treatments that admonished visitors to stay on the paved trail). Strikingly, 55.6 percent of respondents reported this reason for walking off-trail even for the treatment of fencing. The literature suggests that information or education may not be very effective in keeping these visitors on the paved trail (Roggenbuck 1992). All of the treatments in the survey component of the study asked visitors to stay on the paved trail (or on rock surfaces, in the case of treatment 1) and explained the reasons for this desired behavior. Yet, many visitors walked off-trail, apparently because they disagreed with the information or education that was presented or thought that the problem of impacts to soil and vegetation was not important enough to warrant restrictions on freedom of movement by visitors.

Substantial but smaller percentages of respondents (from 20.7 to 30.4 percent, depending on the control/treatment in place) reported that they walked off-trail because they "needed to" (e.g., they had to pass other visitors who were blocking the trail). This generally corresponds to the "unavoidable" type of problem described earlier. Information and education may not be very effective in keeping these visitors on the paved trail.

Substantial percentages of respondents also reported that they walked off-trail for all of the other three reasons included in table 21.2—because respondents were "careless," "unskilled," or "uninformed." As described earlier, the literature suggests that these reasons for problem behaviors may be more amenable to management through information and education programs. The findings reported in table 21.2 are mixed with regard to this hypothesis. Relatively large percentages of respondents fell into the uninformed (18.8 to 42.9 percent) and unskilled (19.1 to 55.2 percent) categories even though they were subject to one of the educational signage treatments. On the other hand, the percentage of respondents in these categories was consistently lower than the percentages in control 1 (in which no information/education on walking off-trail was provided).

Why Visitors Didn't Walk Off-trail

A substantial percentage of visitors (ranging from 32.8 percent for the control to 82.8 percent for treatment 3) reported that they did not walk off-trail. Why not? Insights into this question were derived from the survey question based on the conceptual framework of moral development described earlier. Respondents were asked to indicate why they did not walk off-trail by indicating which of five reasons (corresponding to five stages of moral development) applied to them. Findings are presented in table 21.3. The first statement illustrates the concept of "preconventional morality" and is highly oriented to fear of punishment and/or minimizing pain/maximizing pleasure. The second two statements illustrate the concept of "conventional morality" and are oriented to what others think. The last two statements illustrate the concept of "postconventional morality" and are inwardly oriented toward issues of justice, fairness, and self-respect. It is clear from the findings that the majority of respondents who did not walk off-trail were influenced in their decisionmaking by matters of postconventional morality. Fear of punishment and concern with what others (inside or outside the respondent's social group) think influenced only a small minority of this subset of respondents. This suggests that information and education messages about walking off-trail on the summit of Cadillac Mountain probably should emphasize how walking off-trail affects this area's vegetation and soil, why it is important to protect this area, and why it is everyone's "duty" to help ensure this. At least, this is the case for respondents who did not walk off-trail. Recall that many visitors *did* walk off-trail, even when efforts were made to inform them of the impacts of such behavior. It appears that the population of visitors to the summit of Cadillac Mountain is diverse in their levels of moral development, and that a program of management directed at keeping visitors on the paved trail probably will have to address multiple levels of moral development to reach this broad audience.

Visitor Awareness

Respondents were asked several questions regarding their awareness of the management practices that were in effect when they visited the summit and the degree to which they noticed the environmental impacts of walking off-trail. Respondents were asked if they had noticed trailhead and trailside signage and, if so, to describe briefly the major messages presented by the signs. The vast majority of respondents for all of the treatments reported seeing the trailhead signs. Only about half of respondents reported seeing trailside signs, except for treatment 3 that used prompter signs at visitor-created trails, for which 87.4 percent of visitors reported seeing trailside signs. However, most respondents could not accurately recall important and relevant themes of the content of the messages provided. Less than 30 percent of respondents for all treatments recalled that signage described the fragile character of the summit environment, the need to protect this environment, and management guidelines for visitors to remain on the paved trail (or rock surfaces).

Respondents also were asked if they noticed any damage to soils and/or vegetation on the summit and, if so, how severe they would rate this damage. In the control, only 20.4 percent of respondents reported that they noticed any damage and most (81.4 percent) of the minority who did rated this damage as "minor." However, even under the treatments (where signage informed visitors of the environmental damage of walking off-trail and the resulting ecological impacts occurring on Cadillac Mountain), substantially less than half of respondents reported that they noticed any damage, and most of those who did rated this damage as "minor." The treatment in place had a strong effect on the reported degree of perceived damage. Specifically, as treatments became more aggressive and direct, visitors tended to rate the damage as more severe.

Support for Management Actions

A final battery of questions asked respondents to report whether they would find a range of management practices acceptable for preventing damage to soils and vegetation on the summit of Cadillac Mountain (table 21.5). These management practices were designed to present a full spectrum of approaches that ranged from indirect to direct, and this is the general order of these management practices as shown in table 21.5 and in the questionnaire. For all respondents (regardless of whether they experienced control or treat-

TABLE 21.5 Acceptability of management practices.

Management practice	Percentage of respondents who support management practice
Install educational signs about the damage that can be caused by walking on soils and vegetation	96.5
Install signs asking visitors to stay on the paved summit loop trail or bare rock surface	94.2
Require visitors not to cross fenced boundaries	94.1
Install signs asking visitors to stay on the paved summit trail loop	91.2
Require visitors to stay on the paved summit loop trail or bare rock surfaces	88.7
Pave the summit loop trail	87.6
Prohibit picking blueberries (to discourage visitors from walking off the paved summit loop trail)	85.9
Require visitors to stay on the paved summit loop trail	80.4
Prohibit picnicking (to discourage visitors from walking off the paved summit loop trail)	74.3
Station rangers on the summit to keep visitors on the paved summit loop trail	73.6
Fine visitors for walking off the paved summit loop trail	37.6
Allow walking on the summit only in ranger-led groups	26.1
Require visitors to travel to the summit in busses on which visitors would be told the importance of staying on the paved summit loop trail	23.9
Limit the number of visitors to the summit	21.5
Prohibit all visitors from walking anywhere on the summit (but allow visitors to drive to the summit)	8.2
Completely prohibit all visitor access to the summit	5.5

ment conditions), indirect management practices received the highest acceptability ratings and direct management practices received the lowest acceptability ratings. For example, informational/educational signage was judged as acceptable by over 90 percent of respondents, whereas more restrictive management approaches (e.g., fining visitors for walking off-trail, limiting visitor use) were not acceptable to the majority of respondents. It is interesting to note that the percentage of respondents that found nearly all of these management practices acceptable tended to increase as they experienced some of these management practices in the study treatments.

DISCUSSION

Most of the management practices (in the form of experimental "treatments") applied in this study were effective in reducing the percentage of visitors who walk off-trail on the summit of Cadillac Mountain (as measured by direct observation and visitor self-reports). Without any of these management practices in place, nearly three-quarters (73.7 percent) of visitors were observed to walk off the paved trail. It is important to emphasize that even the "controls" included several management "treatments" designed to encourage visitors to limit the areal extent of their walking and associated impacts. A paved trail was provided, coping stones had been placed along the margin of the trail in strategic places, and fenced exclosures were placed around several large patches of remaining vegetation. Most of the indirect and direct management practices applied in this study reduced the percentage of visitors who walked off-trail to a statistically significant degree.

The direct management practice of fencing the trail was substantially more effective than the indirect management practices. This finding tends to be corroborated generally in the literature (Hammitt and Cole 1998; Cole et al. 1987; McAvoy and Dustin 1983). Moreover, the most aggressive application of indirect management practices (treatment 3) was found to be more effective than less aggressive applications (treatments 1 and 2).

Based on study findings, it is unlikely that indirect management practices will substantially reduce the environmental impacts of visitor use on the summit of Cadillac Mountain. The most effective indirect management practice applied in this study (treatment 3—a relatively aggressive information/education signage program) reduced the observed percentage of visitors walking off-trail to 24.3. However, given the visitor use levels on the summit of Cadillac Mountain (as many as 5,500 visitors per day), reducing the percentage of visitors who walk off-trail to 24.3 still would result in well over a thousand visitors walking off-trail per day. Given the fragile environment of this area, and the findings from the recreation ecology literature that many ecological impacts caused by visitor use tend to occur quickly even under relatively light levels of use, damage to soils and vegetation at the study area likely will continue to grow in extent and severity under a management regime based on indirect practices.

These findings are important because the information/education treatments applied in the study were designed in concert with several principles for their application that have emerged from the professional literature (Manning 2003a). For example, the reasons why visitors should not walk off-trail in this area were included in the messages delivered to visitors, the messages were delivered multiple times, the messages were delivered in both writing (on signs) and in person (by tour bus drivers), and the messages were delivered before visitors arrived on site (on tour busses).

With regard to personal delivery of messages by tour bus drivers, it's possible that this source of information was not considered sufficiently "authoritative" by visitors. Communication theory suggests that nonsubstantive elements of information and education messages, such as message source and medium, can be important in determining effectiveness (Roggenbuck 1992). These types of considerations are sometimes referred to as "the peripheral route to persuasion." If the message about walking off-trail had been delivered by a more authoritative source, such as a uniformed park ranger, it might have been more effective.

Study findings may be suggestive of other issues that might lead to more effective management practices. For example, visitors spent little time reading signs. As noted earlier, this might be exacerbated by visitor crowding around signs. This issue might be factored in as part of the process of considering appropriate use levels (i.e., carrying capacities) of parks and recreation areas. Evidence from both the observational and survey components of the study also suggested that some visitors walked off-trail to pass large numbers of other visitors who had stopped on the trail or were moving very slowly. That is, trail width becomes important relative to allowed use levels. This might be another reason to link the conventional social and ecological dimensions of carrying capacity and park management more broadly (Manning 1999).

Limited attention of visitors to signs also might be related to the fact that most visitors allocate only a short time to spend at sites like the summit of Cadillac Mountain, and they prefer to spend this time seeing the area rather than reading signs. This suggests that information/education might be delivered with more effect before visitors arrive on-site. The park's visitor center, interpretive programs, brochures delivered at the park entrance gate, and announcements on the park's shuttle bus system offer some possible alternatives.

Compared to the observational data, visitors tended to under-report instances of walking off-trail, especially during the study treatments. Several reasons may explain this under-reporting, including social desirability bias and honest confusion over what constitutes "walking off-trail." However, these results suggest that it may be wise to at least spot-check self-reports of visitor behavior through observation.

Both observational and survey data suggest that many visitors who walk off-trail are not highly directed in this activity and are simply "exploring" and "searching for better views." This suggests that walking off-trail might be addressed by providing more maintained trails in the summit area to help satisfy the urge of many visitors to "roam." These additional trails would impact existing soil and vegetation, of course, but ultimately might result in less impact than the current situation. Visitors also might be told more explicitly that other areas in the park are more appropriate (i.e., more ecologically resistant and resilient, less heavily used) for informal exploration.

Some visitors walked off-trail to find a preferred site to take a picture. This suggests that it may be useful to incorporate short spurs along the paved summit loop trail that are posted as "photo points." This would offer visitors opportunities to take good pictures (and pictures without other visitors in the field of view if these photo points are well located and designed) while lessening their need to walk off the paved trail.

Messages concerning appropriate visitor behavior might be targeted more directly at individuals and groups that are more likely to be problematic. In this study, it was found that family and friendship groups (as opposed to couples) were more likely to walk off-trail. Previous research at this site found that children, while making up only 14 percent of all visitors, are responsible for "a higher relative level of off-trail behaviors" (Baldwin and LaPage 2003). Park staff stationed at the summit could focus their personal contacts on these groups.

Study findings suggest that there can be a "synergy" of management practices. For example, adding "prompter" signs at key locations along the trail (treatment 3) to signs at the trailhead (treatment 2) reduced walking off-trail significantly. Moreover, fencing at the beginning of the trail (treatment 4) dramatically reduced the percentage of visitors who stepped over the coping stones that defined the margin of the trail. When the fencing treatment was applied (treatment 4), only 4.8 percent of visitors were observed stepping over coping stones beyond the fencing to leave the trail. However, when treatments 1 and 2 were applied, over 20 percent of visitors stepped over the coping stones. Furthermore, the management practices applied in this study (and management practices more broadly considered) can (and probably should) be used in a complementary manner. For example, fencing was found to be highly effective in reducing walking off-trail, but the educational signage employed in other treatments explains to visitors why it is important to remain on the trail. These two management approaches can be seen to work in a complementary manner, leading to a greater level of effectiveness than either practice could attain independently. More generally, these findings suggest that a "unity" of management messages—a variety of management practices that offer a consistent message—may maximize effectiveness.

A potentially important finding from the observational component of the study concerns the positive relationship between walking off-trail and the number of visitors off-trail. Seeing visitors off-trail may offer "license" to other visitors to walk off-trail. To the extent this is true, it suggests the possibility of a downward spiral in visitor behavior and associated impacts. It also reinforces the importance of keeping visitors on the trail.

As described earlier in this chapter, it has been suggested in the literature that the "type" of recreation management problem can influence the potential effectiveness of information and education as a management practice. Very high percentages of survey respondents reported that the reasons they walked off-trail generally corresponded to "illegal" and "unavoidable" types of problem behaviors as described in the literature. This suggests that information/education (and perhaps other types of indirect management practices) are unlikely to fully address these problems. Moreover, even a majority of respondents reported "illegal" types of problem behaviors under the management practice of fencing (treatment 4)—a very direct management practice. This suggests that more aggressive management practices, perhaps in the form of enforcement, ultimately may be required. Many respondents also reported that their reasons for walking off-trail fell into the "careless," "unskilled," or "uninformed" categories of problem behaviors, and these may be more amenable to information/education (and other indirect approaches). However, all of these respondents who were surveyed during all of the management treatments had been exposed to information/education practices of varying intensity. Yet many of them walked off-trail.

It has been suggested in the literature that visitors may operate at a variety of stages of "moral development," and that this might help guide the application of information/education programs and other management practices. Visitors who did not walk off-trail (as defined by their self-reports) reported that their behavior in this regard was guided most strongly by reasons of "postconventional" morality (i.e., issues of altruism, fairness, and justice). This suggests that information and education programs should be designed to emphasize this type of rationale. However, it is also important to note that many visitors walked off-trail despite the information and education program that was applied. This may suggest that many visitors do not necessarily operate (at least in this context) at such high levels of moral development, and that, therefore, informational/educational messages should be designed and delivered on a variety of moral planes.

Most visitors who were exposed to the management treatments reported remembering trailhead signs (but not trailside signs). However, most could not recall the relevant content of these signs. These findings suggest potentially important limitations to the effectiveness of information/education-based management practices. Moreover, most respondents generally were unaware of the environmental impacts that have occurred on the summit of Cadillac Mountain, and, if they are aware, judge these impacts as "minor." Exposure to management treatments increased the percentage of respondents who noticed visitor-caused damage to soil and vegetation. However, only a minority of respondents perceived these impacts even under treatment conditions. This lack of visitor awareness of impacts is in stark contrast to more objective, informed descriptions of the environmental conditions on the summit of Cadillac Mountain in which such impacts are considered serious (Turner and LaPage 2001). Moreover, it suggests that managers have a great deal of work to do to educate visitors about this issue, and/or that managers will have to take more direct management actions to address this problem even though visitors generally are unaware of this problem and therefore may not support such actions. Both of these tasks are likely to be challenging.

As might have been expected, respondents to the survey tended to support management actions to address walking off-trail that were indirect in nature, and tended to oppose actions that were more direct. However, respondents who had been exposed to the range of indirect and direct management practices included in the experimental treatments tended to be more supportive of the full range of management actions. This suggests that visitors initially might be reluctant to support management practices they have not experienced, but that these management actions are less objectionable when they are applied and actually experienced.

CONCLUSIONS

Findings from the observational and survey components of this study support several conclusions. It is unlikely that indirect management practices such as information and education will satisfactorily solve the problem of visitors walking off-trail at the summit of Cadillac Mountain (and similar sites with relatively fragile natural environments and relatively high visitor use). Information/education-based management practices of increasing intensity, designed on the basis of principles derived from communication theory and the related professional literature, did not reduce the percentage of visitors walking off-trail to a sufficient degree that they are likely to reverse the trend of increasing resource degradation. This is because visitor use levels are so high at this site, soil and vegetation are so fragile, and the types of resource impacts experienced tend to occur relatively quickly even under light levels of use. This problem is exacerbated by the fact that the reasons many visitors walk off-trail can be classified as "illegal" or "unavoidable" and information/education programs (or other indirect management practices) may not be well suited to addressing these behaviors. Even the direct management practice of fencing the paved trail had limited effectiveness beyond its immediate extent (the first 150 feet of trail). Moreover, even though all of the treatments involved information or education about the impacts that are occurring on Cadillac Mountain, the fragile character of the environment, the need to protect this environment, and the impacts of visitors walking off-trail, most visitors could not remember these messages and noticed little or no visitor-caused impacts. And, of course, many visitors continued to walk off-trail.

Based on these and related study findings, we recommend that an integrated suite of direct and indirect management practices be implemented on the summit of Cadillac Mountain. The NPS should require that visitors remain on the paved summit loop trail. Moreover, the summit loop trail could be fenced, though this fencing might be of the "symbolic" type (i.e., low-lying, as unobtrusive as possible). Further, uniformed rangers should be used to enforce (as needed) the regulation to stay on the paved trail. Consideration also should be given to redesigning the paved summit loop trail to extend it, to widen it in key places (e.g., where information/education signs are posted, where visitors tend to congregate), and to include a system of short spur trails to key "photo points." This program of direct management practices should be complemented with a program of aggressive indirect management practices designed to inform visitors of the regulation to stay on the paved trail and the reasons for this regulation. Included in these messages should be identification of opportunities in the park where more informal exploration is allowed or even encouraged. This suite of management practices draws from the broad spectrum of management strategies and tactics outlined earlier in this chapter, and is supported directly by the array of study findings.

Of course, such a program of management should be tested for its effectiveness with a program of research much like the study described in this chapter. Off-trail walking and its environmental impacts should be monitored and management adjusted and refined as resulting data indicate. Surveys to explore how visitors react to these management practices should be included in this program of research. This approach is in keeping with the emerging concept of adaptive management that is being applied increasingly in multiple applications of contemporary environmental management (Lee, 1993; Stankey, Clark, and Bormann 2005).

We also recommend that the management approaches described above be implemented as part of a larger analysis of the carrying capacity of Cadillac Mountain. Moreover, this analysis should include both resource and social components, and the potential interrelationships between these components. In particular, some indications suggest that visitor use levels may be contributing to the problem of visitors walking off-trail. Specific examples include large number of visitors blocking park signage (designed to help address the issue of visitors walking off-trail) and some visitors having to walk off-trail because of congestion along the paved trail. The latter issue is especially important as study findings suggest that seeing visitors off-trail may "give license" to other visitors to do the same. These types of issues should be considered when analyzing the maximum acceptable level of visitor use on the summit of the mountain.

The NPS, like most park and outdoor recreation management agencies, is charged with (1) protecting significant environmental resources, and (2) providing opportunities for public enjoyment and appreciation. Where public demand for parks is high, there can be tension between these two objectives. The summit of Cadillac Mountain is a quintessential manifestation of this tension. Under ideal conditions, visitor-caused impacts to park resources could be addressed satisfactorily through indirect management practices that maintain high levels of visitor freedom. However, research in general, and this study in particular, suggests that this may not be possible. In such cases—and we believe the summit of Cadillac Mountain is one of these cases—some degree of visitor freedom will have to be sacrificed to ensure protection of important park resources. Without a strong program of management that includes forceful, direct practices in combination with complementary indirect practices, large numbers of visitors will continue to walk off-trail on the summit of Cadillac Mountain and associated environmental impacts will continue to expand in extent and severity. As suggested in this study, visitors who walk off-trail will give license to other visitors to walk off-trail, and this will lead to a downward spiral in which park resources will continue to be degraded. Ultimately, the quality of the visitor experience also may be compromised as a function of the aesthetic implications of these resource impacts. We are persuaded that an emerging principle of park and outdoor recreation management—intensive use of parks and outdoor recreation areas requires intensive management—will need wider application as visitor use levels and associated impacts continue to increase in national parks and related outdoor recreation areas.

We believe that the combination of research approaches used in this study—a series of experiments with complementary controls, direct observation of visitor behavior, and follow-up surveys of visitors—was effective in exploring multiple dimensions of the issue of visitors walking off-trail and resulting environmental degradation. The observational component of the study made direct measurements of visitor behavior under control conditions and as visitors reacted to experimental management treatments. The survey component of the study explored how and why management treatments affected visitor decisionmaking and associated behavior, including the acceptability of a range of management practices to visitors. In these ways, the research methods used in the study were complementary by drawing on their respective strengths.

Findings from the multiple methods were also reinforcing, and in this way they offer a check on the validity of study findings. For example, both observation and visitor surveys illustrate the magnitude of the problem of visitors walking off-trail, though visitors tended to under-report this activity. Visitors tended to spend little time reading information/education signage, and this was reflected in their general lack of knowledge of the issue of walking off-trail and the resource-related problems it causes. Both observation and the visitor surveys suggest that many visitors walk off the trail to "explore," to find better photo points, and to avoid other groups, and these findings are suggestive of related management practices, including expanding the trail system, identifying other areas in the park that are more appropriate for "exploration," adding key photo points to the trail system, and widening the trail in strategic locations.

We also should note some potential limitations of the study and implications for future research. First, the professional literature in parks and outdoor recreation suggests that a range of management practices is available as defined by both strategies and tactics. However, this study employed only five management practices, four of which were oriented primarily toward information/education. More study clearly is warranted to test the effectiveness of a fuller range of management practices. Second, the two methodological components of the study (observation and the visitor surveys) did not necessarily (and probably in most cases did not) study the same visitors. Because the samples of visitors included in both components of the study were selected randomly (and were therefore representative of all visitors), we do not feel this affected study findings. However, surveying the visitors who were observed may have been a more powerful research design. Unfortunately, the logistics of doing this would have been considerably more time consuming and expensive. Finally, the observational component of the study required a relatively large staff and was time consuming (a staff member was needed to observe each visitor included in the study and the period of observation sometimes extended to a half hour or more). Moreover, using large numbers of observers presents potential problems of reliability that were not addressed fully in this study. Future research of this nature should explore the feasibility of using technology such as global positioning system (GPS) units to track and record visitor behavior.

22

Using Computer Simulation Modeling to Support Management of Social Carrying Capacity of Ocean Drive

Most visitors to the MDI portion of Acadia use the Park Loop Road to experience the park and access the area's major attractions. The Ocean Drive section of the Park Loop Road starts immediately after the park entrance station and closely follows the coastline for 1.5 miles. Ocean Drive is managed as a one-way road. The road has two lanes, and visitors are allowed to park in the right-hand lane. Several parking lots also are located along Ocean Drive. These parking lots and much of the right-hand lane become filled with vehicles during the peak summer use season. Parking lots and road areas around Sand Beach and Thunder Hole are typically the first to reach their physical capacity.

How many cars ultimately can be accommodated on Ocean Drive before this road becomes too congested? Moreover, how can this road be managed to maximize its capacity? This study used computer simulation modeling to help answer these and related questions.

STUDY METHODS

Simulation Modeling

A simulation model of Ocean Drive was built using Extend, a commercially available, general-purpose simulation software package (Extend 1996). Extend provides users with a library of standard components ("blocks") that may be linked and modified to fit most simulation needs. Extend has been used to simulate recreation use in several national parks and on

---

This chapter is an edited version of the following paper: Jeffrey Hallo and Robert Manning, "Analysis of the Social Carrying Capacity of a National Park Scenic Road," *International Journal of Sustainable Transportation* (forthcoming).

other public lands (Wang and Manning 1999; Manning et al. 2002; Lawson, Kiely, and Manning 2003; Hallo, Manning, and Valliere 2005; Lawson et al. 2006a).

The simulation model treats the road as five continuous zones (labeled A through E), each 0.31 miles in length. For example, Zone A begins immediately after the entrance station and goes for 0.31 miles, where Zone B starts. Each zone represents a length of road four times that shown in the photos in figure 22.1. (These photos were used in a survey of visitors on Ocean Drive to help measure crowding/congestion-related standards of quality; this survey is described later in this chapter.) This length was chosen because it produces zones that correspond well with the visitor attractions and related infrastructure on Ocean Drive, and provides an appropriate level of detail in the analysis of social carrying capacity. A physical capacity of 144 vehicles was set for each zone within the model. This was based on providing 5 meters of linear space per vehicle and a 2-meter buffer per vehicle (to permit practical movement). When this physical capacity is reached for a zone, simulated vehicles are held in a queue in the preceding zone. Larger vehicles (e.g., recreational vehicles or busses) were not included in the model since their numbers on Ocean Drive are low.

Simulated vehicles enter the Ocean Drive model at a frequency generated from a decaying exponential distribution varying around a mean value. Interarrival times (average time between vehicles arriving at the park entrance station) calculated from empirical headway counts (counts of vehicle usage) were used as the mean of this exponential distribution. This approach provides a degree of randomness to when vehicles enter the Ocean Drive model. An exponential distribution has been used to model random or highly variable interarrival times in other contexts (Banks and Carson 1984; Wang and Manning 1999).

As a simulated vehicle is released into the model, it is randomly assigned the attributes of a travel route taken by an actual Ocean Drive visitor. These travel routes were collected using Global Positioning System (GPS) units (described below). Route attributes consist of travel times (delays) for vehicles in each of the five road zones and the parking areas within them. The amount of time a simulated vehicle spends in each zone or parking area is determined by the attributes assigned to it.

In each road zone, a series of blocks test if the simulated use level violates a standard for crowding/congestion. Standards used in these blocks were

Photo 1

Photo 2

Photo 3

Photo 4

Photo 5

Photo 6

Figure 22.1 *Study photos evaluated by Ocean Drive visitors to measure standards of quality for crowding/congestion.*

collected from a visitor survey (described below). Every minute of simulated time, the number of vehicles within a zone is compared against the standard, and the amount of time that the standard is violated is recorded in the model. The model then reports to a spreadsheet the percentage of time that each zone violates the standard for each half-hour period between

9:00 a.m. and 4:00 p.m. Data to check the validity of the model are also measured in Zone D (where the photos in figure 22.1 were taken) by counting at one instant the number of simulated vehicles in that zone. These instantaneous counts were conducted in the model after every five minutes of simulated time.

A management alternative of disallowing parking in the right lane near Sand Beach was built into the simulation model. This was done by defining a minimum average travel speed of 6.3 mph (75 percent below the posted speed limit of 25 mph) that must be maintained by simulated vehicles. This rule for travel behavior was developed based on input from NPS staff at Acadia. The simulation model may be run either with or without this management alternative applied.

The model simulates vehicle use on Ocean Drive for a day (from 9:00 a.m. to 4:00 p.m.). The model is not "primed" with vehicles when it begins; instead, the model starts as if Ocean Drive opens when the simulation begins at 9:00 a.m. Likewise, the generation of vehicles ceases at 4:00 p.m., which is the latest time that data were collected.

The user interface of the simulation model shows a map of the park road and user input fields. These fields allow both the standards for each zone and the use level (as a multiplier of current use levels) to be adjusted by the model operator. The model was run for several potential congestion-related standards at the current Ocean Drive use level, and from 80 to 200 percent of the current use level. This procedure was repeated with the management alternative of "no parking in the right lane near Sand Beach" applied to simulated vehicles. The model was run for fifty simulated days for each standard and for each use level.

Data Collection

Three types of data inputs for the simulation model were collected during the peak summer use season: (1) headway counts, (2) travel routes, and (3) standards of quality. Headway counts were collected by stationing a person at the entrance to Ocean Drive, and having that person record the number of vehicles entering the road for each half-hour period between 9:00 a.m. and 4:00 p.m. Headway counts were collected on five randomly selected days.

Travel routes of vehicles on Ocean Drive were collected (on the same five days as the headway counts) by having a sample of park visitors carry a GPS unit in their vehicle. Vehicles entering Ocean Drive were selected at random (based on the first available vehicle), and the drivers were asked to participate in the study by carrying a GPS unit. Visitors who agreed to participate were given a GPS unit that was turned on but had the display screen covered. This was done to reduce tampering and to minimize the possibility that visitors receiving GPS units would alter their travel behavior because they were carrying the unit. GPS units were collected from study participants at the exit of Ocean Drive, returned to the entrance of Ocean Drive, and then passed out again to other visitors using the same selection protocol. The GPS units collected positional data showing where vehicles traveled. A time was recorded with each GPS datum. GPS was chosen over self-reported map diaries for collecting travel routes because it (1) provides a far more detailed and accurate record of where visitors have gone, (2) results in higher response rates, (3) reduces respondent burden, and (4) leads to less response bias (Hallo et al. 2005).

A separate sample of visitors was selected randomly at the exit of Ocean Drive and asked to participate in a survey. The survey was conducted over seven randomly selected days. The survey was designed to collect data on visitor-based standards of quality for vehicle crowding/congestion on the road. Survey respondents were shown a series of computer-generated photos depicting a range of vehicle use densities on Ocean Drive (figure 22.1). (The issue of visually based research is described more fully in chapter 12.) Six simulated photos showed 0, 4, 8, 12, 16, and 21 vehicles. All respondents were asked to rate each photo by indicating how acceptable it was based on the number of vehicles shown. Respondents rated photos on a scale of −4 ("Very Unacceptable") to +4 ("Very Acceptable"). Survey respondents also were asked to indicate the photo showing the level of use that they (1) would prefer to see, (2) felt that NPS should allow before restricting visitors from using the road, and (3) found so unacceptable that they would no longer use the road. (The issue of question wording and format is described more fully in chapter 13.)

Data used to validate model results were collected on six randomly selected days during the peak summer use season. These data consisted of both headway counts and instantaneous traffic counts. Headway counts were conducted at the same location and using the same techniques as described above for the model input data. Instantaneous counts were conducted by stationing a person at the same location where the study base photo was taken. Instantaneous counts of the number of vehicles on the road section shown in the base photo were taken at five-minute intervals.

DATA INPUTS TO THE SIMULATION MODEL

Headway Counts

Headway counts conducted for the simulation model showed an average of 1,440 vehicles per day ($s = 262.1$) enter Ocean Drive. Vehicle use was lowest from 9:00 to 9:30 a.m., when an average of 43.8 vehicles ($s = 20.3$) entered the road. This corresponds to an interarrival time of 0.68 minutes per vehicle. Peak vehicle use occurred from 11:00 to 11:30 p.m. During this period, an average of 135.0 vehicles ($s = 20.2$) entered Ocean Drive. The interarrival time for this period is 0.22 minutes per vehicle, which means that approximately 4 vehicles enter Ocean Drive per minute. Interarrival times calculated from these counts were used as the mean of an exponential distribution determining the frequency that simulated vehicles were generated in the simulation model.

GPS Routes

A total of 249 Ocean Drive visitors were asked to participate in the study by carrying a GPS unit. Of this number, 208 agreed, representing a response rate of 83.5 percent. When the travel routes were downloaded and reviewed for use in the simulation model, 201 were determined to be usable. These routes contained over 18,000 data points, each with positional coordinates and a time that the point was recorded. Space limitations preclude reporting the road zone and parking lot travel times derived from each GPS travel route. The information below summarizes these data; however, the travel times for each route were used in the simulation model.

The period of time vehicles took to travel through each of the five road zones varied considerably. This variability is likely due to the option that visitors have to park their vehicles on the road. The amount of time a vehicle is parked on the road was included in their travel time for a particular road zone, but any time spent in a parking lot was not. Road Zone B includes Sand Beach and the trailhead for the Beehive Trail. Both are attractions that visitors may spend quite a bit of time experiencing. Travel times for this road zone were the longest, averaging 11.1 minutes ($s = 23.6$). Zone E provides access to the Gorham Mountain trailhead and may provide parking on the road for some visitors to Thunder Hole. The mean travel time for Zone E is 5.2 minutes ($s = 21.8$). A substantial amount of time is required to hike the Gorham Mountain Trail, but only a few minutes are necessary for visitors to see Thunder Hole. Most visitors who park on the road to access Thunder Hole more likely would be in Zone D. The travel time for this zone averaged 4.8 minutes ($s = 7.1$). The mean travel times for Zones A ($\bar{x} = 0.8$ minutes, $s = 1.1$) and C ($\bar{x} = 1.9$ minutes, $s = 6.6$) were the shortest. These zones do not contain major attraction sites where visitors are likely to stop.

Travel times for the entire road also were collected from the GPS route data. The average time taken to travel Ocean Drive was 23.8 minutes ($s = 33.3$). The longest time that anyone in the sample took to travel the length of Ocean Drive was 280.9 minutes. The GPS route that this was associated with showed that the vehicle was stopped on the road near the Gorham Mountain Trail in Zone E for several hours. The shortest time that was taken to travel Ocean Drive was 3.0 minutes, meaning that the vehicle moved at an average speed of 31.5 miles per hour.

GPS data also indicated which parking lots were used along Ocean Drive and for what lengths of time. Five parking lots were used by vehicle drivers in the GPS sample. The Sand Beach parking lot (consisting of two parking loops) in Zone A was used by 64.4 percent of the vehicle drivers for an average of 51.8 minutes ($s = 71.7$). The Thunder Hole parking lot was used by 46.0 percent of vehicle drivers for average time of 24.3 minutes ($s = 24.6$). A parking lot located in Zone C was used by 6.9 percent of vehicles for an average of 12.7 minutes ($s = 15.3$), and a lot in Zone D was used by 2.0 percent of vehicles for an average of 31.4 minutes ($s = 45.2$). These latter two parking lots are relatively small and are not located near any major attraction sites. The Gorham Mountain Trailhead lot received use by 5.0 percent of vehicles for an average of 98.2 minutes ($s = 106.5$).

Crowding Standards

A total of 186 drivers were asked to complete a study questionnaire designed to measure normative standards for the level of vehicle use on Ocean Drive. Of this number, 142 (76.3 percent) agreed to participate. Respondents rated the acceptability of each of the six study photos; average acceptability ratings are plotted in figure 22.2. The point at which average ratings fall out of the acceptable range and into the unacceptable range (the neutral point

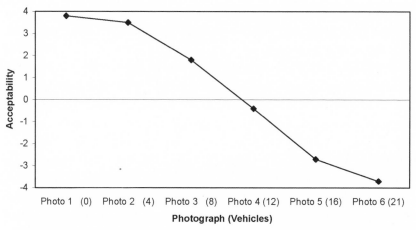

Figure 22.2 *Social norm curve for number of vehicles on Ocean Drive.*

of the acceptability scale) is 11.3 vehicles in the length of road represented in the study photographs. This is called the "acceptability"-based standard. Respondents also were asked to indicate the study photograph that represented the level of use they would prefer to see (called the "preference"-based standard), the photograph that represented the maximum level of use the NPS should allow (called the "management action"–based standard), and the photograph that represented the level of use that was so unacceptable that they would no longer use Ocean Drive (called the "displacement"-based standard). Resulting levels of use were 4.9, 12.5, and 16.0 vehicles, respectively. The four evaluative dimensions used in the study represent a range of potential crowding/congestion standards. (The issue of alternative evaluative standards is described more fully in chapter 13.)

STUDY FINDINGS

Use Levels

Runs of the simulation model at the existing average Ocean Drive use level (1,440 vehicles/day) show the percentage of time that each of the crowding/congestion-related standards was violated for each road zone and for the entire road (table 22.1). Current vehicle use levels violated the preference-based standard 0.6, 79.3, 0.0, 23.0, and 19.3 percent of the time between 9:00 a.m. and 4:00 p.m. for Zones A, B, C, D, and E, respectively. This standard was violated 24.4 percent of the time for the entire road. Current vehicle use levels violated the less-restrictive acceptability and management-action standards in Zone B 13.0 and 2.4 percent of the time. These standards were violated 2.6 and 0.5 percent of the time for the entire road. The least-restrictive displacement standard was not violated for any portion of time at current use levels.

Model runs at 80 to 200 percent of the current average use level produced similar trends in results (table 22.1). Zone B is the area of Ocean Drive where standards were violated most often. Standards based on all four evaluative dimensions were violated in Zone B at use levels from 120 to 200 percent of the current level. Conversely, Zones A and C were the areas where standards were violated the least. In these zones, only the preference standard was ever violated. This occurred in Zone A at a use level 80 percent of current use, and in Zone C it occurred when use is 180 percent of current use. Zones D and E violated the preference standard at all use levels tested. However, these zones did not violate the acceptability standard until use increases to 160 percent of current use. Likewise, the management-action standard was not violated for Zones D and E until use increases to 180 percent of current use. The displacement standard was not violated in Zones D and E at any of the use levels tested.

When the entire road is considered, both preference and acceptability standards were violated for some portion of time at all use levels tested. However, the management-action standard was not violated for the entire road if use drops to 80 percent of current use. The displacement standard was not exceeded for any portion of time until use levels increase to 120 percent of current use.

Applying a management alternative of no parking in the right lane near Sand Beach in the model resulted in a substantial decrease in the percent of time crowding standards were violated in Zone B (which includes Sand Beach) and for the entire road (table 22.2). The preference standard was not violated at the current use level. Both acceptability and management-action standards were not violated until use increases by 80 percent. The displacement standard was not violated at any use level tested.

Social Carrying Capacity

Alternative social carrying capacities were derived for Ocean Drive based on the four standards (preference, acceptability, management action, and

TABLE 22.1   Results from the simulation model showing the percentage of time that portions of Ocean Drive violate standards for crowding/congestion at varying use levels.

	Percentage of current use level	Percentage of time standard is violated					
		Zone A	Zone B	Zone C	Zone D	Zone E	Entire Road
Preference	80	0.5	74.4	0.0	6.6	6.1	17.5
	100	0.6	79.3	0.0	23.0	19.3	24.4
	120	3.1	82.0	0.0	45.2	41.1	34.3
	140	11.7	85.2	0.1	61.8	57.4	43.2
	160	21.7	87.2	0.3	71.9	65.4	49.3
	180	34.3	88.5	0.8	76.2	69.8	53.9
	200	42.2	90.2	2.7	79.5	72.4	57.4
Acceptability	80	0.0	0.4	0.0	0.0	0.0	0.1
	100	0.0	13.0	0.0	0.0	0.0	2.6
	120	0.0	38.6	0.0	0.0	0.0	7.7
	140	0.0	59.1	0.0	0.0	0.0	11.8
	160	0.0	70.0	0.0	0.2	0.1	14.1
	180	0.0	73.9	0.0	1.0	0.7	15.1
	200	0.0	75.9	0.0	4.2	3.6	16.7
Management action	80	0.0	0.1	0.0	0.0	0.0	0.0
	100	0.0	2.4	0.0	0.0	0.0	0.5
	120	0.0	20.3	0.0	0.0	0.0	4.1
	140	0.0	47.3	0.0	0.0	0.0	9.5
	160	0.0	64.0	0.0	0.0	0.0	12.8
	180	0.0	70.4	0.0	0.1	0.1	14.1
	200	0.0	74.2	0.0	0.6	0.4	15.0
Displacement	80	0.0	0.0	0.0	0.0	0.0	0.0
	100	0.0	0.0	0.0	0.0	0.0	0.0
	120	0.0	0.8	0.0	0.0	0.0	0.2
	140	0.0	7.3	0.0	0.0	0.0	1.5
	160	0.0	25.9	0.0	0.0	0.0	5.2
	180	0.0	45.8	0.0	0.0	0.0	9.2
	200	0.0	63.0	0.0	0.0	0.0	12.6

displacement) used in the simulation model. Social carrying capacity was defined in the analysis of simulation results in two ways: (1) the number of vehicles that could use Ocean Drive without violating any zone's crowding/congestion-related standard more than 10 percent of the time, and (2) the number of vehicles that could use the road without violating a crowding/congestion-related standard for the entire road more than 10 percent of the

TABLE 22.2 Results from the simulation model test of a management alternative of no parking in the right lane near Sand Beach.

	Percentage of current use level	Percentage of time standard is violated					
		Zone A	Zone B	Zone C	Zone D	Zone E	Entire Road
Preference	80	0.0	0.0	0.0	7.2	6.1	2.7
	100	1.6	0.1	0.0	25.2	22.9	10.0
	120	3.5	0.4	0.1	48.2	40.7	18.6
	140	12.1	1.7	0.1	64.4	59.2	27.5
	160	20.5	4.9	0.5	73.4	67.4	33.3
	180	37.4	11.1	1.6	77.6	71.9	39.9
	200	42.5	20.8	3.9	80.2	74.2	44.3
Acceptability	80	0.0	0.0	0.0	0.0	0.0	0.0
	100	0.0	0.0	0.0	0.0	0.0	0.0
	120	0.0	0.0	0.0	0.0	0.0	0.0
	140	0.0	0.0	0.0	0.0	0.0	0.0
	160	0.0	0.0	0.0	0.3	0.1	0.1
	180	0.0	0.0	0.0	1.2	1.0	0.4
Management action	200	0.0	0.0	0.0	4.8	3.0	1.6
	80	0.0	0.0	0.0	0.0	0.0	0.0
	100	0.0	0.0	0.0	0.0	0.0	0.0
	120	0.0	0.0	0.0	0.0	0.0	0.0
	140	0.0	0.0	0.0	0.0	0.0	0.0
	160	0.0	0.0	0.0	0.0	0.0	0.0
	180	0.0	0.0	0.0	0.2	0.1	0.1
	200	0.0	0.0	0.0	0.8	0.3	0.2
Displacement	80	0.0	0.0	0.0	0.0	0.0	0.0
	100	0.0	0.0	0.0	0.0	0.0	0.0
	120	0.0	0.0	0.0	0.0	0.0	0.0
	140	0.0	0.0	0.0	0.0	0.0	0.0
	160	0.0	0.0	0.0	0.0	0.0	0.0
	180	0.0	0.0	0.0	0.0	0.0	0.0
	200	0.0	0.0	0.0	0.0	0.0	0.0

time. These definitions allow for infrequent instances (10 percent of the time) when use levels are above average. Extreme peaking of use during holidays is a possible cause of such an instance.

Alternative social carrying capacities were calculated from model results based on the first definition stated above. Model results suggest that 194 vehicles could use Ocean Drive per day (between 9:00 a.m. and 4:00 p.m.)

TABLE 22.3 Social carrying capacity values for Ocean Drive based on four crowding-related standards. Values shown indicate use levels that would cause the most limiting road zone to be out of standard more than 10 percent of the time.

Evaluative dimension	With parking in right lane near Sand Beach		No parking in right lane near Sand Beach	
	Limiting zone	Number of vehicles	Limiting zone	Number of vehicles
Preference	B	194	D	1,197
Acceptability	B	1,371	D[a]	>2,880
Management action	B	1,562	D[a]	>2,880
Displacement	B	2,057	D[a]	>2,880

[a]Limiting zones are based on the zone with the greatest time violating standards at twice the current use level.

according to the preference standard (table 22.3). Ocean Drive has a daily social carrying capacity of 1,371 vehicles based on an acceptability standard, and a capacity of 1,562 vehicles based on a management-action standard. Lastly, 2,057 vehicles could use Ocean Drive per day according to the displacement standard. Zone B is the area of Ocean Drive where these standards are being violated more than 10 percent of the time at these capacities.

Alternative social carrying capacities were calculated based on the second definition stated above, that is, not violating the standard for the entire road more than 10 percent of the time (table 22.4). Model results suggest that 823 vehicles could use Ocean Drive per day according to the preference standard. Ocean Drive has a daily social carrying capacity of 1,889 vehicles based on an acceptability standard and a capacity of 2,060 vehicles based on a management-action standard. The displacement standard is violated 10 percent of the time for the entire road once use levels reach 2,660 vehicles per day.

Social carrying capacity values for Ocean Drive are increased substantially when the management alternative of no parking in the right lane is applied. Based on the preference standard, 1,197 vehicles per day could use the road without use levels in Zone D violating standards more than 10 percent of the time, and 1,440 vehicles could use the road without violating standards for the entire road more than 10 percent of the time. With the management alternative applied, more than twice the current use level could be accommodated on Ocean Drive before a social carrying capacity is reached based on acceptability, management-action, or displacement standards.

TABLE 22.4   Social carrying capacity values for Ocean Drive based on four crowding-related standards. Values shown indicate use levels when the entire road would be out of standard more than 10 percent of the time.

Evaluative dimension	With parking in right lane near Sand Beach	No parking in right lane near Sand Beach
Preference	823	1,440
Acceptability	1,889	>2,880
Management action	2,060	>2,880
Displacement	2,660	>2,880

Model Validation

Empirical and model-derived validation counts of vehicles at one time in the study photo area were plotted and inspected and were found to correspond to each other very well before 12:00 p.m. Less agreement was found among counts later in the sampling day. Substantially more variation occurred in the validation counts than in the model counts, particularly later in the day. Examination of forms use by field staff for the empirical counts showed some confusion about the counting procedures. It is uncertain what influence this had on the empirical validation counts.

The simulation model measured an average of 3.8 simulated vehicles at any one time ($s = 1.7$) in the area of the study photo. Validation counts found an average daily count of 6.0 ($s = 2.7$) vehicles at one time in the area of the study photo. Results of a t-test (for unequal variances) found no statistically significant difference between these mean daily counts.

DISCUSSION

Results from model runs suggest that the current level of vehicle use on Ocean Drive is often higher than visitors reported as being preferred, and occasionally is higher (in Zone B only) than visitors find acceptable or at a point when visitors feel management action should be taken to limit use. Use levels are not at a point that visitors would be displaced from any sections of the road due to crowding/congestion.

Simulation model results also provide estimates regarding the degree to which visitor-reported standards would be violated if the vehicle use level

on Ocean Drive were to increase. If the Ocean Drive use level were to increase by only 20 percent, the simulation model estimates that visitors to
Acadia would begin to be displaced from Zone B on Ocean Drive due to
crowding/congestion. Moreover, a 40 percent increase in the use level on
Ocean Drive would cause standards for preference, acceptability, and management action to be violated for nearly half of the day or more in Zone B.

The simulation model also estimated the number of vehicles that could
use Ocean Drive without violating crowding standards appreciably (more
than 10 percent of the time). However, several considerations need to be
addressed before applying one of these social carrying capacities. First,
should the objective of managing Ocean Drive be to maintain use levels
within standards for the entire road or for segments of the road? Model
runs testing the management alternative of no parking in the right-hand
lane showed that use patterns near Sand Beach and the current policy of
allowing parking in the right lane are the primary causes of standards being
violated. When parking is disallowed on the road and vehicles are kept moving near Sand Beach, preference-based standards are violated only marginally at the current use level. Also, with the management alternative applied,
the road could accommodate substantially increased use without violating
standards based on the other evaluative dimensions. This suggests that by
managing crowding/congestion near Sand Beach, a high-quality visitor experience is created for the entire road.

A second consideration is the choice of a standard based on the range of
evaluative dimensions measured in this study. Social carrying capacities resulting from the model provide a range of vehicle numbers that suggest
what use levels should be (according to visitors) on Ocean Drive. However,
results do not indicate which social carrying capacity is most appropriate
for Ocean Drive. A conceptual model has been explored that suggests that
acceptability or management action–based standards may be more appropriate when high demand for use and the quality of the visitor experience
are in competition (Hallo 2007). Research to test the validity of this conceptual model with NPS mangers and park visitors on Ocean Drive may be an
important next step. This research might examine the tradeoffs that are
made in forming judgments about access and the quality of the experience.
(Research addressing such tradeoffs is described in chapters 14, 23, and 26.)

Other considerations in applying a social carrying capacity to Ocean Drive
are the potential secondary consequences of management actions taken

to reduce crowding/congestion. Simulation model results showed that by prohibiting parking on Ocean Drive near Sand Beach, current issues of crowding/congestion are reduced greatly. However, what will visitors do if they cannot park on the road near Sand Beach and nearby parking lots are full? How will this change the quality of their experience?

Some visitors might react to reduced parking opportunities near Sand Beach by using Acadia's visitor shuttle bus system, the Island Explorer. The Island Explorer provides access to all major sites on Ocean Drive, but only a small minority of visitors to Acadia use it (Daigle and Zimmerman 2004b). To encourage greater ridership on the Island Explorer, availability of parking must be communicated better to visitors before they enter the Ocean Drive section of the Park Loop Road. Intelligent transportation systems (ITS) such as electronic signs are already in use at Acadia that make communicating real-time parking availability information to visitors practical. (The issues of alternative transportation and ITS are described more fully in chapters 9, 20, and 25.)

Undesirable secondary consequences potentially may be seen if the management alternative of disallowing parking on Ocean Drive near Sand Beach is implemented. For example, visitors who do not notice or respond to ITS messages by switching from their personal vehicles to the Island Explorer may not be able to visit Sand Beach because they cannot find parking. Alternatively, these visitors might choose to park farther away and walk to Sand Beach or park illegally. All of these scenarios likely lead to increased frustration for visitors and a decrease in the quality of the visitor experience. Increasing the capacity of the Sand Beach parking lot conceivably could mitigate these negative consequences, though it is uncertain if this is practical or desirable (from both environmental and experiential perspectives). A next step in applying the results from the simulation model might include research to examine these potential secondary consequences.

The simulation model developed for Ocean Drive demonstrates the usefulness of this methodological approach for predictive studies and testing the potential effectiveness of management alternatives. A primary benefit of a simulation model is that, once built, it often can be modified relatively easily to test management alternatives or scenarios. For example, the simulation model could be adapted to determine the number of additional parking spaces in the Sand Beach parking lot required to reduce use levels on the road to comply with visitor-based standards. Also, the behavior of visitors when they cannot park near Sand Beach (e.g., they continue without visiting Sand Beach, take the Island Explorer, or park farther away and walk to Sand Beach) could be built into the model (perhaps based on rules derived from the additional research suggested above) to test what impacts this would have on crowding/congestion on other sections of Ocean Drive.

Simulation modeling also has some potential limitations. Simulation models can be expensive, time consuming, and technically difficult to construct. Also, simulation models, by definition, require using simplifications of processes based on a set of assumptions. Finally, simulation models often rely on static data that may not remain accurate in the context of real-world operations.

CONCLUSIONS

The simulation model of vehicle use on Acadia's Ocean Drive indicates that congestion/crowding-related preference, acceptability, and management-action standards are being violated at current use levels, at least in Zone B. Furthermore, only a modest increase in vehicle use would begin to cause visitors to be displaced from Zone B of Ocean Drive due to crowding/congestion. The simulation model showed that vehicle crowding/congestion could be reduced to below the point where it violates visitor-based standards by disallowing parking in the right lane near Sand Beach. Implementing such a policy might result in consequences both desirable (e.g., increased visitor use of alternative transportation systems) and undesirable (e.g., crowding/congestion issues shifted to other areas). The simulation model built in this study could be a useful tool in further examining the impacts of implementing management alternatives for Ocean Drive.

23

A Comparative Study of Tradeoffs among Trail Attributes at Acadia National Park

The contemporary concepts of carrying capacity and sustainability require managers of national parks and related areas to provide opportunities for high-quality visitor experiences while protecting natural environments from visitor-caused impacts. National parks and related areas are the attractions that serve as the "heart" of outdoor recreation and the basis of related economic benefits (Gunn 1997; Hu and Wall 2005; Swarbrooke 1998). The inherent tension associated with carrying capacity and sustainability of parks requires tradeoffs between the level of visitation, the condition of natural resources, and the type and extent of facility development or site hardening.

Facility development and site hardening often follow increases in visitation, both to improve access to parks and to protect them from visitor-related degradation. Ecological studies have demonstrated a generally curvilinear relationship between visitor-related impacts and amount of use, supporting site-management actions that spatially concentrate and contain use on durable surfaces (Cole 1990; Leung and Marion 1999c). Constructing a well-designed trail or recreation site, surfacing it with gravel, wood, or pavement, and adding fencing to keep visitors from trampling sensitive off-trail environments generally are viewed as potentially effective resource-protection measures. Such facility development and site hardening constitute a core component of sustainable park and tourism management programs internationally (Marion and Leung 1998; Newsome et al. 2002).

However, the benefits associated with achieving important resource protection objectives come with potential costs in the form of changes to the nature of the visitor experience. The experience of negotiating a primitive and

---

This chapter is an edited version of the following paper: Kerri Cahill, Jeffrey Marion, and Steven Lawson, "Exploring Visitor Acceptability for Hardening Trails to Sustain Visitation and Minimize Impacts," *Journal of Sustainable Tourism* 16, no. 2 (2008): 232–45.

challenging trail tread of soil and rock is likely to look, sound, and feel substantially different than walking along a fenced boardwalk—a qualitatively
different recreation experience. Facility-development and site-hardening
practices also may be perceived as artificial and visually obtrusive by some
visitors (Bullock and Lawson 2008). Such developments can constitute a
physical barrier that curtails visitor freedom to explore and experience natural environments. They also may constitute a psychological barrier that
potentially diminishes a visitor's sense of intimacy or connectedness with
the natural environment.

It is important that managers understand the extent to which visitors
notice the use of facility development and site hardening in various types of
recreation settings, and how the application of such resource-protection
practices may affect the nature or quality of visitor experiences. Without a
clear understanding of appropriate and preferred setting conditions and
management strategies in specific locations, it is possible that resources and
visitor-experience opportunities will decline to minimum conditions established for an entire area (Haas et al. 1987; Manning 2003b). Resource-
management policies that fail to account for social acceptability and public
support are inherently tenuous (Shindler, Bunson, and Stankey 2002; Brunson 1993). Thus, if visitors are unsupportive of facility-development and
site-hardening practices in an area, or if these management approaches degrade the quality of visitor experiences, then managers need to consider
alternative measures for ensuring environmental protection.

This study expands previous research of visitor preferences by examining and comparing the opinions of visitors in two different settings at Acadia: Jordan Pond (JP) on Mount Desert Island and Little Moose Island
(LMI) off the Schoodic Peninsula. These areas have very different natural
resource settings, visitor activities, use levels, and facility development. JP is
a main attraction for a large majority of visitors to Acadia, with relatively
high visitation levels and visitor support services. LMI is a small, remote
island with low visitation and almost no visitor support facilities. The focus
of this research was to explore visitor opinions regarding acceptable trail-
development options in divergent recreation settings when faced with
tradeoffs among differing levels of environmental quality, visitation, and
encounters with others. This study used stated-choice analysis to examine
visitor acceptability of trail-development options in the context of these
tradeoffs (Lawson and Manning 2002).

STUDY METHODS

Study Area

Most of the trails on MDI are highly maintained, including the use of gravel, paving, rock steps, wood planking, and bridging. JP was chosen as the representative site on MDI due to its high level of trail development, including substantial use of wood boardwalks and gravel with some stepping stones. JP is a very accessible and popular attraction site within the park.

LMI is located off the tip of the more remote Schoodic Peninsula section of the park. It offers a low-use setting for recreation opportunities, and visitors must cross rocks exposed only at low tide to gain access to the island. On the island, several informal, visitor-created trails are apparent, but there is no designated, signed trail system. There are also no interpretive materials or park rangers on the island. LMI trails are not maintained actively (e.g., no boardwalks or gravel), although some unobtrusive restoration work has been done recently to eliminate unnecessary visitor-created trails.

Stated-Choice Analysis

Stated-choice analysis was used as the primary research method in this study. This research approach was developed in economics and marketing to study consumer preferences for multi-attribute goods (Louviere and Timmermans 1990). Stated-choice studies ask respondents to make a series of choices between competing configurations of multi-attribute goods that often are referred to as profiles or scenarios (Louviere and Timmermans 1990). Within a choice experiment, profiles or scenarios are defined by varying levels of each attribute studied (Mackenzie 1993). For example, respondents may be asked to choose between alternative recreation setting profiles where each profile is described by varying levels of visitor use density, vegetation and soil conditions, and restrictions or regulations imposed on visitors. The choices made by respondents are aggregated and statistically analyzed to estimate preferences for the levels of each of the attributes and the relative importance of each attribute to respondents. Stated-choice models also are used to estimate public support for hypothetical policy or management scenarios, which are represented by varying combinations of the attribute levels (Dennis 1998; Opaluch et al. 1993). Choice experiments have been applied in park and outdoor recreation research and management as a tool to help determine visitor preferences regarding tradeoffs among recreation-related issues. (Louviere and Timmermans 1990; Schroeder et al. 1990; Boxall and Macnab 2000; Bullock, Elston, and Chalmers 1998; Hanley et al. 2002; Morey et al. 2002; Lawson and Manning 2002, 2003; Newman et al. 2005; Cahill et al. 2007).

Selection of Attributes and Levels

A substantial body of research has been conducted on identifying the ecological, social, and management attributes that help define the character of recreation experiences (Manning 1999). Based on a literature review, including park documents, and review of recent park visitor surveys, numerous attributes were considered to define the social, resource, and management conditions related to trail systems in Acadia. In consultation with park managers, four attributes were selected that were considered to be managerially relevant and likely to influence recreation site preferences (table 23.1). The social setting is represented by encounters with other visitors; the resource setting is represented by the condition of the formal trail in terms of widening due to wet soils; and the management setting is represented by level of public access and level of trail development. Four levels were provided for each attribute, representing the range of conditions likely to be encountered in the two park settings. These levels were based on discussions with other researchers and park staff.

Experimental Design

Since each attribute was assigned four levels, a full factorial research design would have produced a total of 4^4 (256) hypothetical recreation settings for respondents to evaluate. This large number of settings was too many choice sets for a survey participant to consider, therefore, a fractional factorial design was used to produce an orthogonal subset of site descriptions (Holmes and Adamowicz 2003). The experimental design combined the four recreation-setting attributes at varying levels to result in 32 paired comparisons blocked into four questionnaire versions. Each questionnaire version included eight paired comparisons. An example of a typical paired comparison is presented in figure 23.1. In each paired comparison question, respondents were asked to indicate whether they preferred Recreation Setting A or Recreation Setting B.

TABLE 23.1   Acadia recreation setting attributes and levels used in the stated-choice survey.

Social Conditions

  Level of Encounters

    1   Visitors encounter no other groups during a hike.

    2   Visitors encounter up to 5 other groups during a hike.

    3   Visitors encounter up to 10 other groups during a hike.

    4   Visitors encounter up to 20 other groups during a hike.

Resource Conditions

  Ecological Condition of Official Trail[a]

    1   Trails show no signs of widening or secondary trails.

    2   Visitor use on trails with wet soils has caused a slight amount of trail widening.

    3   Visitor use on trails with wet soils has caused a moderate amount of trail widening.

    4   Visitor use on trails with wet soils has caused extensive trail widening and formation of secondary trails around wet areas.

Management Conditions

  Public Access

    1   The number of people allowed to hike in this area is not limited.

    2   The number of people allowed to hike in this area is limited—around 75 to 80 percent of interested visitors are able to gain access.

    3   The number of people allowed to hike in this area is limited—about half of interested visitors are able to gain access.

    4   The number of people allowed to hike in this area is limited—around 25 to 30 percent of interested visitors are able to gain access.

  Trail Development[a]

    1   There are no management-constructed features along trails (e.g., stepping stones, wood planking, gravel).

    2   Stepping stones are placed along sections of trails.

    3   Wood planking is placed on sections of trails.

    4   Gravel is placed on sections of trails.

[a]Portrayed in the survey with these narrative statements, as well as photos.

Survey Administration

Surveys were administered during the peak summer use season, generally from 10:00 a.m. to 6:00 p.m. on both weekends and weekdays. The days and times for sampling visitors to LMI varied based on tidal patterns. The stated-choice survey was conducted using self-administered questionnaires. During the survey, respondents were presented with a series of eight pairs of alternative settings defined by varying levels of the four attributes presented in table 23.1. For each pair, respondents were asked to choose the setting

Recreation Setting A	**Recreation Setting B**
The number of people allowed to hike in this area is not limited.	The number of people allowed to hike in this area is limited - around 25-30% of interested visitors are able to gain access.
Visitors encounter up to 5 other groups during a hike.	
Visitor use on trails with wet soils has caused extensive trail widening and formation of secondary trails around wet areas. (See photo below)	Visitors encounter up to 5 other groups during a hike.
	Trails show no signs of widening or secondary trails. (See photo below)
There are no management-constructed features along trails (e.g., stepping stones, wood planking, gravel). (See photo below)	Wood planking is placed on sections of trails. (See photo below)

Figure 23.1 *Example recreation-setting comparison used in the stated-choice survey.*

they preferred. A small number of questions were included at the end of the questionnaire to gather information about visitor characteristics, trip experiences, and visitor assessments of the stated-choice questions.

A total of 399 stated choice surveys were completed at the two study sites. A total of 196 surveys were completed over 19 sampling days at LMI, resulting in an 84.8 percent response rate. At JP, 203 surveys were completed over eight sampling days, with a 66.7 percent response rate.

Stated-Choice Data Analysis

Analysis of the stated-choice responses is based on a model of discrete-choice behavior referred to as random utility theory (Hanemann 1984; Mc-Fadden 1974). According to random utility theory, the attributes of alternatives relevant to a given choice are evaluated in terms of the utility they provide the respondent. Further, the utilities associated with each of the attributes of an alternative are additive, resulting in an overall utility (i.e., desirability) for each alternative, and the alternative with the highest overall utility is selected (Lindberg, Dellaert, and Romer Rassing 1999). Therefore, the parameters of the stated-choice model, which are estimated using logistic regression and maximum likelihood methods, can be interpreted as representing the relative importance of the corresponding attributes to the overall desirability of a given recreation setting (McFadden 1974; Opaluch et al. 1993).

STUDY FINDINGS

Preferences for Social, Resource, and Management Conditions

The coefficient estimates for the setting attributes, along with their standard errors, chi-square values, and p-values for JP and LMI are presented in table 23.2. The public-access and level-of-encounters attributes were entered into the regression model as continuous variables, thus there is a single parameter estimate for each of these two attributes. Due to the ordinal nature of the ecological-condition and trail-development attributes, these were entered into the model using effects coding. Thus, similar to regression analysis with dummy coded variables, parameters were estimated for three of the four levels of each of these attributes. The coefficient for the excluded level of each attribute was calculated as the negative sum of the parameters of the other three levels of the attribute (Holmes and Adamowicz 2003). The strength and direction (positive/negative) of visitor preferences can be interpreted from the coefficient values—levels of attributes with larger coefficients being preferred to levels of attributes with smaller coefficient values. Most of the coefficients are significantly different than zero at the 5 percent level of probability, except Ecological Condition of the Official Trail at levels 2 and 3, and Trail Development at level 1 within the LMI model.

The coefficients reported in table 23.2 provide insight into the preferred levels of each of the study attributes for visitors at JP and LMI, respectively, holding all other attributes constant. The coefficient estimates suggest that visitors to both locations prefer little or no restrictions on public access and few encounters with other visitors, though the strengths of these preferences vary. In addition, visitors to both locations strongly prefer trail conditions with no widening or secondary trails, all else being equal. Of particular interest is the very high strength, in relative terms, of visitor preferences for nonimpacted trail conditions, with minimal variation between visitors to the two very different study sites. The preferred types of trail development differed between the JP and LMI respondents. In particular, JP respondents preferred wood planking to the other trail-development treatments. In contrast, LMI respondents preferred stepping stones, the least

TABLE 23.2 Stated-choice model coefficients for Jordan Pond and Little Moose Island.

Variable	DF	Coefficient estimate	Standard error	Chi-square	p-value
Jordon Pond					
Public access	1	−0.360	0.036	100.233	<0.001
Level of encounters	1	−0.132	0.036	13.714	< 0.001
No trail widening or secondary trails	1	0.470	0.065	52.852	<0.001
Slight trail widening	1	0.220	0.069	10.178	0.001
Moderate trail widening	1	−0.279	0.064	18.948	<0.001
Extensive trail widening, secondary trails[a]	1	−0.411	—	—	—
No management-constructed features	1	−0.478	0.070	46.254	<0.001
Stepping stones	1	0.194	0.066	8.730	0.003
Wood planking	1	0.327	0.067	23.890	<0.001
Gravel[a]	1	−0.043	—	—	—
Little Moose Island					
Public access	1	−0.141	0.035	16.256	<0.001
Level of encounters	1	−0.426	0.040	115.575	<0.001
No trail widening or secondary trails	1	0.458	0.070	42.644	<0.001
Slight trail widening	1	0.008	0.071	0.012	0.912
Moderate trail widening	1	−0.005	0.066	0.005	0.945
Extensive trail widening, secondary trails[a]	1	−0.461	—	—	—
No management-constructed features	1	−0.131	0.076	2.993	0.084
Stepping stones	1	0.435	0.067	41.919	<0.001
Wood planking	1	0.205	0.067	9.426	0.002
Gravel[a]	1	−0.508	—	—	—

[a]Coefficients for the excluded level of the attribute were not estimated by the statistical model, but rather were calculated as the negative sum of the coefficients on the other three levels of the corresponding attribute.

intensive of the trail-development options, other than the "no features" option. Gravel, although not a favorite of respondents at either location, was more preferable to respondents at JP than at LMI, holding all other conditions constant.

Acceptability of Tradeoffs among Conditions

Most management decisions for parks and related areas must be made in the public arena, so it is helpful to examine study data in terms of potential visitor support for management practices in specific settings to identify how respondents would optimize tradeoffs. For example, the statistical models created with study data were used to estimate how park visitors would evaluate tradeoffs between ecological impacts to a trail and alternative levels of trail development designed to minimize ecological impacts. To do this, the LMI and JP models were used to estimate the proportion of visitors who would support alternative configurations of the study attributes (Opaluch et al. 1993). The hypothetical scenarios evaluated in this analysis are based on the assumption that increasing levels of trail development will reduce ecological impacts to the trail. The results of the analysis show that respondents at the two study locations have different notions about acceptable tradeoffs associated with trail management. Respondents at JP would accept more trail development (e.g., gravel and wood planking) to minimize or eliminate ecological impacts to trails. However, LMI respondents clearly prefer that trail development remain more primitive (e.g., stepping stones) even when faced with higher levels of impacts to the ecological condition of trails.

To further examine visitor acceptability for tradeoffs related to trail management at the two sites, two additional management scenarios were evaluated. The objective of the first management scenario was to maximize solitude and naturalness along the trail system using access restrictions and minimal levels of trail development. The objective of the second management scenario was to maximize resource protection and access for visitors of all abilities by pairing unlimited access opportunities (i.e., no restrictions on the number of people allowed to hike in the area) with the highest level of trail development (gravel) that would be the most accessible (to visitors with mobility impairment) of the trail-development options tested. The results of the analysis show that the scenario favored by LMI respondents maximizes solitude and naturalness using the management strategies of access restrictions and minimal site management, with 79 percent of respondents choosing scenario one versus 21 percent choosing scenario two. On the other end of the spectrum, the scenario favored by JP respondents maximizes access for visitors by pairing unlimited access opportunities with the highest level of trail development, with 67 percent of respondents choosing scenario two versus 33 percent choosing scenario one. These results suggest that visitors to LMI are more likely to accept access restrictions to maximize solitude and naturalness, while visitors to JP are more likely to accept higher development and unrestricted access to help ensure hiking opportunities for all visitors. Although these scenarios represent extreme management situations, the results of the analysis provide further evidence of a distinct difference in acceptability for management strategies in the two settings.

CONCLUSION

When making decisions about recreation-facility development and site-hardening actions, park managers should consider carefully how their actions might affect visitor experiences. One valuable form of input to such decisions are surveys of visitors to gauge their preferences regarding alternative actions in different settings and how such actions might affect visitor experiences. This study demonstrates that asking visitors about recreation setting attributes uni-dimensionally (i.e., not in the context of tradeoffs among multiple site attributes), a common approach, can yield incomplete information. At Acadia, visitors to a remote, low-use location (LMI) and to an accessible, high-use location (JP) reported that they prefer trail conditions that include unrestricted access, low levels of encounters, and low levels of ecological impacts. Furthermore, when examined uni-dimensionally, visitor preferences for trail-development options varied only slightly at the two sites. Only through analysis that more explicitly considers trade-offs among trail attributes are divergent opinions clarified. When the attributes of trail development and ecological impacts to trails are analyzed in terms of tradeoffs, it becomes clear that respondents from the two study sites evaluate the potentially competing objectives of maximizing trail development and minimizing ecological impacts to trails differently. Insight on how visitors think these tradeoffs should be balanced provides useful information for management decision making, particularly given the permanency of facility-development and site-hardening actions.

In our study, respondents to a highly visited park attraction site are more willing than respondents to an infrequently visited site to tolerate high levels of trail development (i.e., wood planking and gravel) when needed to address ecological impacts to trails. Such issues are of great importance to park managers, yet they have received relatively little research attention.

This study suggests that visitors have opinions about the acceptability of different levels and types of trail development and that such opinions are related to the type of site under consideration. Trail development can facilitate protection of resource conditions, but it can be perceived as inappropriate in settings that visitors think should be managed in a more primitive or natural state, such as at LMI. In highly visited sites such as JP, trail development may be considered a satisfactory "tradeoff" to allow more visitors the opportunity to enjoy the area, while still protecting resource conditions. Through stated-choice analysis, park managers can better understand the relationship among the attributes that define the character of park settings and the subsequent nature of visitor experiences.

24 A Stated-Choice Analysis of Visitor Preferences on Cadillac Mountain

As noted in earlier chapters, the summit of Cadillac Mountain is a principal visitor attraction at Acadia. This intensive visitor use coupled with a management policy that allows visitors to roam freely and explore the summit has resulted in a substantial loss of vegetation and soils on the mountain (Jacobi 2001a). Over the past several decades, the park has applied a variety of management practices to address the declining resource conditions on the summit of this mountain, including paving the summit loop trail, installing wooden barriers around areas with trampled vegetation and soils, and placing wooden signs along the summit loop trail with a message encouraging visitors to stay on the trail or rock surfaces.

The social, resource, and managerial conditions on the summit of Cadillac Mountain are typical of attraction sites in national parks and related areas, and raise challenging management-related questions. For example, would visitors consent to use limits or strict regulation of their behavior on the summit of Cadillac Mountain in the interest of resource protection? Or, would visitors rather maintain unrestricted access and be allowed to explore the summit freely, irrespective of the resultant resource conditions? Alternatively, would visitors prefer that park managers rely on technical solutions such as site hardening, even if it changes the type of recreation experience provided? The purpose of this study is to use stated-choice analysis, as described in chapter 23, to examine these and related questions.

This chapter is an edited version of the following paper: Steven Bullock and Steven Lawson, "Managing the 'Commons' on Cadillac Mountain: A Stated Choice Analysis of Acadia National Park Visitors' Preferences," *Leisure Sciences* 30, no. 1 (2008): 71–86.

STUDY METHODS

Potential management strategies were represented in this study by a set of three attributes labeled "public access," "freedom of travel," and "structures to minimize off-trail hiking" (see table 24.1). In addition to the management-oriented attributes, additional attributes were included to portray other relevant resource and social conditions on the summit of Cadillac Mountain. In particular, resource conditions on the mountain summit were represented in the visitor survey by an attribute labeled "visitor-caused damage to vegetation and soils." Social conditions were represented by the level of use on the paved summit trail labeled "people on trail," and an attribute concerning visitor behavior labeled "people off-trail on vegetation and soils."

A research design was used to combine a range of levels for the six attributes into eighteen paired comparisons that were blocked into three questionnaire versions, with each containing six paired comparisons (Louviere, Hensher, and Swait 2000). The paired comparisons included a choice of two scenarios that included the six attributes with different combinations of their levels. The design was restricted to exclude unrealistic scenarios such as "many visitors off-trail on vegetation and soils" and "little visitor-caused damage to vegetation and soils." The relative importance of each attribute of the resulting stated-choice model was estimated statistically (Lawson et al. 2006b).

Cadillac Mountain visitors were surveyed on-site after their visit to the summit during a ten-day period of the peak summer use season. Study participants were assigned randomly to complete one of three versions of the questionnaire that differed only in terms of the stated-choice paired comparison questions.

Respondents were presented with information about the impacts of visitor use to vegetation and soils on the Cadillac Mountain summit and potential management strategies to reduce or eliminate visitor-caused resource impacts. Respondents were then instructed to evaluate six paired comparisons. Within each paired comparison, respondents were presented with two alternative scenarios and asked to indicate the scenario they preferred. Figure 24.1 provides an example of a paired comparison included in the study design. Within each scenario included in a paired comparison, the levels of each of the six attributes were described in narrative form with bul-

TABLE 24.1   Cadillac Mountain summit setting attributes and levels.

Type of condition	Attribute	Levels
Resource conditions	Visitor-caused damage to vegetation and soils[a]	*Little* visitor-caused damage to vegetation and soils is present
		Some visitor-caused damage to vegetation and soils is present
		Extensive visitor-caused damage to vegetation and soils is present
Social conditions	People on trail[a]	*Few* other visitors are on the paved trail
		Some other visitors are on the paved trail
		Many other visitors are on the paved trail
	People off-trail on vegetation and soils[a]	*No* visitors are off-trail on vegetation and soils
		Some visitors are off-trail on vegetation and soils
		Many visitors are off-trail on vegetation and soils
Management conditions	Public access[b]	*No* visitors are turned away from visiting the summit of Cadillac Mountain, even during busy times
		A few visitors are turned away from visiting Cadillac Mountain during busy times
		Many visitors are turned away from visiting Cadillac Mountain during busy times
	Freedom of travel[b]	Visitors are *allowed* to roam off-trail
		Visitors are *encouraged* to stay on the paved trail or rock surfaces
		Visitors are *required* to stay on the paved trail
	Structures to minimize off-trail hiking[a]	*No management structures* are used to minimize off-trail hiking
		Signs are used to minimize off-trail hiking
		Rock borders are used to minimize off-trail hiking
		Fencing is used to minimize off-trail hiking

[a]Described narratively and depicted in computer-generated photographs within scenarios.
[b]Described narratively within scenarios.

let points. Each scenario also contained a computer-generated photo depicting the levels of four of the attributes. (Visual research methods are described more fully in chapter 12.) The "public access" and "freedom of travel" attributes did not lend themselves to visual representation and were not included in the photos.

Of 602 visitors contacted, 450 completed the questionnaire, resulting in

Scenario A	Scenario B
• *Many* visitors are turned away from visiting Cadillac Mountain during busy times.	• *A few* visitors are turned away from visiting Cadillac Mountain during busy times.
• Visitors are *encouraged* to stay on the paved trail or rock surfaces.	• Visitors are allowed to roam off-trail.
• *Fencing* is used to minimize off-trail hiking (*see photo*).	• *Signs* are used to minimize off-trail hiking (*see photo*).
• Few other visitors are on the paved trail (*see photo*).	• *Some* other visitors are on the paved trail (*see photo*).
• *No* visitors are off-trail on vegetation and soils (*see photo*).	• *Some* visitors are off-trail on vegetation and soils. (*see photo*).
• Little visitor-caused damage to vegetation and soils is present (*see photo*).	• *Some* visitor-caused damage to vegetaion and soils is present (*see photo*).

Figure 24.1 *An example of one choice set included in the study design. (Visitors were asked to select their preferred scenario of the pair.)*

a 75 percent response rate. The number of respondents was balanced evenly across the three versions of the questionnaire and resulted in 2,636 paired comparisons after accounting for item nonresponse.

STUDY FINDINGS

Relative Importance of Attributes

The magnitude of the chi-square value of "visitor-caused damage to vegetation and soils" suggests that it was the most important of the study attributes to respondents, and that visitors are particularly sensitive to and opposed to extensive resource impacts, while they strongly prefer little resource degradation.

High importance was also placed on "public access" and "people off-trail on vegetation and soils" attributes. Findings from the "public access" attribute suggest that Cadillac Mountain visitors strongly prefer that no visitors be turned away from the area, even during busy times. With respect to the "people off-trail on vegetation and soils" attribute, the findings suggest that visitors prefer some people off-trail more than no people off-trail, but strongly oppose many visitors hiking off-trail onto vegetation and soils. While it appears contradictory that visitors would prefer some people off-trail more than no people off-trail yet prefer little visitor-caused damage to vegetation and soils, it may be that at least some visitors assume that it would be possible to have little damage to vegetation and soils as long as there are not many visitors hiking off-trail. Furthermore, given visitors' sensitivity to the issue of public access to the summit of Cadillac Mountain, visitors may interpret seeing no people off-trail as a manifestation of visitor use limits.

Findings for the attributes representing "structures to minimize off-trail hiking" and "freedom of travel" suggest that these attributes are of moderate importance to Cadillac Mountain visitors. Findings for the "structures to minimize off-trail hiking" attribute suggest that visitors prefer the use of some management structures such as rock borders and signs to help keep visitors on the paved summit trail over using no management structures. However, respondents were indifferent between placing fencing along the trail and using no management structures to keep people on the trail, and were less supportive of using fencing than rock borders or signs along the trail. With respect to the "freedom to travel" attribute, respondents preferred that visitors be required to stay on the paved trail rather than allowed to roam freely off-trail on the mountain summit or simply encouraging them to stay on the paved trail or rock surfaces. Why respondents preferred that visitors be required to stay on the paved trail, yet preferred to see some people off-trail more than no people off-trail is not clear. Possibly visitors assume that many visitors might walk off-trail if the NPS only encouraged visitors to stay on the paved trail and that some visitors would walk off-trail even if they are required to stay on the trail.

Findings suggest that "people on trail" is the least important attribute to visitors. Respondents prefer seeing few visitors on the trail, but are indifferent between moderate and high levels of visitor use on the trail. While it may seem contradictory that people who visit Acadia during the height of the visitor use season would prefer seeing few other visitors on the trail, visitors may be constrained to visiting the park during the peak period of visitor use (e.g., can only vacation during summer months when schools are not in session).

Predicted Support for Potential Management Scenarios

Managing Cadillac Mountain and similar sites requires that management strategies be selected that are not only effective (e.g., prevent further vegetation and soils degradation), but socially acceptable as well. Therefore, the stated-choice model developed in this study was used to predict visitor support for four alternative approaches to managing the summit of Cadillac Mountain (Opaluch et al. 1993).

The first management scenario considered was referred to as the "no-management" alternative and constituted a hands-off approach to the management of Cadillac Mountain. Visitor access to the mountain summit would be unlimited, visitors would be allowed to roam the summit freely, and the park would not use any management structures to keep visitors on the paved summit trail. As a result of these management policies, visitor use on the paved summit trail would be assumed to be relatively high and many people would be walking off-trail, trampling vegetation and soils. Consequently, extensive visitor-caused damage to vegetation and soils would occur.

The second management scenario was referred to as the "education alternative." Visitors are encouraged to stay on the paved trail or rock surfaces through an information program. This policy would be reinforced by placing signs along the trail. In addition, no visitors would be turned away from visiting the summit. Thus visitor use on the paved trail would be assumed to be high. It is assumed that somewhat fewer visitors would be off-trail than under the "no management alternative" and that there would be a corresponding moderate reduction in the amount of visitor-caused damage to vegetation and soils.

The third "site-management" alternative would include a regulation requiring visitors to stay on the paved summit trail and fencing would be installed along the trail to discourage people from going off-trail. Although this policy would result in relatively intensive regulation of visitor behavior, no limit would be placed on the number of people allowed to visit the summit. Thus, it is assumed that there would be many visitors on the paved summit trail, but there would be no visitors walking off-trail and little visitor-caused damage to vegetation and soils.

The fourth management scenario, referred to as the "limited-use" alternative, includes a policy of turning many visitors away from Cadillac Mountain during busy times. As a result of limited public access, it is assumed that there would be few visitors on the paved summit trail and no visitors off-trail. Furthermore, central to this alternative is the assumption that with fewer people allowed on the mountain summit, visitor-caused impacts to vegetation and soils would be reduced without having to rely on intensive site manipulation (e.g., fencing) or regulation of visitor behavior.

Estimates derived from the stated-choice model developed in the study suggest that the site-management alternative would receive the greatest support from Cadillac Mountain visitors, followed by the education alternative and the limited-use alternative. In particular, the stated-choice model estimates that 45 percent of current visitors would support the site-management alternative, while only 20 percent would support the limited-use alternative, even though they both would result in little visitor-caused damage to vegetation and soils and the limited-use alternative would result in lower levels of use along the paved summit trail. According to the results of the stated-choice analysis, moderate support exists among Cadillac Mountain visitors for an education-oriented management approach, with 33 percent of visitors estimated to support this alternative. By far, the least popular alternative considered in this analysis was the no-management alternative, which is estimated to receive support from only about 2 percent of visitors.

DISCUSSION

Results of this study suggest that Cadillac Mountain visitors consider protecting vegetation and soils on the summit to be a high priority, and that they are willing to accept restrictions requiring visitors to stay on the trail and site-management structures such as signs, rock borders, and even fencing if necessary to do so. These findings are consistent with previous research in which visitors were found to be supportive of direct-management practices when needed to control the impacts of recreation use (Anderson and Manfredo 1986; Shindler and Shelby 1993). Further, while respondents were not opposed to relatively large numbers of visitors on the paved summit trail, they preferred not to see many visitors walking off-trail onto vegetation and soils. These results suggest that while crowding may not be a high priority for visitors even at high levels of visitor use on the Cadillac Mountain summit, visitors are sensitive to and concerned with visitor behavior that potentially damages fragile park resources. Furthermore, in contrast to previous suggestions that limiting visitor access is necessary to resolve resource impact problems in national parks (e.g., Hardin 1968; Dustin and McAvoy 1980; Feeny et al. 1990), the results of this study suggest that Cadillac Mountain visitors prefer that no visitors be turned away from visiting the summit, even at busy times.

Results of the analysis of the four management scenarios provide further insight into visitor preferences concerning management of Cadillac Mountain. For example, if adopting a "heavy-handed" management approach to protect and restore resources on the summit of Cadillac Mountain is necessary, our results suggest that visitors would prefer intensive site manipulation (e.g., fencing along the paved summit trail) and regulation of visitor behavior over limiting public access. The analysis suggests that this would be the case even if the limited-use approach would be equally as effective as the site-management approach at addressing resource impact concerns and would result in lower visitor use levels on the trail. Although resource conditions ranked highest among the six study attributes in terms of relative importance to respondents, analysis of the four management scenarios suggests that visitors would tolerate somewhat less-favorable resource conditions coupled with visitor education rather than accept use limits that would result in many people being turned away during busy times. However, the stated-choice model estimates suggest that visitors would prefer the park to adopt strict use limits over an education-oriented management approach, if the educational approach resulted in extensive damage to vegetation and soils. In either case, the stated-choice model estimates that visitors would prefer the site-management alternative to any of the other management alternatives considered in the analysis. Furthermore, analysis of the four management scenarios suggests that while no management alternative is predicted to be supported by a majority of visitors, all three forms of active management (i.e., the "education," "site-management," and "limited-use" alternatives) are much more likely to receive support from visitors than doing nothing and allowing the resources of Cadillac Mountain to become extensively degraded (i.e., the no-management alternative).

While there is a growing body of research on the attitudes and preferences of outdoor recreation visitors, the predominant focus of this work has been on visitors to backcountry and wilderness areas. The findings from our study suggest that results from research on backcountry and wilderness visitors may not be fully applicable to frontcountry attraction sites such as the summit of Cadillac Mountain. In particular, the results of our study suggest that visitors to national park attraction sites may be open to more-intensive management actions that generally would not be supported in backcountry recreation environments, and may be less tolerant of other management actions commonly considered suitable for backcountry areas. For example, our study findings suggest that visitors to the summit of Cadillac Mountain support and prefer the use of management structures such as signs and rock borders to reinforce efforts to keep visitors from walking off the summit loop trail onto vegetation and soils. However, backcountry and wilderness visitors generally prefer low-standard primitive trails with few or no management structures (Manning 1999). Similarly, our study results suggest that Cadillac Mountain visitors prefer regulation of visitor behavior to minimize visitor-caused impacts to resources, while backcountry and wilderness visitors generally prefer unconfined recreation free from management regulation (Cole 2001; Hendee and Dawson 2003; Lawson and Manning 2003). In addition, our study findings suggest that visitors to the summit of Cadillac Mountain are strongly opposed to limiting public access to the mountain summit, even during peak periods when visitor use levels are high. In contrast, findings from studies of visitor preferences and attitudes toward management in backcountry and wilderness areas suggest that use limits generally are supported in areas that are "crowded" (Manning 1999). However, our study results suggest that visitors to national park attraction sites such as Cadillac Mountain are similar to backcountry and wilderness visitors regarding their strong support for protecting natural resource conditions, and while frontcountry visitors may differ from visitors to backcountry areas in terms of the preferred actions and strategies, they favor management to protect park resources (Lawson and Manning 2002; Newman et al. 2005).

This study found that respondents prefer that no visitors be turned away from the summit of Cadillac Mountain. This finding stands in contrast to previous suggestions that limiting visitor access is necessary to effectively manage problems of resource impacts in national parks (Dustin and McAvoy 1980; Feeny et al. 1990; Hardin 1968). However, this finding is consistent with ecological research on the impacts of outdoor recreation, which suggest that limiting use ultimately may not be a viable solution to managing high-use attraction sites like the summit of Cadillac Mountain. Specifically, studies of visitor-caused resource impacts consistently have found that the relationship between the amount of use and impact is curvilinear (Cole 1993; Hammitt and Cole 1998; Leung and Marion 1999c). In particular, these studies have found that the majority of resource impact occurs at low to moderate levels of recreational use with only marginal increases in impact occurring at higher use levels. Consequently, to reduce the trampling impacts from up to 5,500 daily visits on Cadillac Mountain through use limits alone, park managers would have to institute draconian use limits. Further, the curvilinear relationship between impact and use suggests that management methods that concentrate and contain use on durable surfaces ultimately may be more effective for high-use sites, but may be less appealing in low-use wilderness and backcountry sites (Leung and Marion, 2000).

CONCLUSIONS

This study provides insights into visitor preferences concerning the management of national park attraction sites like the summit of Cadillac Mountain. Results of the study suggest that Cadillac Mountain visitors consider protecting vegetation and soils to be a high priority. Respondents indicated a willingness to accept restrictions requiring visitors to stay on the paved summit trail and management structures such as signs and rock borders placed along the trail. While respondents supported visitor regulations and the use of management structures to protect vegetation and soils on the mountain summit, they preferred that the park maintain unlimited public access to the summit. In summary, the results suggest that visitors to Cadillac Mountain support protecting the ecological integrity of the summit of the mountain, and that to achieve this objective, they are willing to accept regulating visitor behavior, but not limitations on public access.

25 Assessing the Effectiveness of Intelligent Transportation System Technology to Manage Visitor Use at Acadia National Park

Intelligent Transportation Systems (ITS) are a combination of information technologies applied to the management of ground transportation and the provision of travel information to outdoor recreation visitors (Sheldon 1997). An ITS can include many different technologies but those most relevant to parks and outdoor recreation are route guidance, traveler information, automated vehicle-location, fleet management, and automated traffic-management systems (Sheldon 1997). The movement of park visitors via ground transportation systems is becoming more challenging as use levels increase. ITS technologies are viewed as potentially important since they can help visitors have safer, faster, and more enjoyable trips. Because of the mix of public and private lands on MDI, it is essential that the NPS work cooperatively with the surrounding communities to maintain a high-quality experience for visitors. In the Acadia National Park General Management Plan, visitor and automobile congestion are identified as areas that need to be addressed in order to maintain the quality of the visitor experience. Also stressed is the need to work with surrounding communities to explore alternative methods for visitors to enter the park because of visitor safety issues resulting from large numbers of cars parked on the sides of roads. A general survey of Acadia visitors also highlighted the problem of congestion; the three things that respondents liked least about their visit were (1) crowds, (2) traffic, and (3) congested parking (Littlejohn 1999). (This study is described more fully in chapter 1.)

As part of a solution to relieve traffic congestion problems, the NPS iden-

---

This chapter is an edited version of the following paper: John Daigle and Carole Zimmerman, "The Convergence of Transportation, Information Technology, and Visitor Experience at Acadia National Park," *Journal of Travel Research* 43, no. 2 (2004): 151–160.

tified public transportation as the preferred approach for both protecting park resources and providing a high-quality visitor experience (National Park Service, 1992). In 1999, the NPS, with the help of several state and federal government agencies, the nonprofit organization Friends of Acadia, and surrounding communities on MDI, introduced the Island Explorer bus. This alternative transportation system used within the park and more broadly on MDI was meant to address the congestion caused by automobiles (Daigle and Lee 2000). From late June through early September of the first season, the buses carried 142,260 passengers over six routes through the park and surrounding MDI towns. The success of the service in its first season led to expansion in the summer of 2000. The Island Explorer received an additional boost in 2002 with a partnership formed with L.L. Bean Company. This partnership involves a $1 million endowment that will help the bus service expand to meet growing demand and enable extension of bus operation into a growing off-peak fall tourist season.

ITS TECHNOLOGY AT ACADIA

The U.S. Department of Interior, the parent agency of the NPS, and the U.S. Department of Transportation entered into a memorandum of understanding in 1997 to work together to address the problems of transportation in national parks. In 1999, Acadia was chosen for a test to determine the effectiveness of ITS in helping to solve park transportation problems. During the summer of 2002, ITS technologies were installed, with many components intended to enhance the operation of the Island Explorer bus system. They included two-way voice communications, automatic vehicle location, electronic bus-departure signs, automated annunciators on-board buses, and automatic passenger counters. ITS traffic-management components within the park included parking lot monitoring and traffic volume recorders at park entrances. These technologies were deployed with the expectation they would have measurable impacts in the form of benefits realized by visitors (e.g., tourists' satisfaction with their visit), organizations (e.g., efficiency of Island Explorer operations), or society at large (e.g., reduce the number of traffic accidents) (Zimmerman, Coleman, and Daigle 2003).

Displays of traveler information utilized real-time data from the ITS components. For example, automatic vehicle-location (AVL) technologies were used with Island Explorer buses to calculate the real-time arrival and departure times for all scheduled bus stops. ITS technologies that could be used directly by visitors included electronic signs that displayed real-time departures of buses. The electronic bus-departure signs were located at the main hub of the bus system in the town of Bar Harbor as well as at two popular destinations in the park, the Visitor Center and Jordan Pond House. Other traveler information integrated with the AVL technology included an automated annunciator on-board busses displaying the location of the next bus stop and announcing the next bus stop. This traveler information was provided for visitors on all Island Explorer buses and scheduled bus stops.

Another ITS technology planned was the status of parking conditions at popular destinations inside Acadia. However, not all the ITS components were operational during the summer of 2002. By mid-June of 2002, the ITS components associated with the Island Explorer all were tested successfully and ready to be put into service for the start of the season. Components within the park, however, proved to be more problematic. Because the loop detectors at the entrance to parking lots were not operational, personal observation was used as an alternative to automated monitors as a way to determine parking lot status of two popular destinations in the park, Sand Beach and Jordan Pond House. This information was communicated to visitors through a website and parking-status signs. The real-time parking-status signs were located at the entrances to the Visitor Center, Blackwoods Campground, and Seawall Campground inside the park. A planned enhancement to the park's web page for displaying real-time traveler information did not take place, but instead was replaced in the second half of the summer season by a temporary web page that was limited to parking-lot status information of the two lots. The parking condition status was updated by NPS staff as conditions changed.

THE STUDY

This chapter reports the results of a survey that examines visitor use of the ITS technologies described above. One objective of the study was to examine the performance of the ITS technologies in providing accurate, understandable, and useable information. Visitors were asked to assess the impact of the ITS technologies on various aspects of mobility, including avoidance of parking problems, traffic congestion, and large crowds; ease of getting around the area; saving time; and changing the time or destination of travel. Also, it was hypothesized that the enhanced visitor experience with the ITS technologies would divert some visitors from using their private vehicles to using the Island Explorer bus. A second objective of the investigation was to examine the self-reported benefits of using the ITS technologies and willingness to use public transit. In addition, an expected benefit of the ITS technologies was that they would contribute to the economic vitality of the region. Specifically, the enhanced experience and increased mobility would contribute to longer visitor stays and increased visitor expenditures.

STUDY METHODS

To ensure that visitors who used the ITS technologies were well represented among the study participants, two sampling methods were employed. Island Explorer bus users were sampled and a total of 514 on-site interviews were conducted on-board buses over the summer peak use season. Other park visitors also were sampled who may or may not have used the ITS technologies and the Island Explorer bus, and a total of 991 on-site interviews were conducted at three sites in the park and the Village Green in Bar Harbor. Following the short interview, visitors were asked to complete a mail-back questionnaire; a 74 percent response rate was attained.

STUDY FINDINGS

Awareness and Use of ITS Technologies

Visitors were asked about their awareness and use of the ITS technologies at Acadia, specifically parking information and technologies associated with the Island Explorer bus. Over half of the visitors (55 percent) who participated in the mail survey reported being aware of the parking availability information. A relatively high proportion of visitors (30 percent) planned to use this travel information. Over one-third of visitors returning mail surveys (37 percent) reported obtaining parking conditions or traffic information provided at the park visitor center, campgrounds, or website.

It should be noted that the parking availability information reflected the designated parking lots at Sand Beach and Jordan Pond only. The status of these parking lots being full did not necessarily restrict visitors from gaining access to these attractions. Visitors could park along the two-lane one-way section of the Park Loop Road and walk to Sand Beach. Visitors also could park along the Park Loop Road and boat access road to gain access to Jordan Pond House. Direct observation of the parking conditions at these locations indicated this was a common practice for visitors when parking lots were full. Some visitors may have realized that these areas were still accessible by privately owned vehicles and, despite knowing that the parking lots were full, did not feel compelled to act on this information.

Nearly half of visitors (49 percent) who participated in the mail survey were aware of the electronic bus-departure signs and more than half of these visitors (28 percent) planned to use this travel technology. Slightly fewer visitors (40 percent) were aware of the Island Explorer automated annunciators, but more (34 percent) planned to use this type of travel information on their visit. Approximately half of visitors reported using the Island Explorer bus during their most recent visit. Caution should be used in projecting the results of awareness and use of ITS technologies to park visitors in general. Answers reflect visitors sampled at many locations providing one or more of the ITS technologies. For example, most visitors contacted on the Island Explorer buses would have been exposed automatically to the automated annunciator.

Visitor Satisfaction with ITS

The survey revealed a high level of satisfaction with the ITS technologies. The vast majority of respondents reported that they found the information provided by the ITS technologies to be accurate and helpful. For example, 93 percent of respondents reported that they could clearly understand the parking and traffic information and nearly all visitors (91 percent) rated the parking information as easy to use. Most visitors (62 percent) thought that the information on parking conditions helped to relieve tension and stress related to travel, and 81 percent believed that using the information in the future would be "a pleasant experience."

Impact of ITS on Mobility

Visitors were asked to assess the impact of ITS technologies on various aspects of mobility, including avoidance of parking problems, traffic congestion, and large crowds; ease of getting around the area; saving time; and changing the time or destination of travel. ITS generally was attributed by users with enhancing their mobility. A relatively high proportion of visitors thought that the real-time parking information helped them avoid parking problems and traffic congestion.

About half of respondents (47 percent) thought the real-time parking information helped to avoid large crowds. However, the most frequently reported response (41 percent) was "neutral." As noted earlier, parking-condition information was given for two of the most popular destinations in the park, Sand Beach and Jordan Pond House. However, there are several other very popular destinations in the park such as Cadillac Mountain. Visitors may have experienced large crowds at other destinations regardless of the status of parking conditions reported at Sand Beach and Jordan Pond House. Of course, with tour busses common at some of the park's destinations, visitors may have experienced crowding at times when traffic or parking was not perceived as a problem.

The mobility of visitors who used the Island Explorer bus and travel-related information during their visit was assessed by asking if the ITS-based information made it easier to get around. A very high percentage of bus users (90 percent) agreed that the real-time bus-departure displays made it easier for them to get around the area. Likewise, a high proportion of bus users (84 percent) agreed that the bus announcements made it easier for them to get around the area.

Enabling visitors to save time based on traveler information was another way in which mobility was assessed. The majority of ITS users agreed that they saved time with the travel information they used, but there was less certainty about the time-saving benefit of the parking information and the on-board bus announcements compared to the real-time bus-departure signs.

Providing visitors enhanced mobility can be achieved by enabling them to make changes to their daily trip planning so they can avoid travel problems. Users of real-time parking information were asked about the impact of this information on their departure times or destinations of travel. Nearly half of respondents (43 percent) reported that they changed the time of day they visited an attraction based upon the real-time parking information. Some visitors (38 percent) changed their minds on what attractions to visit based upon the real-time parking information. These results indicate that a sizable proportion of visitors appeared to take advantage of the parking information to select what destinations to visit and when.

Impact on Visitor Use of the Island Explorer

An important goal of the ITS technologies was to encourage visitors to use the Island Explorer and thereby reduce their use of personal vehicles. Study findings suggest that nearly half (44 percent) of visitors who reported using real-time parking information agreed that the information helped them decide to use the Island Explorer bus. A large majority (80 percent) of visitors who reported using the bus and traveler information reported that the real-time bus-departure displays helped them decide to use the Island Explorer bus. Most visitors (67 percent) who reported using the bus and traveler information reported that the bus on-board announcements helped them decide to use the Island Explorer bus. ITS appears to have been influential in making public transit a comfortable choice as an alternative to use of private vehicles.

Impact of ITS on the Local Economy

An expected benefit of the ITS technologies was that it would contribute to economic vitality in the region, specifically, that the enhanced experience and increased mobility would contribute to longer visitor stays. Based on visitor self-reports of their use of ITS technologies, participants were divided into four groups: (1) visitors who used the traveler information for Island Explorer buses such as the real-time departure of buses but not the availability of parking at Sand Beach and Jordan Pond House (n=273); (2) visitors who used both traveler information related to the Island Explorer buses as well as the availability of parking ($n = 182$); (3) visitors who used parking-availability information but no bus-traveler information ($n = 175$); and (4) visitors who used neither the parking-availability information nor the Island Explorer bus ($n = 279$). Respondents' answers to batteries of questions about length of stay and level of spending during their visit provided a means of assessing the economic implications of ITS.

While the highest proportion of visitors, regardless of visitor group type, stayed in the Acadia/MDI area three to four days, ITS users who used the Island Explorer bus or the bus and parking information reported longer stays than the ITS users of parking information and ITS non-users. More than half of the ITS bus users (58 percent) and 50 percent of ITS users of the bus and parking information reported staying five or more days. In contrast, fewer than half of the ITS users of parking information and ITS non-users reported staying five or more days (44 and 43 percent, respectively). However, the ITS bus user group had the higher mean length of stay (7.2 days) and this was significantly higher than the mean length of stay for ITS parking user group (4.4 days) and ITS non-user group (4.9 days). Thus, the results suggest that there is a correlation between ITS and economic impact as measured by length of stay. ITS users tended to stay longer than non-users, and might be expected to spend more money and have a greater economic impact as a result. In particular, users of the ITS technologies associated with the Island Explorer stayed longer on average than any other ITS users and non-users.

Questions on visitor spending asked respondents to report the amount of money spent on restaurants, purchases such as film, souvenirs, tickets, admissions, tours, rentals, and other tourist-type expenses. Visitors were asked specifically to exclude costs associated with hotels or rental cars so that the data would be generally comparable and not simply reflect large discrepancies in costs between, for example, camping and resort hotels. The highest proportion of visitors, regardless of visitor group type, spent over $500. However, based upon the length of stay reported above for each visitor group, it is not surprising that expenditures were higher for the ITS bus users who used either the bus information alone or the bus and parking information. Over half of the ITS bus users (58 percent) and 55 percent of ITS users of bus and parking information reported spending over $300 during their visit. In contrast, fewer than half of the ITS users of parking information alone and ITS non-users reported spending over $300 during their visit (44 and 46 percent, respectively).

Caution should be exercised in drawing conclusions about the relationship between the use of the ITS traveler information and reported increased length of stay and money spent. On one hand, study data may reflect visitor use of the Island Explorer bus independent of the traveler information. An earlier study of Island Explorer bus passengers (Daigle and Lee 2000) reported similar length of stays compared to general visitors as found in previous studies (Littlejohn 1999). Although money spent was not asked in the 1999 study, it is reasonable to assume that Island Explorer bus passengers would have reported higher amounts of money spent during their visit as compared to visitors in general who reported shorter stays. On the other hand, economic impact may reflect visitor use of the Island Explorer bus related to the ITS traveler information. As noted earlier in this chapter, visitors tended to have a positive experience with the ITS technologies, which in turn helped them to decide to use the Island Explorer. Therefore, to the extent that ITS enhances the experience of visitors using the Island Explorer, and the bus system tends to draw higher-spending visitors, ITS can be seen to have a positive economic impact on the region. Finally, the findings reported above should be viewed in terms of results being correlated and not necessarily as causative. That is, there is no direct evidence that the ITS technologies caused visitors to stay longer and to spend more money. It is possible that those who used ITS more extensively were less familiar with the park and had intended to stay longer than a more "local" visitor. Further research and more direct questioning is warranted to support the positive relationship of ITS with economic impact.

CONCLUSIONS

Study findings are based on one season of ITS deployment. They also are based on a deployment that was not yet fully realized, because not all of the technologies were in place by the summer of 2002. For example, the automated equipment for recording and transmission of the number of vehicles entering and exiting the park and at popular parking areas was unavailable. Nevertheless, the findings lead to a number of conclusions about the benefits of ITS to visitors, the park, and the community of MDI.

The vast majority of visitors (86 percent or more) rated the ITS traveler-information sources very highly on attributes of accuracy, ease of use, and understandability, and reported that the information helped to relieve the stress or uncertainty of travel. The vast majority of users (78 percent or more) believed that using the same ITS information again in a future visit would be a pleasant experience. Particularly promising are reports from ITS users that they plan to use the information again.

The primary benefit of the real-time parking information was that it made it easier for visitors to get around and avoid parking problems and traffic congestion. Parking information influenced when a visit to an attraction was made and what attractions were visited. Moreover, visitors may have used the parking information to see that space existed at a parking lot and, therefore, did not need to change their plans. Study findings suggest that the ability of ITS to influence travel decisions makes it a useful tool for park management.

While awareness of ITS is an essential first step, the survey of visitors revealed that it didn't necessarily translate into use of ITS. The vast majority of visitors contacted on-board Island Explorer buses who reported being aware of one or more of the ITS technologies reported that they used the traveler information. However, only a slight majority of visitors contacted at other locations who reported being aware of one or more of the ITS technologies reported using the traveler information. For example, over half of visitors (55 percent) reported being aware of the information on parking availability, but only 30 percent of visitors reported planning to use the information. The status of parking lots being full did not necessarily restrict visitors from gaining access to these attractions. Some visitors may have realized that these areas were still accessible by privately owned vehicles and, despite knowing the condition of the parking lots, did not plan to use the information. However, if a parking policy were to be implemented to restrict cars from parking outside of designated parking lots, especially at Jordan Pond House, visitors may be more likely to use the parking-availability information. Moreover, heavier promotion of the parking-information and encouraging visitors to act on alternatives might result in greater usage than reported in this study.

Important goals of the ITS technologies were to enhance the visitor experience and to encourage visitors to use the Island Explorer bus. Alleviating visitor travel concerns is seen as important in influencing people's decision to use public transit (Stemerding et al. 1995). ITS technologies appear to be contributing to the overall goal of diverting visitors from personal vehicles to using the Island Explorer bus. ITS technologies make the Island Explorer more attractive to visitors, thereby helping to relieve congestion, parking problems, and improving air quality.

More research is needed in order to understand the benefits and costs associated with visitor use of ITS technologies and alternative transportation modes in national parks and related areas. The reasons why visitors choose to use ITS technologies are not self-evident, and the choice may be closely related to the benefits people derive from using this type of information. Overall, this study demonstrates that visitors who use ITS technologies realize multiple benefits and the technologies contribute to the quality of the park experience.

26 An Experiment in Park Traffic Patterns on the Acadia National Park Loop Road

How many times have you heard it said that there aren't too many people in the national parks, but too many cars? Traffic congestion has become a perennial problem in the parks. There are a number of potential solutions to the problem, including use limits, automobile entrance or parking fees, and public transit systems.

Among the simplest of solutions is creating one-way traffic patterns. Redesignating two-way streets to one-way has been a standard practice of traffic engineers in urban areas for decades. It is well accepted that one-way roads can accommodate heavier traffic flows. But park management is more than engineering. How do one-way roads affect visitors and "the park experience"? For example, do one-way traffic patterns inconvenience visitors to an unacceptable degree? Or, do one-way roads ease congestion enough to allow more attention to be devoted to enjoying the park? It was decided to conduct an experiment to find out the answers to these and related questions.

STUDY METHODS

The experiment was conducted at Acadia. Acadia's popularity, combined with its relatively small size, can result in traffic congestion. This is especially the case along the Park Loop Road, a 20-mile roughly oval roadway constructed by the NPS to connect many of the prime scenic attractions in the park. Many years ago, the NPS designated about half of the Park Loop Road as one-way to ease congestion and improve traffic safety conditions. Recently, the NPS proposed changing the remainder of the road from two-

This chapter is an edited version of the following paper: Robert Manning, "An Experiment in Park Traffic Patterns," *Parks and Recreation* 24 (1989): 6–7, 64.

way to one-way travel (an approximately one-half mile section of the road connecting to the spur road on Cadillac Mountain would remain two-way under this proposal).

The experiment involved a test implementation of the proposed road changes. During one week in August, the proposed road changes were put into effect. During the following week, the road system was returned to its normal traffic pattern. During both weeks, road users were surveyed about their reaction to the road system. Variables addressed in the questionnaire included visitor perceptions of traffic congestion and safety, enjoyment and appreciation of the park, and attitudes about the proposed traffic changes. Sampling was conducted each day over the two-week period from 7:00 a.m. to 7:00 p.m., interviewing 858 motorists and 184 bicyclists.

STUDY FINDINGS

The vast majority of both motorists and cyclists were visitors to the park and not residents of MDI. Moreover, the percentage of residents using the Park Loop Road did not decline to a statistically significant degree when the traffic pattern was changed to one-way. This is important because some of the concern over the proposed road changes involved residents of MDI. Residents of communities on MDI sometimes use portions of the Park Loop Road for business or other travel around the island.

Some residents felt that the proposed road changes would inconvenience them to the extent that it no longer would be feasible to use the Park Loop Road for such travel. Results from the experiment indicate that this may be true only to a very limited extent. The percentage of MDI residents using the road under one-way conditions declined approximately 5 percent, but this was not a statistically significant change. Some residents who use the road for purely business or other nonrecreational purposes may have shifted to other non-park roads due to the experimental one-way traffic pattern. But many residents use the Park Loop Road for recreational purposes and this use apparently is unaffected by the proposed road changes.

Visitors were stopped and administered the study questionnaire at the point where they had just finished traveling the section of road affected by the proposed one-way change. They were asked to consider the questions as they applied to the section of road they had just traveled. Results show that the one-way traffic pattern substantially enhances the quality of the park experience for visitors. Motorists, for example, evaluated traffic congestion and safety conditions as better, to a statistically significant degree, under the one-way traffic pattern as opposed to the normal two-way pattern. They also felt that their ability to stop, park, and view the scenery was enhanced with the one-way traffic flow. And, in fact, motorists did report stopping more often to enjoy the park under one-way road conditions.

The same relationship held with other evaluation variables, including ability to relax and enjoy the park, problems in getting "caught" or "stuck" behind very slow-moving vehicles, sharing the road with bicyclists, pleasantness of trip, and attractiveness of the affected section of Park Loop Road. Motorists also felt that the proposed change in the road inconvenienced them less, as they actually experienced this change, rather than having it explained to them in a hypothetical way.

The only two variables not rated more favorably by motorists in the one-way experiment were problems in sharing the road with hikers or people walking and the attractiveness of the road overall. However, responses to these two variables were so uniformly high for the sample as a whole that statistically significant differences between subsamples would be difficult to detect.

Bicyclists' evaluations of Park Loop Road conditions were similar to those of motorists. Bicyclists who travelled the road under one-way conditions rated their experience as significantly better on five of the evaluation items than did those who travelled the road under the two-way traffic pattern. The five evaluation items were traffic congestion; safety conditions; ability to stop, park, and view the scenery; ability to relax and enjoy the park; and problems in sharing the road with automobiles.

CONCLUSIONS

Several conclusions can be drawn from this study. First, one-way traffic patterns can enhance the quality of the visitor experience substantially. Under the one-way traffic pattern, visitors to Acadia felt less congested and perceived traffic conditions as safer. Visitors were less likely to experience the frustration of getting "stuck" behind very slow-moving vehicles and fewer conflicts arose between motorists and bicyclists. And visitors were able to stop and enjoy the park more often and more intensely. In other words, the one-way traffic pattern reduced the distraction of automobile traffic and allowed visitors to place more attention on enjoying the park.

Second, visitor impressions of one-way traffic patterns seem to improve markedly as they actually experience these conditions. Although most visitors favored the one-way traffic pattern as it was described to them, their favorability rating increased substantially as they drove the Park Loop Road in its proposed one-way pattern. Visitors also found the one-way traffic pattern to be less inconvenient than they originally had thought. Experiments like this may give more accurate readings of visitor feelings toward proposed park changes.

Finally, one-way traffic patterns may cause some inconvenience to local residents. Residents of MDI viewed the proposed road changes less favorably than did park visitors. However, use of the road by residents did not decrease significantly during the one-way experiment. Moreover, resident use of the road constitutes a small minority of all traffic carried by the road. Some inconvenience caused to local residents may be a small price to pay for a substantial enhancement in the quality of the visitor experience. This is especially so considering the underlying purpose of the Park Loop Road and national parks more broadly.

Based on this study, it is recommended that serious consideration be given to one-way traffic patterns in parks where such patterns are feasible. One-way traffic patterns can not only reduce traffic congestion from an engineering standpoint, but can also substantially enhance the quality of the park experience.

Conclusion
Managing Parks and People

The preceding chapters present a wide-ranging program of research designed to support management of outdoor recreation at Acadia. These studies address the primary geographic units of the park, including Mount Desert Island, Schoodic Peninsula, and Isle au Haut; principal visitor attractions, including the Park Loop Road and Ocean Drive, Cadillac Mountain, the carriage roads, the trail system, Sand Beach, and Jordan Pond House; major visitor activities, including sightseeing/driving for pleasure, hiking, camping, and biking; and a range of management issues, including crowding, conflict, coping, traffic congestion, parking, public transportation, impacts to park resources, and the effectiveness and acceptability of alternative management practices.

These chapters were organized into the three principal components of the National Park Service's Visitor Experience and Resource Protection (VERP) framework as described in the Introduction: (1) formulation of management objectives/desired conditions and associated indicators and standards of quality, (2) monitoring indicator variables, and (3) management actions designed to maintain standards of quality for indicator variables. However, some studies have implications for more than one of these three components. The research described in these chapters (as well as related components of research that could not be included in the book) was designed to support application of the VERP framework at Acadia and to help guide management of outdoor recreation more generally.

This research has contributed to an ongoing program of planning and management at Acadia. Initial components of research focused on the park's carriage roads and a plan for this popular and historic system of multi-use trails has been developed, adopted, and implemented (Jacobi and Manning 1997). Using findings from research, an interdisciplinary team of park staff formulated a set of crowding and conflict-oriented indicators and standards of quality for the visitor experience on two recreation opportunity zones comprising this area. Indicators of quality are monitored at regular intervals and management actions have been undertaken to help ensure that standards of quality are maintained.

Research addressing the Schoodic Peninsula, Isle au Haut, and broader MDI sections of the park has been conducted more recently and plans for these areas are now being developed. This is in keeping with NPS policy that requires all parks to have General Management Plans, and recent changes in this policy that require such plans to adopt central elements of the VERP framework, including formulation of indicators and standards of quality.

Of course, similar research has been conducted at a number of other parks and related areas, and all of this work has contributed to a substantive and growing body of knowledge about parks and people, including the impacts that visitors can cause to park resources and the quality of the visitor experience and how outdoor recreation might best be managed (Hammitt and Cole 1998; Manning 1999, 2007). This body of knowledge can be organized and presented in a series of emerging principles that can be used to guide planning and management of outdoor recreation at Acadia and related parks and outdoor recreation areas. This final chapter presents these principles and illustrates how they might be applied using examples from the program of research at Acadia.

PRINCIPLES OF MANAGING OUTDOOR RECREATION

1. Outdoor recreation management should be guided by a three-fold framework of resource, social, and managerial concerns. Visitor use of parks and protected areas can impact vital natural and cultural resources, can degrade the quality of the visitor experience, and can lead to management practices that are inappropriate in type and intensity. Moreover, potentially important linkages exist among these components of outdoor recreation management. For example, visitor-caused impacts to natural resources can have aesthetic implications that degrade the quality of the visitor experience and lead to management practices that are unacceptable to some visitors. Comprehensive analysis and management of outdoor recreation requires explicit consideration of its resource, social, and managerial components.

The program of research at Acadia illustrates this three-fold framework of concerns in several ways. It's clear that visitor use of Acadia results in associated impacts to (1) park resources (e.g., widening and erosion of park trails, trampling of soils and vegetation at campsites and the summit of Cadillac Mountain), (2) the quality of the visitor experience (e.g., crowding at attraction sites and along trails and the carriage roads, automobile traffic congestion, lack of parking, conflict among visitor groups), and (3) park management (e.g., the need for more direct and intensive management practices, the acceptability and effectiveness of a range of management alternatives). These issues ultimately must be addressed in the form of management objectives and desired conditions and associated indicators and standards of quality that range across the three-fold framework (this is discussed more fully under Principle 6).

The potential linkages among these components are also evident. For example, visitors can impact soil and vegetation along park trails leading to trail widening and deepening and exposure of rocks and roots. These issues constitute potentially important impacts to park resources, but also can degrade the quality of the visitor experience through their aesthetic implications and the degree to which they make trails rougher and hiking more challenging. Resource impacts to trails often can be managed by various forms of site management (e.g., surfacing trails) and by encouraging or even requiring visitors to stay on formal trails, but these management practices themselves can alter the type and quality of the visitor experience in inappropriate and unacceptable ways.

The stated preference and verbal protocol methods adopted in several studies are additional manifestations of the multiple and interrelated components of outdoor recreation management. In these studies, visitors were asked implicitly and explicitly to consider and make tradeoffs among selected resource, experiential, and managerial components of outdoor recreation management. All three of these components were judged as important, but relative importance varied by study context (e.g., level of use and development), and many respondents were conscious of the inherent tension and tradeoffs among these issues.

2. Outdoor recreation management should be considered within a rational, inclusive, transparent, and traceable framework. Analysis and management of outdoor recreation can be complex and even contentious. It involves consideration of resource, social, and managerial components; relies on scientific information, social values and norms, and management judgment; and ultimately balances the inherent tension between providing public access to parks and protecting park resources and the quality of the visitor experience. A structured framework should be used to help guide the inherent complexity of analyzing and managing outdoor recreation, and this framework should be rational and internally consistent, as open and transparent as possible, and fully traceable to stakeholders. VERP is an example of this type of framework and is used widely throughout the national parks and related areas. Similar management frameworks are used in other places by other agencies and organizations.

VERP is being used to guide analysis and management of outdoor recreation at Acadia, and the program of research outlined in this book was designed to help inform this process. Management of outdoor recreation at Acadia (and elsewhere) can be challenging, especially when considering carrying capacity-related issues and the inherent tension between public use and protection of park resources and the quality of the visitor experience. The VERP framework provides a systematic and rational process within which to make such management decisions through a series of linked steps: (1) formulation of management objectives/desired conditions and associated indicators and standards of quality, (2) monitoring indicator variables, and (3) application of management practices designed to maintain standards of quality. This framework helps to ensure that an underlying logic and internal consistency is applied in outdoor recreation management. Moreover, the program of natural and social science research designed to support application of VERP helps inform the process by determining existing resource and social conditions, identifying management issues and potential indicators and standards of quality, developing and applying monitoring protocols, and testing the acceptability and effectiveness of management actions.

Application of VERP and the associated programs of research at Acadia were designed to be inclusive by offering opportunities for participation by major stakeholders. In particular, the program of research directly involved a range of park visitors (including current and "displaced" visitors, visitors participating in multiple and sometimes conflicting activities, visitors at peak and off-peak locations and times), residents of neighboring towns, and the business community.

This program of research and management under guidance of the VERP framework is resulting in a traceable "record of decision" at Acadia that can be used to explain and support management. Experience with the park's carriage roads offers a good example. Based on the park's program of planning and associated research, a plan for the carriage roads was prepared that identifies management objectives and associated indicators and standards of quality that are being applied at this area. A long-term program of monitoring is being conducted on crowding and conflict-related indicators, and management practices are being applied to help ensure that standards of quality are being maintained.

3. Outdoor recreation management should focus on the impacts of visitor use, management objectives/ desired conditions, and associated indicators and standards of quality. Early studies of outdoor recreation management, and carrying capacity in particular, focused on the relationships between visitor use and resulting impacts as illustrated in figure C.1. It was thought that the maximum acceptable level of visitor use (as represented on the X axis of this figure) could be determined inherently from these relationships. However, it became apparent that this could not be determined without appropriate consideration of the limits of acceptable change on impacts and desired conditions of park resources and the type and quality of the visitor experience (as represented on the Y axis of figure C.1). If the limits of acceptable change (as informed by desired conditions) are set as represented by point Y_1, then the maximum acceptable level of visitor use is represented by point X_1. But if the limits of acceptable change are set at the point Y_2 (or any other point along the Y axis), then the maximum acceptable level of visitor use is represented by some other point along the X axis. Management objectives/ desired conditions and associated indicators and standards of quality ultimately must guide decisions about the types and levels of visitor use that can be accommodated in parks and related areas.

Undue focus on maximum acceptable use levels tends to confuse management practices with management objectives. Establishing a maximum level of visitor use (i.e., limiting visitor use) is a management practice, not a management objective. In cases where no strong and direct relationships exist between amount of visitor use and visitor-caused impacts (such as when impact is more related to visitor behavior than number of visitors), limits on visitor use levels may be ineffective in achieving management objectives

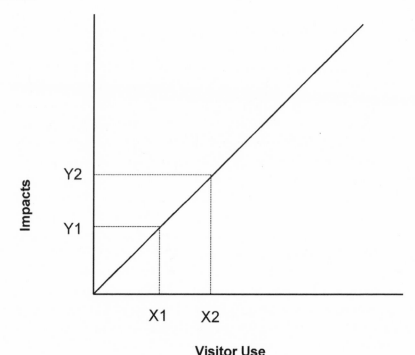

Visitor Use

Figure C.1 *Relationship between visitor use and impacts.*

or desired conditions. An important exception to this reasoning may be when visitor use level is the impact under consideration (as it often is with concern over crowding).

The program of natural and social science research at Acadia was useful in identifying a range of impacts of outdoor recreation and related issues and helping to formulate associated indicators and standards of quality that could guide outdoor recreation management. Natural science and related research methods inventoried and assessed resource conditions and found that visitor use was creating substantive impacts in the form of trampling of fragile vegetation, damage to trees, and soil compaction and erosion along park trails, at campsites, and at attraction sites such as at the summit of Cadillac Mountain. Social science research also identified a range of visitor-caused impacts to the quality of the park experience, including crowding at attraction sites and along trails and the carriage roads, traffic congestion on the Park Loop Road, lack of parking at attraction sites, conflict between visitor groups, degradation of scenic quality caused by resource impacts, and unacceptable management practices. This program of research also supported formulation of a series of indicators and standards of quality that can be used to guide management of these issues.

In some cases, visitor-caused impacts were found to be associated more strongly with type of visitor use or other issues rather than amount of visitor use. For example, conflict between visitor activities (hiking and biking) on the carriage roads is related to visitor behavior, including riding bicycles too fast, bicycles passing hikers from behind without warning, walking abreast thereby blocking passage of bicycles, and dogs off-leash. Likewise, unwarranted impacts to soils and vegetation along trails and on the summit of Cadillac Mountain are caused by visitors walking off designated trails. In these cases, management practices were designed to modify visitor behavior rather than impose limits on visitor use levels.

However, in other cases the amount of visitor use is strongly related to problem issues such as multiple forms of crowding and congestion. In these cases, limits on visitor use ultimately may be needed. However, there may be important exceptions to this case. For example, the number of cars on the Park Loop Road and elsewhere in the park is a primary cause of traffic congestion and lack of parking. But one-way traffic patterns and encouraging visitor use of the Island Explorer shuttle bus may be effective approaches to managing these types of crowding-related problems.

4. Outdoor recreation management has descriptive and prescriptive components.
As illustrated in figure C.1, the relationships between visitor use and associated impacts constitute an important part of the descriptive component of outdoor recreation management: they are factual, objective, and scientifically derived. However, there is also an important prescriptive component that is more subjective and involves decisions about management objectives/desired conditions, the maximum acceptable level of impacts to park resources and the quality of the visitor experience, and the indicators and standards of quality that should guide outdoor recreation management. This prescriptive component requires some element of management judgment, but this judgment should be as "informed" as possible.

The program of research at Acadia includes both descriptive and prescriptive elements. Baseline data on resource and social conditions in the park constitute the most fundamental form of descriptive information. Examples are wide-ranging and include measures of soil and vegetation conditions along trails, at campsites and attraction sites; visitor use levels and activity patterns; and visitor perceptions of resource and experiential impacts of increasing outdoor recreation. This type of information is vital as a foundation for park planning and management. Resulting data can be used to determine relationships between level and type of visitor use and resulting resource and social impacts. For example, a positive and generally linear relationship has been found between amount of use on the trails of Isle au Haut and resulting trail impacts. Similarly, the computer simulation model of vehicle use on Ocean Drive illustrates the way in which vehicles-per-viewscape rise with increasing traffic levels.

While these types of descriptive information are important in informing park management, more prescriptive information is also needed to help assess limits of acceptable change and ultimately formulate standards of quality. Normative and related types of research were used at Acadia to support the prescriptive component of park management. For example, visitors and other stakeholders were asked to render judgments about the acceptability of a range of resource, social, and managerial conditions, including impacts to trails and campsites, crowding along trails and at attraction sites, and type and intensity of management practices. These "social norms" can help inform management judgments about appropriate limits of acceptable change and associated indicators and standards of quality.

5. Outdoor recreation management requires decisions about the "limits of acceptable change." Research on outdoor recreation demonstrates that visitor-caused impacts can occur quickly even under relatively low levels of use. For example, much of the ecological impact at wilderness campsites tends to happen within the first few years of use, even when use levels are relatively low (Hammitt and Cole 1998). Moreover, many wilderness visitors prefer to camp out of sight and sound of other visitors, so crowding also can occur under relatively low levels of use (Manning 1999). This research suggests that it is not practical to adopt management objectives/desired conditions in such a way as to suggest that no visitor-caused impacts will be permitted, at least not at parks where substantial public use is allowed. From a practical standpoint, the operative decision is usually not whether visitor-caused impacts will be allowed, but what the acceptable level of impacts will be (Stankey et al. 1985).

Research at Acadia documents a number of recreation-related impacts, including degradation of park resources and reduction of the quality of the visitor experience. Examples include trampling of vegetation, soil compaction and erosion, damage to trees, crowding and congestion, and conflicting uses. Moreover, these impacts are found even in the relatively low-use portions of the park such as Isle au Haut, the Schoodic Peninsula, low-use areas on MDI, and during off-peak periods. Several studies documented the generally positive relationship between use and impact. Examples include (1) increasing levels of trail impacts at Isle au Haut associated with higher numbers of hikers, (2) increasing numbers of visual encounters among groups of hikers and bikers on the carriage roads and vehicles on Ocean Drive as use levels rise, (3) declining levels of acceptability and associated measures of the quality of the visitor experience with increasing levels of social and environmental impacts as illustrated in the social norm curves derived from several studies, and (4) the declining acceptability of increasingly direct and regulatory management practices. These impacts and relationships suggest that management decisions must be rendered on the maximum acceptable level of such impacts and the associated changes they cause to the resource, social, and managerial components of the park.

6. Outdoor recreation management should be guided by management objectives/ desired conditions and associated indicators and standards of quality. As noted above, management objectives/desired conditions are needed to guide analysis and management of outdoor recreation, including decisions about the levels and types of visitor use that can be accommodated appropriately in parks and related areas. Management objectives/desired conditions should be developed for resource, social, and managerial conditions. Without guidance of management objectives/desired conditions, decisions about outdoor recreation management appear (and probably are) arbitrary and uninformed. Management objectives/desired conditions often are expressed in a broadly conceptual form (e.g., maintain "natural environments," provide "opportunities for solitude"). They provide essential direction for analysis and management of outdoor recreation, but they ultimately must be stated in quantifiable terms that can be used to measure management success (or failure). Indicators of quality are measurable, manageable variables that are used as proxies for management objectives/desired conditions. Standards of quality define the minimum acceptable condition of indicator variables.

Much of the research at Acadia was designed to help guide formulation of management objectives/desired conditions and associated indicators and standards of quality. For example, assessment of resource conditions associated with recreation use identified several types of impacts, such as loss of groundcover vegetation, soil compaction and erosion, and creation of social or visitor-caused trails, that can be used as indicator variables. Moreover, surveys of visitors, community residents, and the business community identified a number of potential indicators of the quality of the visitor experience, including the resource impacts noted above, multiple manifestations of crowding and congestion (including people-per-viewscape on the carriage roads, people-at-one-time at attraction sites, vehicles-per-viewscape on park roads, encounters with other groups along trails), conflicting uses, and the level and type of management practices designed to mitigate these impacts. This research also identified where and when these indicators are most relevant.

A companion program of research was directed at guiding formulation of standards of quality for these indicator variables. In some cases, inflection points inherent in the relationships between recreation use and associated impacts can help isolate appropriate standards of quality (or limits of acceptable change as described in Principle 5). However, standards often can be guided by societal values and related social norms, and this is addressed in Principle 7.

7. Outdoor recreation management is more normative than deterministic. Early exploration of outdoor recreation was based on an assumption that there were inherent thresholds of resource impacts that would determine the maximum acceptable level of visitor use (Wagar 1964). However, more-contemporary analysis suggests that an important societal component of carrying capacity is manifested in social values and related norms. Visitors and other stakeholders often have normative standards for the resource, social, and managerial conditions in parks and related areas, and these normative judgments can be used to help formulate indicators and standards of quality to guide analysis and management of outdoor recreation. Social norms have been measured for the resource, social, and managerial components of outdoor recreation (Shelby and Heberlein 1986; Vaske et al. 1986; Whittaker and Shelby 1988; Shelby, Bregenzer, and Johnson 1988; Patterson and Hammitt 1990; Williams et al. 1991; Vaske, Donnelly, and Petruzzi 1996; Manning, Lime, and Hof 1996a; Manning, Lime, et al. 1996; Manning 1997b; Manning, Valliere, Ballinger, et al. 1998a; Jacobi and Manning 1999).

Research at Acadia placed a considerable emphasis on guiding formulation of standards of quality for a number of indicator variables. This research relied heavily on the personal and social norms of several stakeholder groups, including visitors and community residents. In this approach, survey respondents were asked to judge the acceptability of a range of visitor-caused impacts to resource, social, and managerial conditions in selected areas of the park. The personal norms of individuals were aggregated to examine social norms of various types of respondents as defined by recreation activity, park location, and time period. Several question formats and "evaluative dimensions" ("preference," "acceptability," "management action," and "displacement") were incorporated into these studies, resulting in a range of potential standards. Where appropriate, visual simulations were used to enhance the clarity of questions. Several studies also incorporated questions that asked respondents to make tradeoffs between the park conditions they wished to maintain and desired public access. Study findings help provide an empirical basis for formulating standards of quality and addressing the closely related normative issues of the prescriptive component of park and outdoor recreation and defining the limits of acceptable change as described in Principles 4 and 5, respectively.

8. Outdoor recreation management requires a long-term commitment to monitoring. Outdoor recreation management frameworks such as VERP rely on an explicit program of monitoring indicator variables. This is a long-term commitment for the duration of the planning/management horizon (although monitoring usually is conducted only periodically during this time period). Findings from the monitoring program suggest the extent to which standards of quality are being maintained (and therefore whether carrying capacity has been exceeded), the success (or failure) of management practices, and whether levels and types of visitor use need to be adjusted.

Research at Acadia has helped advance a program of monitoring that is focused on managing outdoor recreation. This research has helped demonstrate the potential usefulness of a range of monitoring techniques, including direct observation and measurement by field and research staff, automatic traffic counters, remote sensing, visitor surveys, and computer simulation modeling. For some indicators of quality, such as crowding and congestion, computer simulation modeling can be used to estimate the maximum number of visitors that can be accommodated without violating standards of quality, and this might constitute a form of "proactive" monitoring (Lawson, Manning, et al. 2003). A long-term program of monitoring has been designed and implemented at Acadia, and experience suggests that (1) the number of indicator variables incorporated in park and outdoor recreation management should be kept to a minimum to help ensure the feasibility of monitoring, (2) indicators that are relatively easy to monitor should be selected, and (3) indicators that are "synthetic"—that are proxies for more than one management objective/desired condition—are especially useful.

9. Outdoor recreation management should consider a broad range of management practices. It was noted in Principle 3 that limits on the number of visits to parks and related areas is more appropriately considered a management practice than a management objective. That is, it is a means to an end (maintaining management objectives/desired conditions and standards of quality for associated indicator variables) rather than an end in itself. Use limits are only one of many potential management practices, and all of these alternatives should be considered when analyzing and managing outdoor recreation. Management practices can be classified on the basis of strategic purpose (e.g., limit demand, increase supply, reduce impacts by changing visitor behavior, and "hardening" park resources) (Manning 1979) and their "direct" or "indirect" nature (Gilbert et al. 1972; Lime 1977a; Peterson and Lime 1979). Decisions about the most appropriate management practices to apply should be based on the type of park and outdoor recreation opportunity, the character of the impacts to be managed, the potential effectiveness of alternative management practices, and the acceptability of management practices to visitors and other stakeholders. Use limits often are considered to be an undesirable management practice because they inherently deny public access to parks and outdoor recreation areas and this runs counter to one of the basic mandates of most parks and related areas.

The program of research at Acadia is suggestive of the spectrum of management practices that can be applied to outdoor recreation. Management practices addressed include the strategies of hardening park resources through proper location, design, and maintenance of facilities such as trails and campsites, reducing the resource and social impacts of visitor use through information/education and rules and regulations, and imposing limits on use when and where necessary. Within these broad strategies, a spectrum of direct and indirect management practices are considered, applied, and tested. Study findings help guide management by indicating the relative effectiveness of management practices in maintaining standards of quality and the degree to which these management practices are acceptable to visitors and other stakeholders in a range of park and outdoor recreation contexts. Suites of reinforcing management practices designed to present a unified message to visitors may be especially powerful in minimizing impacts, and intensive visitor use may require concomitant intensive management.

10. Outdoor recreation management is a form of adaptive management. Adaptive management has emerged as important concept in contemporary environmental management (Lee 1993; Stankey, Clark, and Bormann 2005). Adaptive management advocates proactive decisionmaking based on the best information available, but then revising and refining management as new information becomes available. Embedded in adaptive management is the notion of monitoring environmental and associated social conditions to help judge the effectiveness of management practices and adjusting management accordingly. In this way, outdoor recreation management is less of a linear process and more of an iterative, evolving framework for decisionmaking.

Research at Acadia supports the fundamentally adaptive nature of outdoor recreation management. The descriptive and prescriptive information developed in these studies helps guide formulation of management objectives/desired conditions and associated indicators and standards of quality (this is described more fully in Principle 12). Monitoring helps determine the extent to which standards of quality are being maintained, the need for management actions, and the effectiveness of these management practices.

11. Outdoor recreation management should be applied within a "recreation opportunity spectrum" framework. Management of outdoor recreation usually is conducted at the park or even site level. However, such management should be considered within a more contextual perspective, taking into account the role of specific places within the greater system of parks and outdoor recreation opportunities. Public tastes in outdoor recreation (e.g., activities, norms, attitudes) can be diverse, and there should be a corresponding diversity of opportunities (Manning 1999). Moreover, high-quality visitor experiences can and should be found within all of these types of opportunities. Analysis and management of outdoor recreation, or sites within parks, should be based at least partially on the need to provide a diversity of park and outdoor recreation conditions and opportunities. The Recreation Opportunity Spectrum framework has been developed in the professional literature to help guide this analysis (Brown, Driver, and McConnell 1978; Clark and Stankey 1979; Manning 1985).

Research at Acadia supports the design and management of a diverse system of park and outdoor recreation opportunities. Empirical studies conducted at multiple locations and time periods suggest a range of indicators and standards that can be applied across the park. This ultimately is manifested by the broad-scale divisions of the park into the MDI, Schoodic Peninsula, and Isle au Haut sections of the park, representing generally increasing levels of remoteness, naturalness, and solitude. This is represented at smaller scales as well with respect to the spatial and temporal "zoning" of the carriage roads in deference to demand for competing types of recreation opportunities. The desirability of alternative types of recreation opportunities is supported explicitly in the stated-choice studies in which variations in visitor preferences are related strongly to specific sites. More generally, the social norms and related evaluative dimensions used and developed in several studies (e.g., "preference," "acceptability," "management action," and "displacement") offer a spectrum of potential standards of quality that can be used empirically to guide the design of a corresponding spectrum of opportunities. In this way, each site within the park is not an island unto itself, but part of a thoughtful and deliberative system of park and outdoor recreation opportunities. The need for such a system is evident in the diversity of park visitors and values ranging from first-time visitors who want to see the park's iconic features and who may not be observant of resource and social impacts to more experienced visitors who are especially sensitive to such impacts and who may be (and some of whom already have been) displaced from the park by increasing environmental and social impacts.

12. Outdoor recreation management requires some element of management judgment. Analysis and management of outdoor recreation can be guided in many ways, including legal mandates, agency policy, resource conditions, and social values and norms. However, all of this information ultimately must be fashioned together. In this way, management of outdoor recreation can be seen to be a blend of science and art. The science is comprised of descriptive information such as baseline conditions of visitor use levels and patterns and park resources, and the relationships between visitor use and associated impacts. The art is comprised of judgments about appropriate management objectives/desired conditions and associated indicators and standards of quality that will be used to guide outdoor recreation management. Outdoor recreation will always require some element of management judgment, but such judgments should be as "informed" as possible by science and related considerations (Manning and Lawson 2002).

The research program at Acadia was designed to support the exercise of management judgment. Studies addressed both the descriptive and the sometimes more challenging prescriptive components of outdoor recreation management. Resulting data can help guide application of contemporary park and outdoor recreation management frameworks such as VERP by empirically supporting formulation of management objectives/desired conditions and associated indicators and standards of quality, designing and implementing monitoring programs, and assessing the acceptability and efficacy of management practices designed to maintain standards of quality. Data derived from these studies must be integrated with other considerations in the planning and management process. For example, the overarching General Management Plan for the park, based on legislative directives and assessment of the park's natural and cultural resources, supports the range of contexts represented by the park's three major geographic regions (MDI, Schoodic Peninsula, and Isle au Haut) and specifies the special role of selected park sites such as the carriage roads and the especially high-quality visitor experience this area is designed to offer. There will always be an inescapable role for management judgment in assessing and synthesizing the multiple sources of information inherent in managing parks and outdoor recreation. The program of research at Acadia was designed to "inform" these types of judgments and to help move management along the continuum from art to science.

RESEARCH IMPLICATIONS

The program of research conducted at Acadia was designed to support management of outdoor recreation. However, there are potentially important implications of this work for research itself. The studies conducted at

Acadia (many components of which could not be included in this book) illustrate the range of research methods that can be applied depending on the issues under study and available expertise and funding. At the broadest level, these methods can be characterized as representing the natural and social sciences. Natural science is represented by a variety of field-oriented techniques to inventory, assess, and monitor resource conditions as affected by visitor use. Primary methods include direct observation and measurement and remote sensing. Social science is represented by a number of methods designed to inventory, assess, and monitor visitor use and users and associated experiential impacts and conditions. Specific methods vary widely and include qualitative interviews, quantitative surveys, direct counts and observations, normative research, importance-performance analysis, tradeoff analysis, visual simulations, and computer-based simulation modeling.

All of these methods can be applied in a variety of research designs, including exploratory research, descriptive studies, analytical approaches, cross-sectional designs, longitudinal studies, and experiments and associated controls. All of these research designs have potential strengths and weaknesses and can complement one another when used in comparative ways. For example, cross-sectional designs (e.g., a resource inventory or a visitor survey) can provide a detailed assessment of current conditions, while longitudinal designs (e.g., monitoring protocols applied over time) help identify trends in conditions. Simulation models can estimate current and future resource and social conditions and these estimates can be validated through on-the-ground counts and inventories and through remote sensing.

Several studies illustrate the potential benefits of integrating the natural and social sciences where appropriate. Developing relationships between resource impacts and types and levels of visitor use requires application of resource inventory and assessment and measurement of visitor use levels and behavior. Indicators and standards of quality for resource conditions can be informed by the thresholds at which park visitors and other stakeholders notice and object to selected manifestations of visitor-caused resource degradation. Surveys designed to measure such thresholds or normative standards must be informed by natural science that reveals the patterns and rates at which such impacts occur.

Many of the studies described in this book rely on a variety of social science methods and this research is designed to engage people—visitors, residents of neighboring communities, business managers, society more broadly—in the management of parks. It would be foolish to deny the importance of environmental constants and related natural science on management considerations in parks and related areas, and the first principle of park and outdoor management as outlined above reinforces this point. But such environmental constraints are often broadly ranging, and society has an important role to play in considering and ultimately determining the appropriate conditions that should be maintained in parks and related areas.

Just as natural and social science can be complementary, so too can social science methods. Qualitative methods (e.g., in-depth interviews) can be especially useful when relatively little is known about the issue under study, and resulting findings can help inform more-quantitative and generalizable methods (e.g., surveys of representative samples of visitors). Direct observations of visitor behavior can help test the validity of visitor self-reports and attitudinal surveys. Stated-choice modeling and other forms of tradeoff analysis ask park visitors and other stakeholders to reveal preferences among competing goods and services, issues that may not be addressed adequately in more descriptive surveys. Computer simulation modeling can estimate the effectiveness of alternative management practices without the need for often difficult experimental approaches.

The program of research described in this book clearly is applied in character (as opposed to basic research). Theory and methods developed in the natural and social science disciplines are borrowed and adapted by researchers and applied to help address the issues faced by park planners and managers. This is ultimately a collaborative process between scientists and managers that can help inform and guide management of parks and people.

References Cited

Abbe, D., and R. E. Manning. 2007. Wilderness day use: Patterns, impacts, and management. *International Journal of Wilderness* 13, no. 2:21–25, 38.

Adelman, B., T. Heberlein, and T. Bonnickson. 1982. Social psychological explanations for the persistence of a conflict between paddling canoeists and motorcraft users in the Boundary Waters Canoe Area. *Leisure Sciences* 5:45–61.

Alexandre, C., and W. Eleonore. 2007. Change detection for updates of vector database through region-based classification of VHR satellite data. *ISPRS Workshop on Updating Geo-spatial Databases with Imagery, 5th ISPRS Workshop on DMGISs*, August 28–29, 2007, China.

Alpert, L., and L. Herrington. 1998. An interactive information kiosk for the Adirondack Park visitor interpretive center, Newcomb, N.Y. *Proceedings of the 1997 Northeastern Recreation Research Symposium*, USDA Forest Service General Technical Report NE-241, 265–67.

Altman, I. 1975. *The environment and social behavior: Privacy, personal space, territory, crowding*. Monterey, Calif.: Brooks/Cole Publishing Company.

Anderson, D. H., and P. J. Brown. 1984. The displacement process in recreation. *Journal of Leisure Research* 16:61–73.

Anderson, D. H., and M. J. Manfredo. 1986. Visitor preferences for management actions. In *Proceedings—National Wilderness Research Conference: Current Research*, USDA Forest Service General Technical Report INT-212, 314–19.

Anderson, L., R. Manning, and W. Valliere. 2009. Indicators and standards of quality across space and time. *Proceedings of the 2008 Northeastern Recreation Research Symposium*. USDA Forest Service General Technical Report NRS-P-42, 170–76.

Anderson, M. A., M. H. Stewart, M. V. Yates, and C. P. Gerba. 1998. Modeling the impact of body-contact recreation on pathogen concentrations in a source drinking water reservoir. *Water Research* 32, no. 11:3293–3306.

Aust, M. W., J. L. Marion, and K. Kyle. 2005. *Research for the development of best management practices for minimizing horse trail impacts on the Hoosier National Forest*. Management report, U.S. Department of Agriculture, U.S. Forest Service, Final Report, Bedford, Indiana.

Bacon, J., R. Manning, S. Lawson, W. Valliere, and D. Laven. 2003. Indicators and standards of quality for the Schoodic Peninsula section of Acadia National Park. *Proceedings of the 2002 Northeastern Recreation Research Symposium.* USDA Forest Service General Technical Report NE-302, 279–85.

Baldwin, E., and W. LaPage. 2003. Visitor behaviors and resource impacts at Cadillac Mountain, Acadia National Park, Part II: Sign comparison study summer 2002. Technical Report for Acadia National Park Natural Resources Division.

Banks, J., and J. S. Carson. 1984. *Discrete-event system simulation.* Englewood Cliffs, N.J.: Prentice Hall.

Bateson, J., and M. Hui. 1992. The ecological validity of photographic slides and videotapes in simulating the service setting. *Journal of Consumer Research* 19:271–81.

Bayfield, N. G., and R. J. Lloyd. 1973. An approach to assessing the impact of use on a long distance footpath—the Pennine Way. *Recreation News Supplement* 8:11–17.

Becker, R. 1981. Displacement of recreational users between the lower St. Croix and upper Mississippi Rivers. *Journal of Environmental Management* 13:259–67.

Becker, R., B. Niemann, and W. Gates. 1981. Displacement of users within a river system: Social and environmental tradeoffs. In *Proceedings of the Second Conference on Scientific Research in the National Parks,* USDA Forest Service General Technical Report NC-63, 33–38.

Borrie, W., W. Freimund, M. Davenport, and R. Manning. 2001. Crossing methodological boundaries: Assessing visitor motivations and support for management actions at Yellowstone National Park using quantitative and qualitative research approaches. *The George Wright Forum* 18:72–84.

Boxall, P., and B. Macnab. 2000. Exploring the preferences of wildlife recreationists for features of boreal forest management: A choice experiment approach. *Canadian Journal of Forest Resources* 30:1931–41.

Bratton, S. P., M. G. Hickler, and J. H. Graves. 1979. Trail erosion patterns in Great Smoky Mountains National Park. *Environmental Management* 3:431–45.

Brewer, L., and D. Berrier. 1984. Photographic techniques for monitoring resource change at backcountry sites. USDA Forest Service General Technical Report NE-86, 13.

Brown, P., B. Driver, and C. McConnell. 1978. The opportunity spectrum concept in outdoor recreation supply inventories: Background and application. *Proceedings of the Integrated Renewable Resource Inventories Workshop,* USDA Forest Service General Technical Report RM-55, 73–84.

Brown, T., M. Richards, T. Daniel, and D. King. 1989. Recreation participation and the validity of photo-based preference judgments. *Journal of Leisure Research* 21:40–60.

Brunson, M. 1993. "Socially acceptable" forestry: What does it imply for ecosystem management? *Western Journal of Applied Forestry* 8, no. 4:116–19.

Budruk, M., and R. Manning. 2003. Crowding related norms in outdoor recreation:

U.S. versus international visitors. *Proceedings of the 2002 Northeastern Recreation Research Symposium*, 216–21.

Bullock, C., D. Elston, and N. Chalmers. 1998. An application of economic choice experiments to a traditional land use: Deer hunting and landscape change in the Scottish Highlands. *Journal of Environmental Management* 52:335–51.

Bullock, S. D., and R. Lawson. 2008. Managing the "commons" on Cadillac Mountain: A stated choice analysis of Acadia National Park visitors' preferences. *Leisure Sciences* 30, no. 1:71–86.

Burrus-Bammel, L. L., and G. Bammel. 1984. Applications of unobtrusive methods. In *Proceedings of a workshop on unobtrusive techniques to study social behavior in parks*, ed. J. D. Paine. National Park Service Southeast Regional Office, Natural Science and Research Division.

Cahill, K., J. Marion, and S. Lawson. 2007. Enhancing the interpretation of stated choice analysis through the application of a verbal protocol assessment. *Journal of Leisure Research* 39, no. 2:201–21.

———. 2008. Exploring visitor acceptability for hardening trails to sustain visitation and minimize impacts. *Journal of Sustainable Tourism* 16, no. 2:232–45.

Carmines, E., and R. Zeller. 1979. *Reliability and validity assessment*. Thousand Oaks, Calif.: Sage Publications.

Chavez, D. J. 1996. Mountain biking: Issues and actions for USDA Forest Service managers. Research Paper PSW-RP-226. Pacific Southwest Research Station, USDA Forest Service, Albany, Calif.

Christensen, H., and D. Dustin. 1989. Reaching recreationists at different levels of moral development. *Journal of Park and Recreation Administration* 7, no. 4:72–80.

Clark, R. N., J. D. Hendee, and F. L. Campbell. 1971. Values, behavior, and conflict in modern camping culture. *Journal of Leisure Research* 3:145–49.

Clark, R. N., and G. H. Stankey. 1979. The recreation opportunity spectrum: A framework for planning, management, and research. General Technical Report PNW-98. Portland, Ore.: U.S. Department of Agriculture, Forest Service, Pacific Northwest Forest and Range Experiment Station.

Coffey A., and P. Atkinson. 1996. *Making sense of qualitative data: Complimentary research strategies*. Thousand Oaks, Calif.: Sage Publications.

Cohen, J., B. Sladen, and B. Bennett. 1975. The effects of situational variables on judgments of crowding. *Sociometry* 38:278–81.

Cole, D. N. 1983. Assessing and monitoring backcountry trail conditions. USDA Forest Service Research Paper INT-303, 10 p.

———. 1989. Wilderness campsite monitoring methods: A sourcebook. General Technical Report INT-259. Ogden, Utah: USDA Forest Service, Intermountain Research Station.

———. 1990. Ecological impacts of wilderness recreation and their management. In *Wilderness management*, ed. J. C. Hendee and C. P. Dawson, 413–59. 2nd ed. Goldon, Colo.: Fulcrum Publishing.

————. 1991. Changes on trails in the Selway-Bitterroot Wilderness, Montana, 1978–89. USDA Forest Service Research Paper INT-450.

————. 1993. Wilderness recreation management. *Journal of Forestry* 91:22–24.

————. 2001. Day users in wilderness: How different are they? Research Paper RMRS-RP-31. Ogden, Utah: USDA Forest Service, Rocky Mountain Research Station.

————. 2004. Impacts of hiking and camping on soils and vegetation: A review. In *Environmental impacts of ecotourism*, ed. R. Buckley, 41–60. Cambridge, Mass.: CABI Publishing.

Cole, D. N., M. E. Petersen, and R. C. Lucas. 1987. Managing wilderness recreation use: Common problems and potential solutions. USDA Forest Service General Technical Report INT-230.

Crist, E. P. 1985. A TM tasseled cap equivalent transformation for reflectance factor data. *Remote Sensing of Environment* 17:301–6.

Daigle, J. J., and B. Lee. 2000. Passenger characteristics and experiences with the Island Explorer Bus: Summer 1999. Technical Report NPS/BSO-RNR/NRTR/00-15. Boston: Department of Interior, National Park Service, New England System Support Office.

Daigle, J. A., and C. A. Zimmerman. 2004a. Alternative transportation and travel information technologies: Monitoring parking lot conditions over three summer seasons at Acadia National Park. *Journal of Park and Recreation Administration* 22:82–103.

————. 2004b. The convergence of transportation, information technology and visitor experience at Acadia National Park. *Journal of Travel Research* 43, no. 2:151–60.

Daniel, T., and R. Boster. 1976. Measuring landscape esthetics: The scenic beauty estimation method. Research Paper RM-167. Fort Collins, Colo.: USDA Forest Service, Rocky Mountain Forest and Range Experiment Station.

Davenport, M. A., W. Borrie, W. Freimund, and R. E. Manning. 2002. Assessing the relationship between desired experiences and support for management actions at Yellowstone National Park using multiple methods. *Journal of Park and Recreation Administration* 20, no. 3:51–64.

Dennis, D. F. 1998. Analyzing public inputs on national forests using conjoint analysis. *Forest Science* 44, no. 3:421–29.

Denzen, N. K. 1970. *Sociological methods: A sourcebook.* 2nd ed. New York: McGraw-Hill.

Denzen, N. K., and Y. S. Lincoln. 1994. Handbook of qualitative research. Thousand Oaks, Calif.: Sage Publications.

Desor, J. 1972. Toward a psychological theory of crowding. *Journal of Personality and Social Psychology* 21:79–83.

Desvousges, W. H., V. K. Smith, and M. P. McGivney. 1983. A comparison of alternative approaches for estimating recreation and related benefits of water quality improvements. U.S. Environmental Protection Agency, EPA 230-05-83-001.

Dillman, D. 1978. *Mail and telephone surveys: The total design method.* New York: John Wiley and Sons.

Dissmeyer, G. E., and G. R. Foster. 1984. A guide for predicting sheet and rill erosion on forest land. USDA Forest Service Technical Publication R8 TP 6.

Ditton, R., A. Fedler, and A. Graefe. 1983. Factors contributing to perceptions of recreational crowding. *Leisure Sciences* 5:273–88.

Donnelly, M., J. Vaske, and B. Shelby. 1992. Measuring backcountry standards in visitor surveys. In *Defining wilderness quality: The role of standards in wilderness management—A workshop proceedings.* USDA Forest Service General Technical Report PNW-305, 38–52.

Driver, B. L., and J. Bassett. 1975. Defining conflicts among river users: A case study of Michigan's Au Sable River. *Naturalist* 26, no. 1:19–23.

Dustin, D. L., and L. H. McAvoy. 1980. Hardening national parks. *Environmental Ethics* 2, no. 1:39–44.

Ericsson, K., and H. Simon. 1993. Protocol analysis: Verbal reports as data. Cambridge, Mass.: MIT Press.

Eroglu, S., and D. Harrell. 1986. Retail crowding: Theoretical and strategic implications. *Journal of Retailing* 62:347–63.

Evans, C. B. 2002. Summit steward 2002 season report. Acadia National Park.

Extend. 1996. Version 3.2.1. [Computer software] Imagine That, San Jose, Calif.

Farrell, T. A., and J. L. Marion. 2002. Trail impacts and trail impact management related to ecotourism visitation at Torres del Paine National Park, Chile. *Leisure/Loisir* 26:31–59.

Feeny, D., F. Berkes, B. J. McCoy, and J. M. Acheson. 1990. The tragedy of the commons: Twenty-two years later. *Human Ecology* 18, no. 1:1–19.

Festinger, L. 1957. *A theory of cognitive dissonance.* Stanford, Calif.: Stanford University Press.

Forman, R. T. T., D. Speiling, J. A. Bissonette, A. P. Clevenger, C. D. Cutshall, and V. H. Dale. 2003. *Road ecology: Science and solutions.* Washington, D.C.: Island Press.

Freimund, W., J. Vaske, M. Donnelly, and T. Miller. 2002. Using video surveys to access dispersed backcountry visitors' norms. *Leisure Sciences* 24:349–62.

Frissell, S. S., and D. P. Duncan. 1965. Campsite preference and deterioration in the Quetico-Superior canoe country. *Journal of Forestry* 65:256–60.

Fritz, J. D. 1993. Effects of trail-induced sediment loads on Great Smoky Mountains National Park high gradient trout streams. M.S. thesis. Cookville: Tennessee Technological University.

Gilbert, G., G. Peterson, and D. Lime. 1972. Towards a model of travel behavior in the Boundary Waters Canoe Area. *Environment and Behavior* 4:131–57.

Gilligan, C. 1982. *In a different voice.* Cambridge, Mass.: Harvard University Press.

Godbey, G. 1984. Some reactions to nonreactive research in park and recreation settings. In *Proceedings of a workshop on unobtrusive techniques to study social behavior in parks,* ed. J. D. Peine. National Park Service Southeast Regional Office, Natural Science and Research Division.

Goonan, K., R. Manning, and W. Valliere. 2009. Research to guide trail management at Acadia National Park. *Proceedings of the 2008 Northeastern Recreation Research Symposium*, USDA Forest Service General Technical Report NRS-P-42, 266–74.

Graefe, A., and E. Drogin. 1989. Factors affecting boating satisfaction at Raystown Lake. *Proceedings of the 1989 Northeastern Recreation Research Symposium*, USDA Forest Service General Technical Report NE-132, 31–38.

Green, J. C., V. J. Caracelli, and W. F. Graham. 1989. Towards a conceptual framework for mixed-method evaluation designs. *Educational Evaluation and Policy Analysis* 11, no. 3:255–74.

Gross E. J., R. R. Nemani, W. Turner, and F. Melton. 2006. Remote sensing for the national parks. *Park Science* 24, no. 1:30–36.

Gunn, C. A. 1997. *Vacationscape: Developing tourist areas.* 3rd ed. New York: Taylor & Francis.

Haas, G., B. Driver, P. Brown, and R. Lucas. 1987. Wilderness management zoning. *Journal of Forestry* 85, no. 12:17–21.

Haas, G., and C. Jacobi. 2002. Final report: A visitor capacity charrette for Acadia National Park, August 1–3, 2001. Acadia National Park Natural Resources Report Number 2002-5.

Hall, C. N., and F. R. Kuss. 1989. Vegetation alteration along trails in Shenandoah National Park, Virginia. *Biological Conservation* 48:211–27.

Hall, T., and J. Roggenbuck. 2002. Response format effects in questions about norms: Implications for the reliability and validity of the normative approach. *Leisure Sciences* 24:325–38.

Hallo, J. C. 2007. Understanding and managing vehicle use as a component of the visitor experience in national parks. Unpublished doctoral dissertation, University of Vermont, Burlington, Vt.

Hallo, J. C., and R. E. Manning. Forthcoming. Transportation and recreation: A case study of visitors driving for pleasure at Acadia National Park. *Journal of Transport Geography.*

———. Forthcoming. Use of computer simulation modeling to support analysis of social carrying capacity for a scenic road at Acadia National Park. *Journal of Sustainable Transportation.*

Hallo, J. C., R. E. Manning, and W. A. Valliere. 2005. Acadia National Park scenic roads: Estimating the relationship between increasing use and potential standards of quality. In *Computer simulation modeling of recreation use: Current status, case studies, and future direction,* ed. D. N. Cole, 55–57. USDA Forest Service General Technical Report RMRS-GTR-143.

Hallo, J. C., R. E. Manning, W. A. Valliere, and M. Budruk. 2005. A case study comparison of visitor self-reported and GPS recorded travel routes. *Proceedings of the 2004 Northeastern Recreation Research Symposium*, USDA Forest Service General Technical Report NE-326, 172–77.

Hammitt, W. E., and D. N. Cole. 1998. *Wildland recreation: Ecology and management.* 2nd ed. New York: John Wiley & Sons.

Hammitt, W. E., and J. L. Hughes. 1984. Characteristics of winter backcountry use in Great Smoky Mountains National Park. *Environmental Management* 8:161–66.

Hammitt, W. E., and M. E. Patterson. 1991. Coping behavior to avoid visual encounters: Its relationship to wildland privacy. *Journal of Leisure Research* 23:225–37.

Hammitt, W. E., and W. M. Rutlin. 1995. Use encounter standards and curves for achieved privacy in wilderness. *Leisure Sciences* 17:245–62.

Hanemann, W. 1984. Welfare evaluations in contingent valuation experiments with discrete responses. *American Journal of Agricultural Economics* 66:332–41.

Hanley, N., R. Wright, and G. Koop. 2002. Modeling recreation demand using choice experiments: Climbing in Scotland. *Environmental Resource Economics* 22:449–66.

Hardin, G. 1968. The tragedy of the commons. *Science* 162:1243–48.

Harmon, D. 1992. Using an interactive computer program to communicate with the wilderness visitor. *Proceedings of the Symposium on Social Aspects and Recreation Research*, USDA Forest Service General Technical Report PSW-132, 60.

Havlick, D. G. (2002). *No place distant: Roads and motorized recreation on America's Public Lands.* Washington: Island Press.

Heberlein, T. 1977. Density, crowding, and satisfaction: Sociological studies for determining carrying capacities. *Proceedings: River Recreation Management and Research Symposium*, USDA Forest Service General Technical Report NC-28, 67–76.

Heberlein, T., and B. Shelby. 1977. Carrying capacity, values, and the satisfaction model: A reply to Greist. *Journal of Leisure Research* 9:142–48.

Hendee, J. C., and C. P. Dawson. 2003. *Wilderness management: Stewardship and protection of resources and values.* 3rd ed. Golden, Colo.: Fulcrum Publishing.

Hendee, J. C., G. H. Stankey, and R. C. Lucas. 1990. *Wilderness management.* Golden, Colo.: North American Press.

Hesselbarth, W., and B. Vachowski. 2000. Trail construction and maintenance notebook. Publication 0023-2839-MTDC-P. USDA Forest Service, Technology and Development Program, Missoula, Montana.

Heywood, J. 1993a. Behavioral conventions in higher density day use wildland/urban recreation settings: A preliminary case study. *Journal of Leisure Research* 25:39–52.

———. 1993b. Game theory: A basis for analyzing emerging norms and conventions in outdoor recreation. *Leisure Sciences* 15:37–48.

———. 1996a. Convention, emerging norms, and norms in outdoor recreation. *Leisure Sciences* 18:355–63.

———. 1996b. Social regularities in outdoor recreation. *Leisure Sciences* 18, no. 1:23–27.

Hof, M., J. Hammitt, M. Rees, J. Belnap, N. Poe, D. Lime, and R. Manning. 1994.

Getting a handle on carrying capacity: A pilot project at Arches National Park. *Park Science* 14, no. 1:11–13.

Hollenhorst, S., S. Brock, W. Freimund, and M. Twery. 1993. Predicting the effects of gypsy moth on near-view aesthetic preferences and recreation behavior intentions. *Forest Science* 39:28–40.

Holmes, T., and W. Adamowicz. 2003. Attribute-based methods. In *A primer on non-market valuation*, ed. P. Champ, K. Boyle, and W. Adamowicz, 171–220. Dordrecth, the Netherlands: Kluwer Academic Publishers.

Hooper, L. 1998. *National Park Service trails management handbook*. Denver, Colo.: U.S. National Park Service Denver Service Center.

Hornback, K., and R. Manning. 1992. When is a visit really a visit? Public use reporting at Acadia National Park. *Park Science* 13:13, 23.

Hu, W., and G. Wall. 2005. Environmental management, environmental image and the competitive tourist attraction. *Journal of Sustainable Tourism* 13, no. 6:617–35.

Ingle, C. M., Y. Leung, C. Monz, and H. Bauman. 2004. Monitoring visitor impacts in coastal national parks: A review of techniques. In *Protecting our diverse heritage: The role of parks, protected areas, and cultural sites. Proceedings of the George Wright Society/National Park Service Joint Conference*, April 14–18, 2003, San Diego, California.

Jacobi, C. 1997. Monitoring carrying capacity on Acadia National Park carriage roads: 1997. Acadia National Park Natural Resources Report 97-11, December 1997.

———. 2001a. A census of vehicles and visitors to Cadillac Mountain, Acadia National Park, August 14, 2001. Acadia National Park Natural Resources Report 2001-11.

———. 2001b. Monitoring carrying capacity on Acadia National Park carriage roads: 2000 (crowding and behaviors). Acadia National Park Natural Resources Report Number 2001-1, February 2001.

———. 2003. A census of vehicles and visitors to Cadillac Mountain, Acadia National Park, August 1, 2002. Acadia National Park Natural Resources Report 2002-05.

———. 2007. Monitoring visitor capacity for Acadia National Park carriage roads: 2006 (crowding and behaviors). Acadia National Park Natural Resources Report Number 2007-1, February 2007.

———. 2008. Monitoring visitor capacity for Acadia National Park carriage roads: 2007 (crowding). Acadia National Park Natural Resources Report Number 2008-2, February 2008.

Jacobi, C., and R. Manning. 1997. Applying the Visitor Experience and Resource Protection Process to Acadia National Park Carriage Roads: A Summary of Research and Decision-Making. Acadia National Park Natural Resources Report Number 97-10.

———. 1999. Crowding and conflict on the carriage roads of Acadia National Park:

An application of the Visitor Experience and Resource Protection framework. *Park Science* 19:22–26.

Jensen, J. R. 2005. *Introductory digital image processing: A remote sensing perspective.* 3rd ed. Upper Saddle River, N.Y.: Prentice Hall.

Kasworm, W. F., and T. L. Monley. 1990. Road and trail influences on grizzly bears and black bears in northwest Montana. In *Bears: Their biology and management: Proceedings of the 8th International Conference,* ed. L. M. Darling and W. R. Archibald, 79–84. Victoria, B.C.: International Association for Bear Research and Management.

Kim, M. 2009. Monitoring vegetation impact using remote sensing technology: Cadillac Mountain Summit, Acadia National Park. Ph.D. dissertation, University of Maine.

Kirk, J., and M. Miller. 1986. *Reliability and validity in qualitative research.* Beverly Hills, Calif.: Sage Publications.

Knight, R. L., and D. N. Cole. 1995. Wildlife responses to recreationists. In *Wildlife and recreationists: Coexistence through management and research,* ed. R. L. Knight and K. J. Gutzwiller, 51–70. Washington, D.C.: Island Press.

Kohlberg, L. 1976. Moral stages and moral development. In *Moral development and behavior: Theory, research and social issues.* New York: Holt, Rinehart, and Winston.

Kuentzel, W. F., and T. A. Heberlein. 1992. Cognitive and behavioral adaptations to perceived crowding: A panel study of coping and displacement. *Journal of Leisure Research* 4:377–93.

Law, A. M., and W. D. Kelton. 1991. *Simulation modeling and analysis.* New York: McGraw-Hill.

Lawson, S. R., R. Itami, R. Gimblett, and R. Manning. 2006a. Benefits and challenges of computer simulation modeling of backcountry recreation use in the Desolation Lake Area of the John Muir Wilderness. *Journal of Leisure Research* 38:187–207.

———. 2006b. A conjoint analysis of preference heterogeneity among day and overnight visitors to the Okefenokee Wilderness. *Journal of Leisure Research* 38, no. 4:575–600.

Lawson, S. R., A. M. Kiely, and R. E. Manning. 2003. Computer simulation as a tool for developing alternatives for managing crowding at wilderness campsites on Isle Royale. *George Wright Forum* 20:72–82.

Lawson, S. R., and R. E. Manning. 2002. Tradeoffs among social, resource and management attributes of the Denali Wilderness experience: A contextual approach to normative research. *Leisure Sciences* 24:297–312.

———. 2003. Research to inform management of wilderness camping at Isle Royale National Park: Part II—Prescriptive research. *Journal of Park and Recreation Administration* 21, no. 3:43–56.

Lawson, S. R., R. E. Manning, W. A. Valliere, and B. Wang. 2003. Proactive monitoring and adaptive management of social carrying capacity in Arches

National Park: An application of computer simulation modeling. *Journal of Environmental Management* 68:305–13.

Lee, K. N. 1993. *Compass and gyroscope: Integrating science and politics for the environment.* Washington, D.C: Island Press.

Leonard, R. E. and A. M. Whitney. 1977. Trail transect: A method for documenting trail changes. Research Paper NE-389. Upper Darby, Penn.: USDA Forest Service, Northeastern Forest Experiment Station.

Leung, Y. F., and J. L. Marion. 1996. Trail degradation as influenced by environmental factors: A state-of-knowledge review. *Journal of Soil and Water Conservation* 51:130–36.

———. 1999a. Assessing trail conditions in protected areas: An application of a problem-assessment method in Great Smoky Mountains National Park, USA. *Environmental Conservation* 26:270–79.

———. 1999b. The influence of sampling interval on the accuracy of trail impact assessment. *Landscape and Urban Planning* 43:167–79.

———. 1999c. Spatial strategies for managing visitor impacts in national parks. *Journal of Park and Recreation Administration* 17, no. 4: 20–38.

———. 2000. Recreation impacts and management in wilderness: A state-of-knowledge review. In *Proceedings: Wilderness science in a time of change,* vol. 5: *Wilderness ecosystems, threats, and management,* ed. D. N. Cole et al. May 23–27, 1999, Missoula, Montana. Proceedings RMRS-P-15-Vol-5, 23–48. Ogden, Utah: USDA Forest Service, Rocky Mountain Research Station.

———. 2004. Managing impacts of campsites. In *Environmental impact of tourism,* ed. R. Buckley, 245–58. Cambridge, Mass.: CABI Publishing.

Leung, Y., and C. Monz. 2006. Visitor impact monitoring: Old issues, new challenge —An introduction to this special issue. *George Wright Forum* 23, no. 2:7–10.

Leung, Y. F., N. Shaw, K. Johnson, and R. Duhaime. 2002. More than a database: Integrating GIS data with the Boston Harbor Islands Visitor Carrying Capacity Study. *George Wright Forum* 19:69–78.

Levin, S. A. 1992. The problem of pattern and scale in ecology. *Ecology* 73, no. 6:1943–67.

Lime, D. W. 1972. Large groups in the Boundary Waters canoe area: Their number, characteristics, and impact. USDA Forest Service Research Note NC-142.

———. 1977a. Research for river recreation planning and management. In *Proceedings: River Recreation Management and Research Symposium,* January 24–27. USDA Forest Service North Central Experiment Station GTR NC-28. Minneapolis.

———. 1977b. When the wilderness gets crowded…? *Naturalist* 28:1–7.

Lindberg, K., B. Dellaert, and C. Romer Rassing. 1999. Resident tradeoffs, A choice modeling approach. *Annals of Tourism Research* 26, no. 3:554–69.

Littlejohn, M. 1999. Acadia National Park visitor study: Summer 1998. U.S. National Park Service Visitor Services Project Report 108. Moscow: University of Idaho, Cooperative Park Studies Unit.

Louviere, J., D. A. Hensher, and J. D. Swait. 2000. *Stated choice methods: Analysis and application.* Cambridge: Cambridge University Press.

Louviere, J., and H. Timmermans. 1990. Stated preference and choice models applied to recreation research. *Leisure Sciences* 12:9–32.

Loveland, T. R., T. Sohl, S. Stehman, A. Gallant, K. Sayler, and D. Napton. 2002. A strategy for estimating the rates of recent United States land-cover changes. *Photogrammetric Engineering and Remote Sensing* 68, no. 10:1091–99.

Lucas, R. 1964a. The recreational capacity of the Quetico-Superior Area. USDA Forest Service Research Paper LS-15.

———. 1964b. Wilderness perception and use: The example of the Boundary Waters Canoe Area. *Natural Resources Journal* 3, no. 3:394–411.

Lunetta, R. L., J. F. Knight, J. Ediriwickrema, J. G. Lyon, and L. Dorsey Worthy. 2006. Landcover change detection using multi-temporal MODIS NDVI data. *Remote Sensing of Environment* 105:142–54.

MacConnell, W. P., and P. G. Stoll. 1968. *Use of aerial photographs to evaluate the recreational resources of the Connecticut River in Massachusetts.* College of Agriculture, Bulletin No. 573, University of Massachusetts, Amherst.

Mackenzie, J. 1993. A comparison of contingent preference models. *American Journal of Agricultural Economics* 75:593–603.

Manning, R. E. 1979a. Impacts of recreation on riparian soils and vegetation. *Water Resources Bulletin* 15, no. 1:30–43.

———. 1979b. Strategies for managing recreational use of national parks. *Parks* 4:13–15.

———. 1985. Crowding norms in backcountry settings: A review and synthesis. *Journal of Leisure Research* 17, no. 2:75–89.

———. 1986. *Studies in outdoor recreation.* Corvallis: Oregon State University Press.

———. 1989. An experiment in park traffic patterns. *Parks and Recreation* 24:6–7, 64.

———. 1990. Do parks make good neighbors? *Park Science* 11:19–20.

———. 1997a. Visitors and neighbors of Acadia National Park: Planning for the future—Study completion report. Burlington: University of Vermont.

———. 1997b. Social carrying capacity of parks and outdoor recreation areas. *Parks and Recreation* 32:32–38.

———. 1999. *Studies in outdoor recreation: Search and research for satisfaction.* 2nd ed. Corvallis: Oregon State University Press.

———. 2001. Visitor experience and resource protection: A framework for managing the carrying capacity of national parks. *Journal of Park and Recreation Administration* 19:93–108.

———. 2003a. Emerging principles for using information/education in wilderness management. *International Journal of Wilderness* 9, no. 1:20–27.

———. 2003b. What to do about crowding and solitude in parks and wilderness? A reply to Stewart and Cole. *Journal of Leisure Research* 35, no. 1:107–19.

———. 2007. *Parks and carrying capacity: Commons without tragedy*. Washington, D.C.: Island Press.

Manning, R. E., J. Bacon, D. Laven, S. Lawson, and W. Valliere. 2004. Research to support carrying capacity analysis at Isle au Haut, Acadia National Park. University of Vermont Park Studies Laboratory.

Manning, R. E., and C. Ciali. 1980. Recreation density and user satisfaction: A further exploration of the satisfaction model. *Journal of Leisure Research* 12:329–45.

Manning, R. E., and W. A. Freimund. 2004. Use of visual research methods to measure standards of quality for parks and outdoor recreation. *Journal of Leisure Research* 36, no. 4:557–79.

Manning, R. E., C. Jacobi, and J. Marion. 2006. Recreation monitoring at Acadia National Park. *George Wright Forum* 23, no. 2:59–72.

Manning, R. E., C. Jacobi, W. Valliere, and B. Wang. 1998. Standards of quality in parks and recreation. *Parks and Recreation* 33:88–94.

Manning, R., D. Johnson, and M. Vande Kamp. 1996. Recreation management in natural areas: Problems and practices, status and trends. *Natural Areas Journal* 16, no. 2:142–46.

Manning, R. E., and S. Lawson. 2002. Carrying capacity as "informed judgment": The values of science and the science of values. *Environmental Management* 30:157–68.

Manning, R. E., S. Lawson, P. Newman, M. Budruk, W. Valliere, and D. Laven. 2004. Visitor perceptions of recreation-related resource impacts. In *Environmental impacts of ecotourism*, 259–272. London: CAB International.

Manning, R. E., S. Lawson, W. Valliere, J. Bacon, and D. Laven. 2002. Schoodic Peninsula, Acadia National Park Visitor Study 2000–2001. University of Vermont: Park Studies Laboratory.

Manning, R. E., and D. Lime. 1996. Crowding and carrying capacity in the national park system: Toward a social science research agenda. In *Crowding and congestion in the national park system: Guidelines for management and research*. St. Paul: University of Minnesota Agricultural Experiment Station Publication 86, 27–65.

Manning, R. E., D. Lime, W. Freimund, and D. Pitt. 1996. Crowding norms at frontcountry sites: A visual approach to setting standards of quality. *Leisure Sciences* 18:39–59.

Manning, R. E., D. Lime, and M. Hof. 1996. Social carrying capacity of natural areas: Theory and application in the U.S. national parks. *Natural Areas Journal* 16, no. 2:118–27.

Manning, R. E., D. Lime, M. Hof, and W. Freimund. 1995. The visitor experience and resource protection process: The application of carrying capacity to Arches National Park. *George Wright Forum* 12:41–55.

Manning, R. E., D. W. Lime, R. F. McMonagel, and P. Nordin. 1993. Indicators and standards of quality for the visitor experience at Arches National Park: Phase 1 research. University of Minnesota Cooperative Park Studies Unit.

Manning, R. E., J. Morrissey, and S. Lawson. 2005. What's behind the numbers? Qualitative insights into normative research in outdoor recreation. *Leisure Sciences* 27:205–24.

Manning, R. E., C. Negra, W. Valliere, and C. Jacobi. 1996. Acadia National Park carriage road study: Phase I research. U.S. National Park Service, Technical Report NPS/NESORNR/NRTR/96-07.

Manning, R. E., P. Newman, W. Valliere, B. Wang, and S. Lawson. 2001. Respondent self-assessment of research on crowding norms in outdoor recreation. *Journal of Leisure Research* 33, no. 3:251–71.

Manning, R. E., and F. I. Potter. 1984. Computer simulation as a tool in teaching park and wilderness management. *Journal of Environmental Education* 15:3–9.

Manning, R. E., and W. Valliere. 2001. Coping in outdoor recreation: Causes and consequences of crowding and conflict among community residents. *Journal of Leisure Research* 33:410–26.

Manning, R. E., W. Valliere, N. Ballinger, and C. Jacobi. 1998b. Acadia National Park carriage road study: Phase III research. Technical Report NPS/ NESO-RNR/NRTR/98-1.

Manning, R. E., W. Valliere, B. Minteer, B. Wang, and C. Jacobi. 2000. Crowding in parks and outdoor recreation: A theoretical, empirical, and managerial analysis. *Journal of Park and Recreation Administration* 18, no. 4:57–72.

Manning, R., W. Valliere, B. Wang, N. Ballinger, and C. Jacobi. 1997. Acadia National Park carriage road study: Phase I research. Boston: U.S. National Park Service Technical Report NPS/NESO-RNR/NRTR/97-3.

———. 1998. Acadia National Park carriage road study: Phase II research. Technical Report NPS/NESO-RNR/NRTR/98-3.

Manning, R. E., W. Valliere, B. Wang, and C. Jacobi. 1999. Crowding norms: Alternative measurement approaches. *Leisure Sciences* 21, no. 2:97–115.

Marion, J. L. 1991. Developing a natural resource inventory and monitoring program for visitor impacts on recreation sites: A procedural manual. Natural Resources Report NPS/NRVT/NRR-91/06. Denver, Colo.: USDI National Park Service, Natural Resources Publication Office.

———. 1994. An assessment of trail conditions in Great Smoky Mountains National Park. Research/Resources Management Report. Atlanta, Ga.: USDI National Park Service, Southeast Region.

———. 1995. Capabilities and management utility of recreation impact monitoring programs. *Environmental Management* 19:763–71.

———. 2007. Development and application of trail and campsite monitoring protocols in support of visitor experience and resource protection decision making at Isle Au Haut, Acadia National Park. Blacksburg, Va: USDI, U.S. Geological Survey, Virginia Tech Field Unit.

Marion, J. L., and D. N. Cole. 1996. Spatial and temporal variation in soil and vegetation impacts on campsites. *Ecological Applications* 6:520–30.

Marion, J. L., and Y. F. Leung. 1997. An assessment of campsite conditions in Great

Smoky Mountains National Park. Research/Resources Management Report. Atlanta, Ga.: USDI National Park Service, Southeast Regional Office.

———. 1998. International impact research and management. In *Wildland Recreation: Ecology and Management*, ed. W. E. Hammitt, and D. N. Cole, 328–46. 2nd ed. New York: John Wiley & Sons.

———. 2001. Trail resource impacts and an examination of alternative assessment techniques. *Journal of Park and Recreation Administration* 19:17–37.

Marion, J. L., Y. Leung, and S. K. Nepal. 2006. Monitoring trail conditions: New methodological considerations. *George Wright Forum* 23:36–49.

Marion, J. L., and N. Olive. 2006. Assessing and understanding trail degradation: Results from Big South Fork National River and Recreational Area. Research/Resources Management Report. Oneida, Tenn.: USDI National Park Service, Big South Fork National River and Recreation Area.

Marion, J. L, J. Roggenbuck, and R. Manning. 1993. Problems and practices in backcountry recreation management: A survey of National Park Service managers. Denver, Colo.: U.S. National Park Service Natural Resources Report NPS/NRVT/NRR-93/12.

Marion, J. L., J. Wimpey, and L. Park. (forthcoming). Monitoring protocols for characterizing trail conditions, understanding degradation, and selecting indicators and standards of quality, Acadia National Park, Mount Desert Island. Blacksburg, Va.: USDI, U.S. Geological Survey, Virginia Tech Field Station.

Marshall, M. N. 1996. Sampling for qualitative research. *Family Practice* 13:522–24.

Martin, S., S. McCool, and R. Lucas. 1989. Wilderness campsite impacts: Do managers and visitors see them the same? *Environmental Management* 13:623–29.

Martinson, K., and B. Shelby. 1992. Encounter and proximity norms for salmon anglers in California and New Zealand. *North American Journal of Fisheries Management* 12:559–67.

McAvoy, L. H., and D. L. Dustin. 1983. Indirect versus direct regulation of recreation behavior. *Journal of Park and Recreation Administration* 1, no. 4:12–17.

McCool, S. F., and N. A. Christensen. 1996. Alleviating congestion in parks and recreation areas through direct management of visitor behavior. In *Congestion and crowding in the national park system: Guidelines for management and research*, ed. D. W. Lime. MAES Misc. Pub. 86-1996. St. Paul, Minn.: Department of Forest Resources and Minnesota Agricultural Experiment Station, University of Minnesota.

McCool, S. F., D. W. Lime, and D. H. Anderson. 1977. Simulation modeling as a tool for managing river recreation. In *River Recreation Management and Research Symposium proceedings*, 202–9. USDA Forest Service General Tech. Rep. NC-28, North Central Forest Experiment Station, St. Paul, Minnesota.

McFadden, D. 1974. Conditional logic analysis of qualitative choice behavior. In *Frontiers in econometrics*, ed. P. Zarembka, 105–42. New York: Academic Press.

Merigliano, L. L. 1990. Indicators to monitor wilderness conditions. In *Managing America's enduring wilderness resource*, ed. D. W. Lime, 205–9. St. Paul: University of Minnesota, Agricultural Experiment Station and Extension Service.

Michener, W. K., and P. F. Houhoulis. 1997. Detection of vegetation changes associated with extensive flooding in a forested ecosystem. *Photogrammetric Engineering and Remote Sensing* 63:1363–74.

Miles, M. B., and M. A. Huberman. 1994. Qualitative data analysis: An expanded sourcebook. 2nd ed. Thousand Oaks, Calif.: Sage Publications.

Milgram, S. 1970. The experience of living in cities. *Science* 167:1461–68.

Moore, S., J. Schockey, and S. Brickler. 1990. Social encounters as a cue for determining wilderness quality. In *Social science and natural resource recreation management*, 69–79. Boulder, Colo.: Westview Press.

Morey, E., T. Buchanan, and D. Waldman. 2002. Estimating the benefits and costs to mountain bikers of changes in trail characteristics, access fees, and site closures: Choice experiments and benefits transfer. *Journal of Environmental Management* 64:411–22.

Myeong, S., D. J. Nowak, and M. J. Duggin. 2006. A temporal analysis of urban forest carbon storage using remote sensing. *Remote Sensing of Environment* 101:277–82.

Nassauer, I. J. 1990. Using image capture technology to generate wilderness management solutions. In *Managing America's enduring wilderness resource*, ed. D. W. Lime, 553–62. St. Paul: University of Minnesota, Agricultural Experiment Station and Extension Service.

National Park Service. 1992. General Management Plan—Acadia National Park. Bar Harbor, Me.: U.S. Department of Interior, National Park Service.

———. 1997. VERP: The visitor experience and resource protection (VERP) framework—A handbook for planners and managers. Technical Report Denver, Colo.: National Park Service.

National Survey on Recreation and the Environment. 2000–2002. The Interagency National Survey Consortium, Coordinated by the USDA Forest Service, Recreation, Wilderness, and Demographics Trends Research Group, Athens, Georgia, and the Human Dimensions Research Laboratory, University of Tennessee, Knoxville, Tennessee.

Naylor, T. H., and J. M. Finger. 1967. Verification of computer simulation models. *Management Science* 14:92–101.

Newman, P., R. E. Manning, D. F. Dennis, and W. McKonly. 2005. Informing carrying capacity decision making in Yosemite National Park, USA using stated choice modeling. *Journal of Park and Recreation Administration* 23, no. 1:75–89.

Newsome, D., S. A. Moore, and R. K. Dowling. 2002. *Natural area tourism: Ecology, impacts and management*. Clevedon, England: Channel View Publications.

Nielson, J., and R. Endo. 1977. Where have all the purists gone? An empirical examination of the displacement hypothesis in wilderness recreation. *Western Sociological Review* 8:61–75.

Nielson, J., and B. Shelby. 1977. River-running in the Grand Canyon: How much and what kind of use. *Proceedings: River Recreation Management and Research Symposium.* USDA Forest Service General Technical Report NC-28, 168–77.

Noe, F. 1992. Further questions about the measurement and conceptualization of backcountry encounter norms. *Journal of Leisure Research* 24:86–92.

Nunnally, J. 1978. *Psychometric theory.* New York: McGraw-Hill.

Opaluch, J. J., S. Swallow, T. Weaver, C. Wessells, and D. Wichelns. 1993. Evaluating impacts from noxious facilities: Including public preferences in current siting mechanisms. *Journal of Environmental Economics and Management* 24:41–59.

Park, L., R. Manning, J. Marion, S. Lawson, and C. Jacobi. 2008. Managing visitor impacts in parks: A multi-method study of the effectiveness of alternative management practices. *Journal of Park and Recreation Administration* 26:97–121.

Patterson, M. E., and W. E. Hammitt. 1990. Backcountry encounter norms, actual reported encounters, and their relationship to wilderness solitude. *Journal of Leisure Research* 22, no. 3:259–75.

Patton, M. Q. 2002. *Qualitative research and evaluation methods.* 3rd ed. Thousand Oaks, Calif.: Sage Publications.

Peterson, G., and D. Lime. 1979. People and their behavior: A challenge for recreation management. *Journal of Forestry* 77:343–46.

Pidd, M. 1992. *Computer simulation in management science.* New York: John Wiley & Sons.

Potter, F. I., and R. E. Manning. 1984. Application of the wilderness travel simulation model to the Appalachian Trail in Vermont. *Environmental Management* 8:543–50.

Price, M. F. 1983. Management planning in the Sunshine area of Canada's Banff National Park. *Parks* 7, no. 4:6–10.

Reid, S. E., and J. L. Marion. 2005. A comparison of campfire impacts and policies in seven protected areas. *Environmental Management* 36:48–58.

Robertson, R., and J. Regula. 1994. Recreational displacement and overall satisfaction: A study of central Iowa's licensed boaters. *Journal of Leisure Research* 26:174–81.

Rochefort, R., and D. Swinney. 2000. Human impact survey in Mount Rainier National Park: Past, present, and future. USDA Forest Service Proceedings RMRS-P-15-VOL-5.

Roggenbuck, J. W. 1992. Use of persuasion to reduce resource impacts and visitor conflicts. In ed. *Influencing human behavior,* ed. M. Manfredo. Champaign, Ill.: Sagamore.

Roggenbuck, J. W., and D. Berrier. 1982. A comparison of the effectiveness of two communication strategies in dispersing wilderness campers. *Journal of Leisure Research* 14:77–89.

Roggenbuck, J. W., D. Williams, S. Bange, and D. Dean. 1991. River float trip encounter norms: Questioning the use of the social norms concept. *Journal of Leisure Research* 23:133–53.

Rohrmann, B., and I. Bishop. 2002. Subjective responses to computer simulations of urban environments. *Journal of Environmental Psychology* 22, no. 4:319–30.

Rowe, R. D., R. C. d'Arge, and D. S. Brookshire. 1986. An experiment on the economic value of visibility. *Journal of Environmental Economics and Management* 7:1–19.

Russo, J., E. Johnson, and D. Stephens. 1989. The validity of verbal protocols. *Memory & Cognition* 17:759–69.

Sader, S. A. 1987. Digital image classification approach for estimating forest clearing and regrowth rates and trends. In *International Geoscience and Remote Sensing Symposium*, Ann Arbor, Michigan, May, 18–21, 209–13.

SAIC. 2003. *Quality of service and customer satisfaction on arterial streets—final report*. Science Applications International Corporation (SAIC), George Mason University, Volpe National Transportation Systems Center. Available from http://www.itsdocs.fhwa.dot.gov/JPODOCS/REPTS_TE/13849.html [accessed March 28, 2007].

Schechter, M., and R. C. Lucas. 1978. *Simulation of recreation use for park and wilderness management*. Baltimore: Johns Hopkins University Press.

Schkade, D. A., and J. W. Payne. 1994. How people respond to contingent valuation questions: A verbal protocol analysis of willingness to pay for environmental regulation. *Journal of Environmental Economics and Management* 26:88–109.

Schneider, I., and W. Hammitt. 1995. Visitor response to outdoor recreation conflict: A conceptual approach. *Leisure Sciences* 17:223–34.

Schroeder, H. W., J. F. Dwyer, J. J. Louviere, and D. H. Anderson. 1990. Monetary and nonmonetary trade-offs of urban forest site attributes in a logit model of recreation choice. In *Forest resource value and benefit measurement: Some cross-cultural perspectives*, ed. B. L. Driver and G. L. Peterson, 41–51. General Technical Report RM-197. Fort Collins, Colo.: Rocky Mountain Forest and Range Experiment Station.

Shelby, B., N. Bregenzer, and R. Johnson. 1988. Displacement and product shift: Empirical evidence from Oregon rivers. *Journal of Leisure Research* 20:274–88.

Shelby, B., and R. Colvin. 1982. Encounter measures in carrying capacity research: Actual, reported, and diary contacts. *Journal of Leisure Research* 14, no. 4:350–60.

Shelby, B., and R. Harris. 1985. Comparing methods for determining visitor evaluations of ecological impacts: Site visits, photographs, and written descriptions. *Journal of Leisure Research* 17:57–67.

Shelby, B., and T. A. Heberlein. 1986. Carrying capacity in recreation settings. Corvallis: Oregon State University Press.

Shelby, B., and B. Shindler. 1992. Interest group standards for ecological impacts at wilderness campsites. *Leisure Sciences* 14:17–27.

Shelby, B., and J. Vaske. 1991. Using normative data to develop evaluative standards for resource management: A comment on three recent papers. *Journal of Leisure Research* 23, no. 2:173–87.

Shelby, B., J. Vaske, and M. Donnelly. 1996. Norms, standards, and natural resources. *Leisure Sciences* 18:103–23.

Sheldon, P. J. 1997. *Tourism information technology*. New York: Cab International.

Shindler, B., M. Bunson, and G. Stankey. 2002. Social acceptability of forest conditions and management practices: A problem analysis. General Technical Report PNW-GTR-537. Portland, Ore.: Pacific Northwest Research Station.

Shindler, B., and B. Shelby. 1993. Regulating wilderness use: An investigation of user group support. *Journal of Forestry* 91:41–44.

———. 1995. Product shift in recreation settings: Findings and implications from panel research. *Leisure Sciences* 17:91–104.

Smith, K. V., and R. L. Headly. 1975. The use of computer simulation models in wilderness management. In *Management science applications to leisure time,* ed. S. Ladany. North Holland, Amsterdam: Elsevier.

Smith, K. V., and J. V. Krutilla. 1976. *Structure and properties of a wilderness travel simulator.* Baltimore: Johns Hopkins University Press.

Song, C., C. E. Woodcock, K. C. Seto, M. P. Lenney, and S. A. Macomber. 2001. Classification and change detection using Landsat TM data: When and how to correct atmospheric effects? *Remote Sensing of Environment* 75:230–44.

Stankey, G. H. 1973. Visitor perception of wilderness recreation carrying capacity. USDA Forest Service Research Paper INT-142.

———. 1980. A comparison of carrying capacity perceptions among visitors to two wildernesses. USDA Forest Service Research Paper INT-242.

———. 1989. Solitude for the multitudes: Managing recreational use in the wilderness. In *Public places and Spaces,* 277–99. New York: Plenum Press.

Stankey, G. H., R. N. Clark, and B. T. Bormann. 2005. *Adaptive management of natural resources: Theory, concepts, and management institutions.* Portland, Ore.: U.S. Department of Agriculture.

Stankey, G. H., D. Cole, R. Lucas, M. Peterson, S. Frissell, and R. Washburne. 1985. The limits of acceptable change (LAC) system for wilderness planning. General Technical Report INT-176. Ogden, Utah: U. S. Department of Agriculture, Forest Service, Intermountain Forest and Range Experiment Station.

Stankey, G. H., and S. McCool. 1984. Carrying capacity in recreational settings: Evaluation, appraisal, and application. *Leisure Sciences* 6:453–73.

Stemerding, M. P., H. Oppewal, H. J. P. Timmerman, and T. A. M. Beckus. 1995. An experimental constraints/preference approach for the management of leisure mobility. In *Proceedings of the Fourth International Outdoor Recreation and Tourism Trends Symposium and the 1995 National Recreation Resource Planning Conference,* compiled by J. L. Thompson, D. W. Lime, B. Gartner, and W. M. Sames. St. Paul: University of Minnesota, College of Natural Resources and Minnesota Extension Service.

Stewart, W., and D. Cole. 2003. On the prescriptive utility of visitor survey research: A rejoinder to Manning. *Journal of Leisure Research* 35:119–27.

Stokols, D. 1972a. On the distinction between density and crowding: Some implications for future research. *Psychological Review* 79:275–77.

———. 1972b. A social psychological model of human crowding phenomena. *Journal of the American Institute of Planners* 38:72–83.

Sutherland, S. 1996. *The international dictionary of psychology*. New York: Crossroad.

Swarbrooke, J. 1998. *Sustainable tourism management*. Wallingford, U.K.: CABI.

Tarrant, M., H. Cordell, and T. Kibler. 1997. Measuring perceived crowding for high-density river recreation: The effects of situational conditions and personal factors. *Leisure Sciences* 19:97–112.

Tashakkori, A., and C. Teddlie. 1998. Mixed methodology: Combining qualitative and quantitative approaches. Thousand Oaks, Calif.: Sage Publications.

Thayer, M. A. 1981. Contingent valuation techniques for assessing environmental impacts: Further evidence. *Journal of Environmental Economics and Management* 8:27–44.

Titre, J., and A. S. Mills. 1982. Effect of encounters on perceived crowding and satisfaction. In *Forest and river recreation: Research update*, 146–53. University of Minnesota Agricultural Experiment Station Miscellaneous Publication 18.

Transportation Research Board. 2000. *Highway capacity manual*. Washington, D.C.: National Research Council.

Turnbull, K. F. 2003. Transport to nature: Transportation strategies enhancing visitor experiences of national parks. *TR News* 224:15–21.

Turner, G. M., R. H. Gardner, and R. V. O'Neill. 2001. *Landscape ecology in theory and practice*. New York: Springer-Verlag.

Turner, R., and W. LaPage. 2001. Visitor behaviors and resource impacts at Cadillac Mountain, Acadia National Park. Report of Research for the United States Department of the Interior, 1–113. Cooperative Agreement 1443CA4520-A-0015.

Tyser, R. W., and C. A. Worley. 1992. Alien flora in grasslands adjacent to road and trail corridors in Glacier National Park, Montana (U.S.A.). *Conservation Biology* 6:253–62.

Vander Stoep, G. A., and J. Roggenbuck. 1996. Is your park being loved to death? Using communications and other indirect techniques to battle the park "love bug." In *Congestion and crowding in the national park system*. ed. D. W. Lime, 85–132. Minnesota Agricultural Experiment Station Miscellaneous Publication 86-1996.

van Someren, M., Y. Barnard, and J. Sandberg. 1994. *The think aloud method: A practical guide to modeling cognitive processes*. New York: Academic Press.

Vaske, J., M. Donnelly, and T. Heberlein. 1980. Perceptions of crowding and resource quality by early and more recent visitors. *Leisure Sciences* 3:367–81.

Vaske, J., M. Donnelly, and J. Petruzzi. 1996. Country of origin, encounter norms, and crowding in a frontcountry setting. *Leisure Sciences* 18:165–76.

Vaske, J., A. Graefe, B. Shelby, and T. Heberlein. 1986. Backcountry encounter norms: Theory, method and empirical evidence. *Journal of Leisure Research* 18, 3:137–53.

Vaske, J., and D. Whittaker. 2004. Normative approaches to natural resources. In *Society and national resources: A summary of knowledge*. 283–94. Jefferson, Mo.: Modern Litho.

Wagar, J. A. 1964. *The carrying capacity of wild lands for recreation*. Forest Science Monograph 7. Washington, D.C.: Society of American Foresters.

Wang, B., and R. Manning. 1999. Computer simulation modeling for recreation management: A study on carriage road use in Acadia National Park, Maine, USA. *Environmental Management* 23:193–203.

Watson, A. 1995. Opportunities for solitude in the Boundary Waters Canoe Area wilderness. *Northern Journal of Applied Forestry* 12:12–18.

Weis, M., S. Muller, C. E. Liedtke, and M. Pahl. 2005. A framework for a GIS and imagery data fusion in support of cartographic updating, *Information Fusion* 6:311–17.

Wenjun, L., G. Xiaodong, and L. Chunyan. 2005. Hiking trails and tourism impact assessment in protected area: Jiuzhaigou Biosphere Reserve, China. *Environmental Monitoring and Assessment* 108:279–93.

West, P. C. 1981. On-site social surveys and the determination of social carrying capacity in wildland recreation management. USDA Forest Service Research Note NC-264.

———. 1982. Effects of user behavior on the perception of crowding in backcountry forest recreation. *Forest Science* 28, no. 1:95–195.

Whittaker, D., and B. Shelby. 1988. Types of norms for recreation impacts: Extending the social norm concept. *Journal of Leisure Research* 20, no. 4:261–73.

Wilderness Act. 1964. Act of September 3, 1964. Public Law 88-577.78 Stat. 890.

Williams, D., J. W. Roggenbuck, and S. P. Bange. 1991. The effect of norm-encounter compatibility on crowding perceptions, experience and behavior in river recreation settings. *Journal of Leisure* 23:154–72.

Wing, M., and B. Shelby. 1999. Using GIS to integrate information on forest recreation. *Journal of Forestry* 97, no. 1:12–16.

Wohlwill, J., and H. Heft. 1977. A comparative study of user attitudes toward development and facilities in two contrasting natural recreation areas. *Journal of Leisure Research* 9:264–80.

Wolper, J., S. Mohamed, S. Burt, and R. Young. 1994. Multisensor GPS-based recreational trail mapping. In *Proceedings of ION GPS 1994* vol. 7/V1, 237–44. Alexandria, Va.: Institute of Navigation.

Xavier, A. C., and C. A. Vettorazzi. 2004. Monitoring leaf area index at watershed level through NDVI from Landsat-7/ETM+ data. *Science Agriculture* 61, no. 3:243–52.

Young, J., D. Williams, and J. Roggenbuck. 1991. The role of involvement in identifying users' preferences for social standards in the Cohutta Wilderness.

Proceedings of the 1990 Southeastern Recreation Research Conference. USDA
Forest Service General Technical Report SE-67, 173–83.

Zimmerman, C. A., T. G. Coleman, and J. Daigle. 2003. Evaluation of Acadia
National Park ITS Field Operational Test: Final report. Report DOT FHWA-
OP-03-130. ITS Joint Program Office, U.S. Department of Transportation.

Zimmerman, C. A., J. Daigle, and J. Pol. 2004. Tourism business and intelligent
transportation systems: Acadia National Park, Maine. *Transportation
Research Record: Journal of the Transportation Research Board* 1895:182–87.

Index